20

# Land-Grant Universities
# for the Future

# LAND-GRANT UNIVERSITIES *for the* FUTURE

Higher Education for the Public Good

STEPHEN M. GAVAZZI
and
E. GORDON GEE

Foreword by C. Peter Magrath

Johns Hopkins University Press
*Baltimore*

Johns Hopkins University Press
2715 North Charles Street
Baltimore, Maryland 21218-4363
www.press.jhu.edu

Library of Congress Cataloging-in-Publication Data

Names: Gavazzi, Stephen M., author. | Gee, E. Gordon
(Elwood Gordon), 1944–author.
Title: Land-grant universities for the future : higher education for the
public good / Stephen M. Gavazzi and E. Gordon Gee.
Description: Baltimore : Johns Hopkins University Press, [2018] |
Includes bibliographical references and index.
Identifiers: LCCN 2018007461 | ISBN 9781421426853 (hardcover : alk. paper) |
ISBN 9781421426860 (electronic) | ISBN 1421426854 (hardcover : alk. paper) |
ISBN 1421426862 (electronic)
Subjects: LCSH: State universities and colleges—United States. |
Agricultural colleges—United States. | Agricultural education—United States. |
Education, Higher—Aims and objectives—United States.
Classification: LCC LB2329.5 .G38 2018 | DDC 378/.05—dc23
LC record available at https://lccn.loc.gov/2018007461

A catalog record for this book is available from the British Library.

*Special discounts are available for bulk purchases of this book. For more information,
please contact Special Sales at 410-516-6936 or specialsales@press.jhu.edu.*

Johns Hopkins University Press uses environmentally friendly book materials,
including recycled text paper that is composed of at least 30 percent post-consumer
waste, whenever possible.

# CONTENTS

Universities that are not engaged with their communities in the twenty-first century will soon find themselves disengaged from any meaningful relevance to the citizenry of the United States. And that applies most particularly to the land-grant universities, which are the most creative and valuable universities in this country. There are two reasons for this. First, it is their heritage, their core commitment, going back to their birth thanks to Justin Morrill and Abraham Lincoln during this nation's worst war—the Civil War—and greatest crisis. Today we face an equally challenging crisis—a deeply polarized nation in a troubled world awash in nuclear weapons. Second, our nation's communities—rural, urban, and in between—urgently need to partner as equals with the land-grant universities so that together they can work on solutions to the problems of their communities.

Just as the entire community should be involved, so too should the entire university be committed to robust action aimed at trying to solve their common—community—problems. It must be emphasized that land-grant universities are intensely practical, not only because of their valuable vocational programs but also because of their liberal arts programs. Contrary to an often-cited misconception, the liberal arts are really practical arts! Why? Because they educate persons to think, to conceptualize, to imagine possibilities. Put another way, they prepare people for life, which always brings change and the need for adjustments. The liberal arts are practical arts that prepare people to face life's challenges by being flexible in a world that constantly changes.

The partnership between land-grant universities and communities begins with the partners—the collaborators—recognizing their shared interests. On the university side it begins with the attitude, as a member of the Kellogg Commission on the Future of State and Land-Grant Universities expressed it, "If it's part of the community's agenda, we want to think about how can we make it part of ours." On the community side, it begins with the recognition that the university, a part of the community, also has talents to contribute. Further, the engaged land-grant university does three things:

1. It organizes itself to respond to the needs of today's students and tomorrow's, not yesterday's.
2. It enriches students' experiences by bringing research and engagement into the curriculum and offering practical opportunities for students to prepare for the world they will enter.
3. It puts its critical resources (knowledge and expertise) to work—in partnership with the community—on the problems they face.

If the partnerships are to succeed, the land-grant students don't simply "graduate" from their school; they remain lifelong members of their university and community, forever contributing and serving. And this—and not just by the way—will make these "students for life" men and women whose lives will be enriched and fulfilled. We should all be students for life, because the enriched life is one that always includes learning and serving.

The land-grant university–community partnership does not just simply or magically develop. It requires leadership, and that means leaders from both the community and the university. These are men and women who care about their world and how it can be improved—as it so clearly can—by their vision and hard work. Again, put simply, leaders lead; they have ideals and vision—and are willing to takes risks, perhaps fail, but perhaps also succeed in improving that part of the world in which their university and community resides.

As we contemplate the critical questions involving land-grant universities for the future before us, universities that serve the public—not just the private—good, it is well to baldly state that the last thing university leaders should ever, even for a nanosecond, concern themselves with is the ridiculous rankings game that ensnares some of them. The rankings game, a truly stupid game, is—BS!

My conclusion is that the eternal core mission of our stimulating land-grant universities is today as it was in 1862: it is to serve people, just as we should do as individuals. We serve ourselves best when we serve others and our communities.

C. Peter Magrath

Throughout the course of compiling the material for this book, we were overwhelmed by the offers of assistance we received from a variety of individuals and organizations. Without the guidance they provided, there would be no book.

First and foremost, we wish to thank our friend and colleague, Ohio State University president Michael V. Drake, MD, for his unqualified support and assistance in jump-starting the research project on which this book is based. In addition to having agreed to coauthor a letter sent to all land-grant university presidents and chancellors announcing the launch of the Ohio State University–West Virginia University study of land-grant universities, Dr. Drake served as an important sounding board during our analysis of the interview data collected from those higher education leaders.

We are indebted to Peter McPherson, current president of the Association of Public and Land-Grant Universities (and former president of Michigan State University), for his overall encouragement of this project and, as will be recounted in chapter 2, his willingness to be interviewed on the history of the Kellogg Commission on the Future of State and Land-Grant Universities. Similar fond sentiments also are held by us regarding the assistance we received from C. Peter Magrath, a former president of APLU (when it was still known as NASULGC) whose land-grant ties include presidencies at the University of Minnesota, West Virginia University, and the University of Missouri higher education system. Dr. Magrath was kind enough to speak at length about his own recollections of the Kellogg Commission efforts, also recounted in chapter 2. On a similar note, we deeply appreciated the remembrances of Dick Stoddard and James Harvey, who were keen eyewitnesses to the events and individuals surrounding the activities of the Kellogg Commission.

We also wish to thank APLU vice president for economic development and community engagement James Woodell, who, in addition to having agreed to speak on the record regarding the Innovation and Economic Prosperity Universities Designation developed by his organization (as discussed in chap. 2), made himself available for countless informal conversations on land-grant issues throughout the time this book was being written. Another important source of information was Paul LeMahieu, senior vice president of programs and operations at the Carnegie Foundation for the Advancement of Teaching, who was instrumental in helping us construct the historical background of the Carnegie Classification for Community Engagement designation, also found in chapter 2.

We wish to recognize the contributions of three additional presidents of organizations dedicated to issues of great importance to higher education. This includes Barbara Gellman-Danley, current president of the Higher Learning Commission, whose discussion of the impact of accrediting bodies on the land-grant mission can be found in chapter 4. This same chapter also holds the insights of Rick Legon, current president of the Association of Governing Boards of Universities and Colleges, who spoke to us at length regarding the critical role played by governing board members as land-grant universities worked to meet the needs of the communities they were designed to serve. And in chapter 6, readers will be treated to the thoughts of Andrew Seligsohn, current president of Campus Compact, who provided his thoughts about the critical impact land-grant institutions must have on the development of a healthy civic culture.

We were delighted to have so many additional leaders and experts in the higher education field agree to speak to us on record about the important issues and concerns identified through our analysis of data pertaining to the present strengths, weaknesses, opportunities, and threats faced by land-grant universities. In alphabetical order, these included Hiram Fitzgerald (Michigan State University), Daniel M. Fogel (University of Vermont), Donald Heller (University of San Francisco), Barbara Holland (University of Nebraska Omaha), Nathan Sorber (West Virginia University), Richard Vedder (Ohio University), David Weerts (University of Minnesota), and Daniel Wheeler (University of Nebraska at Lincoln). The insightful remarks of these thought leaders are sprinkled throughout the pages of this book.

We would be remiss if we did not also acknowledge the early assistance we received from Michael Barone of the *Washington Examiner*. His keen insights regarding contemporary American culture were instrumental in providing us with an initial framework for organizing our thoughts about the relation between the land-grant mission and the current political climate of our nation. In addition to being gracious with his time, Mr. Barone also led us directly to the work of Washington State's Ryne Rohla, whose cartographical expertise directly aided us in presenting and dissecting the voting patterns of polling sites proximate to land-grant institutions during the 2016 US presidential election. The thoughts of both Mr. Barone and Mr. Rohla can be found in chapter 1, setting the stage for all that is to follow.

In conclusion, we wish to recognize those individuals who provided critical behind-the-scenes support throughout the writing process. This includes the efforts of Bonnie Anderson and the rest of the West Virginia University Office of the President staff, who ably managed our correspondence with the land-grant presidents and chancellors contacted for inclusion in the interview component of our land-grant study. The infectious enthusiasm of our editor at Johns Hopkins University Press, Gregory M. Britton, cannot be overstated, nor can we exaggerate the amount of close attention we believe he gave to this project. And finally, we are grateful for the devoted support we have received from our loved ones—Courtney Gavazzi and Laurie Erickson—who kept the home fires burning while we completed this work.

# Land-Grant Universities
# for the Future

# Whither the Land-Grant?

"I would have learning more widely disseminated," said Justin S. Morrill, the Vermont legislator and author of the land-grant movement.

We have disseminated it.

Our institutions should be "the public's universities," in the words of Abraham Lincoln, one of the fathers of public higher education. They have been.

The ideals of Morrill and Lincoln beckon us still.

—Kellogg Commission on the Future of State and Land-Grant Universities

We are passionate—nay, zealous—about public higher education. And we are radical adherents to the idea that land-grant universities—based as they are on the ideals put forward by Senator Justin Morrill, President Abraham Lincoln, and the other social and political giants of their time—continue to set the bar for performance excellence in the realm of public higher education. We are, you might say, fiercely land-grant in our orientation. Yet we are also rather matter-of-fact in our assessment that not all is well in land-grant land these days.

How exactly did your authors arrive at this place and time to extoll the virtues of land-grant institutions while simultaneously examining their warts? By explanation, we begin this book with our personal land-grant stories, the transformative events from our lives which, in combination, brought us together to write this homage and critique of the land-grant university. After these personal vignettes, we provide our readers with a brief description of the strengths, weaknesses, opportunities, and threats (SWOT) analysis that we conducted through interviews with 27 of the presidents and chancellors of the 1862 land-grant universities located in the 48 continental United States. To a person, these presidents and chancellors were brimming with enthusiasm about the strengths and opportunities of present-day land-grant universities, just as surely as they were deeply concerned about some of the weaknesses and threats facing these institutions of higher learning.

Next, we include some critical commentary about the political climate within which these interviews were conducted. We had contact with approximately half of the presidents and chancellors in the months preceding the 2016 US presidential election, with the remainder interviewed after Donald Trump was declared the electoral victor over Hillary Clinton. The impacts of the campaigns that these candidates had chosen to run were significant and unmistakable for many of the presidents and chancellors we interviewed. We believe that there are many important lessons to be extracted from the electoral process and its aftermath which can serve as teachable moments for land-grants and other public universities, and we provide some preparatory remarks about those critical elements in this introduction. Most importantly, we believe that this evolving political context provides us with important information regarding the very definitions of those *communities* with whom colleges and universities should be engaging (spoiler alert: there is no one all-encompassing community that institutions of higher learning can approach with a single, unified message).

We also introduce our readers to a marital metaphor we will employ to describe the most desirable type of relationship that should be developed and maintained between campuses and the communities they are designed to serve. Marriages are thought to be most satisfying and stable—termed "harmonious relationships"—when partners are actively making efforts to meet each other's needs in ways that create a sense of overall comfort. On the other hand, marital partners find themselves in more difficult circumstances when one or both spouses are displaying less effort in maintaining the relationship and/or when those efforts are counterproductively creating greater degrees of discomfort. Sounding a similar note, we assert that universities will regain the high ground only when it is certain that the public at large is experiencing a more harmonious relationship with its land-grant institutions. Here we mean to say that the efforts undertaken by each university must generate a sense of reassurance that the immediate interests of different communities are being served in tandem with those activities being recognized as vital to the future well-being of those communities.

This primary orientation toward meeting the needs of communities rests on the decisive determination that land-grant institutions must position themselves as standing for distinctly different values than all other universities, both public and private. In higher education, there has been a long-standing drive to make institutions more homogenized. We believe that exactly the opposite should be the case, in large part because we know that the strength of the American higher educational system historically has rested on its diversity. For that reason, we are aggressive in insisting that the march toward becoming more fiercely land-grant in orientation coincides with the adoption of a servant leadership mentality on campus—in essence, trumpeting the cause of the servant university, or the people's university, if you will—as we explain in more detail in chapter 1.

## Land-Grant Born and Raised

Stephen Gavazzi has spent his entire adult life either studying at or working for a land-grant institution. He was an undergraduate student at Pennsylvania State University, received his master's degree and PhD from the University of Connecticut, and has been a faculty member for the past 27 years at The Ohio State University. At each point in his life, the land-grant mission and traditions have affected him in a variety of different ways.

Gavazzi came into this world slightly more than 24 hours before the bicentennial year of the 1862 Morrill Land-Grant Act. He was born in State College, Pennsylvania, while his father, John, was completing his master's degree in Penn State's school psychology program. John Gavazzi was the first person in his family to obtain a college degree, graduating from what was then Wilkes College (now Wilkes University) in Northeast Pennsylvania. A Korean War veteran, John Gavazzi used the GI Bill to support his undergraduate work. His entrance into a graduate program at Penn State as a man of very modest means (and with his first child on the way), however, occurred only because he had access to an affordable higher education made possible by his home state's land-grant institution.

As a legacy to this family history, Stephen Gavazzi entered Penn State with aspirations to become a psychologist like his father. As common with other land-grant programs in the social sciences, Penn State faculty members in the psychology department strongly suggested that their students become involved in community-based volunteer efforts. Gavazzi was given the opportunity to serve as a crisis intervention worker in a suicide prevention clinic, providing him with a set of experiences in the mental health realm which would forever change his life plans. Most specifically, his exposure to clients desperate to end their lives as a reaction to intimate relationship difficulties and family problems firmed his resolve to become a marriage and family therapist.

As a result, Gavazzi entered the master's program in marriage and family therapy at the University of Connecticut immediately upon graduation from Penn State. This graduate program demanded that students involve themselves in two separate internships—one on campus and one in the community—as marriage and family therapy interns. There were consistent and clearly articulated expectations communicated to students about giving back to the communities that supported the university and its programs through their tax dollars. Therefore, Gavazzi gave nary a second thought to the fact that all this work was unpaid. It was what students at land-grant institutions did, plain and simple.

Fortunately, what comes around usually goes around in the land-grant world, at least during the time covered by Gavazzi's doctoral program. His dissertation project, which focused on community-based mental health issues, was supported in part by a modest research grant made possible through the Hatch Act. Discussed in more detail in chapter 2 of this book, this congressional appropriation (originally formulated in 1887) was designed to support research efforts undertaken by land-grant institutions. Without access to this sort of funding, Gavazzi's dissertation study would not have been able to be implemented at the same level of empirical sophistication.

As a long-time faculty member at Ohio State, where he was hired immediately after graduating from UConn, Gavazzi established a long track record of empirical work spun off of that funded dissertation work. His research program mainly examined the relation between family issues and child and adolescent behavioral problems, results he used to create prevention and intervention initiatives for use in clinically based work. This sort of applied research is, as is discussed more extensively in chapters 3 and 5 of this book, one of the hallmarks of a land-grant faculty member.

Even more integrally linked to the land-grant mission was the set of experiences he acquired as the result of the six and a half years he spent as the dean and director of Ohio State's Mansfield regional campus. During a period when admission to the Columbus campus had become increasingly selective, Ohio State's regional campuses continued to operate as open enrollment facilities. By design, these campuses were providing access to affordable educational opportunities for all of Ohio's citizens, regardless of their prior level of preparation.

This last point deserves more attention. Gavazzi worked with countless numbers of students who, but for the Mansfield regional campus, would never have been able to obtain a college degree. Ten different degrees were offered that could be finished completely on the Mansfield regional campus, something that was particularly attractive to those students who were place-bound in that North Central Ohio geographic region. Further, tuition was set at two-thirds the cost of the Columbus campus, making the regional campuses an attractive alternative for those students who were more financially challenged. And with a year's worth of modest success (30 credit hours and a 2.0 grade point average or better), students from the regional campuses also earned the right to transfer to the Columbus campus and complete any of the degree programs offered there.

Both of your authors believe that the most noble hallmark of the land-grant university is its ability to educate the "sons and daughters of toil," comparable wording to that used in describing those offspring of working-class parents who were supposed to benefit most from the 1862 Morrill Act. Disappointingly, those were not the typical students being educated on Ohio State's Columbus campus by the second decade of the twenty-first century. As it turns out, the family income levels of four out of every five incoming freshmen admitted to the main campus were at or above the national median. Compare this to the Mansfield regional campus, where almost 50% of their first-year students were eligible for Federal Pell Grants, a form of financial aid that is used as one of the most common markers of lower family income levels.

The drive toward greater selectivity on the main campus in Columbus was understandable within the context of the university's desire to increase its stature in national rankings, among other things. More will be said about the pursuit of ever-higher placement in these standings in chapter 3. However, for present purposes this meant that the responsibility for creating and maintaining access to an affordable education for those sons and daughters of toil was shifted largely to the regional campuses of this specific university. As a result, Gavazzi became more and more convinced that Ohio State's land-grant mission was most alive and well in Mansfield and on the other smaller campuses. This only served to increase his desire to shine a spotlight on the need for land-grant institutions to be more mindful of their original purpose and attentive to their intended audience.

## Once upon a Land-Grant

E. Gordon Gee felt the distinct privilege of growing up in rural America, on the eastern border of the state of Utah in a small town named Vernal. At that time, it was the largest city between Salt Lake City and Denver, a vast distance if one measures by cities in the East. As he was growing up, Gee had no access to a television. Vernal did not have a movie theater, and so his time was spent reading, listening to a Clear Channel radio station out of Salt Lake City, being heavily involved in the Boy Scouts of America, and being equally involved as a member of 4-H. So, his roots are, of the era, typically land-grant—a small-town boy in rural America exposed to only two opportunities to explore the wider world: through Scouting and 4-H.

When Gee went to the University of Utah as an undergraduate, he discovered a whole other life in a larger city where many of his fellow students had been exposed to neither small towns nor rural life. Although he acclimated well, what he came to realize was that the value system of urban America was not always reflective of the value system that he found in his hometown and among his family and friends. That value system was one of patriotism, spiritual commitment, love of family, and belief in community. And it was also all about community building.

Gee had no idea that the Extension agents and 4-H agents and 4-H volunteers with which he regularly had contact were a part of the land-grant history and mission. All he knew was that these were his friends and neighbors, members of his church, and people with whom he went to school. And he experienced them as good people who cared about each other. They had a solidity among themselves that he had rarely experienced since.

Gee left the University of Utah and went into the wider world, first having completed a mission for the Mormon Church in Germany. He was educated in the East at Columbia University and then worked for the federal court system and ultimately for the US Supreme Court and its chief justice. Gee spent time at some of America's most prestigious law firms, and though he found all these extraordinary opportunities both exciting and fulfilling, he never found them totally connecting with his land-grant roots and his understanding of community building.

After serving as associate dean of the Law School at Brigham Young University, Gee was named dean of the Law School at West Virginia University, and shortly thereafter he was named president. It was at that moment that he truly discovered the power of the land-grant university. Almost immediately,

Gee set out to learn about the state through his university's eyes and ears, that is, through contact with the Extension faculty who were assigned to each of the 55 counties constituting West Virginia. He quickly learned that West Virginia was one of the cradles of both 4-H and Cooperative Extension Services, seen especially in the operation of Jackson's Mill, one of the nation's truly remarkable centers for 4-H.

Gee left West Virginia for the presidency at the University of Colorado, wanting to do many of the same things in terms of community building. Unfortunately for Gee, Colorado State was the land-grant institution, and they had abilities to connect and contribute way beyond those of the University of Colorado. Whereas Colorado State was beloved, Gee thought, the University of Colorado was merely tolerated. Finally, seeking to rekindle a spirit of support for the University of Colorado, Gee aligned himself with the president of Colorado State University, traveling the state together to tell a common story. Even then, he thought that the land-grant narrative was more powerful, and it was always better received.

The essence of the land-grant mission and the power of the land-grant university were truly clarified for Gee when he went to The Ohio State University as president in 1990. There were 88 counties in the state, all loaded with Extension faculty and programs. Gee believed that this presented an enormous set of opportunities to see the good work of the university in every corner of the state and to feel its power reverberate through rural and urban communities alike.

Gee then made the decision to join the Ivy League by becoming president of Brown University, a place he found at once to be a wonderful, intellectually lively liberal arts institution. Brown is located in Providence, Rhode Island, but as far as the university was concerned, Gee thought it could have resided in Keokuk, Iowa. When he gave his opening press conference, he stated that he believed that private universities ought to be in the public service. Gee was shocked by the resulting criticism he received for trying to change the image of the university into that of a public institution.

Gee eventually resigned himself to the belief that the mantra of the private university was isolationism, arrogance, and self-engagement. At first, he thought that it was an artifact of being at Brown, but his next stint at Vanderbilt felt much the same. Nashville, Tennessee, in the year 2000 had a clear fault line in its body politic. The music community, largely characterized as country music, stood apart from the community of solid southern families. Indeed, these two worlds lived in different parts of the city, and they were philosophically distinct from each other. Gee did a great deal of work to try to bring them together. However, the private institution of Vanderbilt was focused on ratings, rankings, and significant achievements conforming to the standards of *U.S. News and World Report* and other such entities.

So, one fine morning Gee woke up and asked himself, "Why in the world am I at Vanderbilt?" It wasn't as if he was miserable. He truly enjoyed his work, the people in the community, and his board, and he was the highest-paid university president in the country at that time. And yet, as he would think about his life, he realized there was a hole, framed by a question as to why he was doing what he was doing at Vanderbilt. Because Gee was never able to adequately answer that question, he found himself agreeing to return to Ohio State in 2007, and he immediately reconnected with the public university, the land-grant tradition, and the power of community building. He felt, again, a life of purpose, largely because he saw the power of the university to make a difference in people's lives.

And now the circle of presidencies is complete in the life of E. Gordon Gee. For the past three years, Gee has served again as the president of West Virginia University. Having returned, he has come to recognize that, if possible, West Virginia has an even stronger land-grant tradition than does Ohio State. The university is particularly important to a state that has immense economic challenges. To thrive, Gee believes that the state must change the arc of its existence and the culture surrounding its communities. In this instance, he insists that the university is and must be the driving force for improving the quality of the average citizen's life, in large part because of the rural nature of the state and the fact that the university is its most visible and powerful entity. So as Gee wakes up in the morning now, he knows his purpose, and he knows his responsibility. He feels the state and its people calling for the university to be both wise and good. Indeed, this university, this land-grant university, is the people's servant.

## What Lies Ahead in This Book

Chapter 1 explains the study we conducted regarding the strengths, weaknesses, opportunities, and threats that land-grant universities faced as they attempted to meet the needs of the communities they were designed to serve. Here we provide details of our interviews with 27 presidents and chancellors of the 1862 land-grant institutions. We then describe the political context of the 2016 US presidential election, which took place amid these interviews. Politically oriented comments made by the senior administrators we interviewed at that time, along with campus unrest around free speech issues, led us to an exploration of the voting patterns of citizens living on and near land-grant university campuses. We report on the left-leaning skew of many of these campuses across the nation as a prelude to our discussion of the importance of building harmonious campus–community relationships across the political spectrum. This chapter ends with our call for land-grant institutions to adopt the mantle of the "servant university"—of the people's university, if you will—establishing a context and tone defined by stewardship and sacrifice.

In chapter 2, we provide a brief and concise narrative about how the land-grant universities were created, as well as how these institutions of higher learning developed over time. The centerpiece of this narrative is the notion of a covenant, a bilateral bond that exists between land-grant institutions and the communities they were designed to serve. Discussion of the Morrill Acts of 1862 and 1890, the Hatch Act of 1887, and the Smith-Lever Act of 1914 set the backdrop for a historical recitation of the land-grant university's tripartite mission of teaching, research, and service. This is followed by an examination of more recent efforts to codify community engagement, including the work of the Kellogg Commission on the Future of State and Land-Grant Universities, the Carnegie Foundation for the Advancement of Teaching Classification for Community Engagement, and the Innovation and Economic Prosperity Universities Designation developed by the Association of Public and Land-Grant Universities (APLU).

Chapter 3 covers the responses given by the 27 presidents and chancellors of the 1862 US land-grant universities who participated in semi-structured interviews by answering questions about the various strengths, weaknesses, opportunities, and threats faced by land-grant institutions as their representatives attempted to meet the needs of community stakeholders. The bulk of this chapter involves our coverage of the seven main themes that emerged from our analysis of the qualitative data generated from the presidents' and chancellors' responses to our interview questions. These themes include concerns about funding declines versus the need to create efficiencies, striving for research prowess versus teaching and service excellence, pursuing knowledge for knowledge's sake versus a more applied focus to research, the focus on rankings versus an emphasis on access and affordability, meeting the needs of rural communities versus the needs of a more urbanized America, the global reach of universities versus closer-to-home impact, and assessing the benefits of higher education versus the devaluation of a college diploma.

In chapter 4, we begin by focusing specifically on the impact that governing board members, elected officials, and accrediting bodies have on the land-grant institution's ability to meet the needs of communities. Overall, the presidents and chancellors we interviewed portrayed governing board members as struggling to understand the value of higher education in the context of the land-grant mission. Other comments made by these senior administrators touched on some of the themes that emerged in chapter 3, including the portrayal of governing board members as being focused on issues related to the financial stresses and strains of universities, as well as being more heavily invested in research-related activities. Also, when board members were perceived to be more knowledgeable about rural and agricultural issues, they were thought to be more sensitive to the needs of communities. We go on to discuss other levels of governance in this chapter, including the impact of state legislators and policymakers, as well as the influence of higher education accreditation bodies.

Chapter 5 focuses attention on the critical role that faculty members play in meeting the needs of communities. Faculty efforts to involve themselves in outreach and engagement activities are the predominant subject matter that emerges from the comments made by the presidents and chancellors we interviewed, and there was large-scale acknowledgment that the land-grant spirit was alive and well in much of this work. At the same time, however, we also note that many of these senior leaders were openly concerned about the unequal distribution of these efforts across the different disciplines of the university. Further, we provide a specific examination of issues surrounding promotion and tenure, which as often as not create complexity for faculty members who become heavily engaged in outreach and engagement activities. All of this sets the stage for a discussion of the evolving nature of the land-grant university's tripartite mission of teaching, research, and service as carried out by faculty members.

In chapter 6, we focus attention on the role students play in meeting the needs of communities. The viewpoints of presidents and chancellors regarding student involvement largely concentrate on service-learning and civic engagement activities. Student activism and the promotion of democratic ideals also were mentioned by the senior administrators we interviewed, and so are discussed accordingly.

In chapter 7, we provide a thorough interpretation of the interview data through the lens of our marital metaphor and the servant university framework, and then we offer a platform for the creation of a compelling narrative about the role of land-grant universities in terms of their orientation toward meeting the needs of various community constituencies. As we synthesize the material covered in this book, we offer ideas we believe can contribute to a reboot of Mr. Lincoln's universities for the remainder of this century and beyond. Because we believe so strongly that our students need to be as knowledgeable about the land-grant mission as they are about every other subject matter our universities offer in their general education curricula, we also propose a course that can routinely be offered to our students as one intentional way of building the land-grant advocates and leaders of the twenty-first century.

## In Closing: Standing on the Shoulders of Giants

In closing the introductory section of this book, we wish to explicitly acknowledge the scholarship on land-grant institutions which has preceded our own writing, much of which has formed the very foundation of our interpretation of the interview material we gathered. We begin by noting our reliance on one of the most recently published works on land-grant institutions, *The Modern Land-Grant University*, edited by Robert Sternberg,[1] as well as his follow-up book entitled *What Universities Can Be*.[2] A second edited volume that served as a primary resource for us was Daniel M. Fogel and Elizabeth Malson-Huddle's book *Precipice or Crossroads?*, published in 2012 as part of the nation's sesquicentennial celebration of the Land-Grant Act.[3]

There are many other splendid works on land-grant institutions and issues that must be mentioned here as well, even if they received less of our direct attention. This includes *The Land-Grant Colleges and the Reshaping of American Higher Education*, edited by Roger Geiger and Nathan Sorber, a volume that provides an extensive historical perspective on the land-grant university's development over time.[4] Two volumes edited by Alan Marcus, entitled *Science and Service* and *Service as Mandate*, also provide us with rather extensive historical information about American land-grant institutions.[5] Our interest in engagement activities compels us to include reference to *Engaging Campus and Community*, edited by Scott Peters and colleagues, although it more broadly addresses all public institutions of higher learning.[6] Finally, no bibliography on the land-grant mission would be complete without mention of George McDowell's *Land-Grant Universities and Extension into the 21st Century*, a book that provides a more focused examination of the role played by Cooperative Extension Services in American society.[7]

Further, there are several books on more general higher education issues which also deserve honorable mention here. This includes the excellent *Higher Education for the Public Good* volume edited by Adrianna Kezar, Tony Chambers, and John Burkhardt, whose chapters are cited extensively throughout our writing, and whose title became our subtitle.[8] We also relied heavily on the contents of the most recent editions of two books published by Johns Hopkins University Press. Readers undoubtedly will recognize how we were influenced both by the fourth edition of *American Higher Education in the Twenty-First Century*, edited by Michael Bastedo, Philip Altbach, and Patricia Gumport, and by the second edition of *The States and Public Higher Education Policy*, edited by Donald Heller.[9]

We are grateful to have stood on the shoulders of these scholarly giants as we have peered into the land-grant horizon. Our attempt to build on this accumulated knowledge base regarding land-grant institutions, however, coincides with our determination also to forge a new path forward that might seem a bit less well traveled. It is our hope, therefore, that we will have balanced what is well known about land-grant institutions with some tantalizing new thoughts that might not be readily located in the existing literature.

# The Land-Grant Study, Campus–Community Relationships, and the Servant University

Studying the strengths, weaknesses, opportunities, and threats facing land-grant institutions as they attempted to meet the needs of the communities they were designed to serve was thought to be the natural extension of a comprehensive conversation that had taken place between Gavazzi and Gee in early 2016. At that time, Gavazzi was writing a book on campus–community (i.e., town–gown) relationships,[1] and he had consulted Gee to gain feedback on some themes that had been developed out of interviews conducted with university presidents and city managers. That consultation had resulted in an entire chapter's worth of commentary, much of it focused on the development of "intentional leadership" within town–gown relationships, a viewpoint that placed primary emphasis on the critical role that senior university and municipal leaders play in establishing and maintaining healthy campus–community connections.

Many of the issues raised in that specific chapter seemed to be predicated on the type of university in question, that is, whether it was a larger or smaller campus, whether it was situated in a larger or smaller municipality, and, perhaps most importantly, whether it was a public or private institution. These qualifiers created a dialogue that went far beyond the confines of the campus–community chapter. One particularly poignant discussion point was our shared concern that the special role that land-grant institutions played in community engagement efforts was becoming forgotten, or at the very least was being diluted in the words and actions of other public institutions of higher learning.

We began to wonder what other land-grant presidents and chancellors were thinking when it came to community engagement efforts. Did these higher education leaders believe that their universities were meeting the needs of their community stakeholders? Were they prioritizing community engagement efforts, or instead were they downplaying such pursuits in favor of other activities? We certainly had some clues about the viewpoints of some senior administrators of land-grant institutions of higher learning, thanks in large part to the written contributions these individuals were making to the literature (much of which is reviewed in chaps. 2 and 3). What we felt we needed, however, was a more systematic understanding of the community engagement zeitgeist among land-grant presidents and chancellors.

This chapter begins with a description of the study we conducted investigating the various strengths, weaknesses, opportunities, and threats that land-grant universities were facing as they attempted to meet the needs of the communities they were designed to serve. The backbone of this study included the interviews we facilitated with 27 presidents and chancellors of the 1862 land-grant institutions in the continental United States. Because we carried out this study amid the 2016 US presidential election, we also examine the political context in which land-grant universities find themselves at present. We end the chapter with a discussion of campus–community relationships and an exploration of servant leadership concepts.

## The Strengths, Weaknesses, Opportunities, and Threats (SWOT) Analysis

A research proposal was developed that called for university presidents and chancellors of land-grant institutions to be recruited for participation in a semi-structured interview designed to capture information about the strengths, weaknesses, opportunities, and threats faced by modern-day land-grant universities. Special emphasis was placed on how well these institutions of higher learning were carrying out the land-grant mission of meeting the needs of the communities they were designed to serve. The research proposal was submitted to The Ohio State University's institutional review board in March 2016 and approved (determined exempt) later that month.

As the next step in this process, a letter from West Virginia University president E. Gordon Gee and Ohio State University president Michael V. Drake was sent to all 1862 and 1890 land-grant presidents and chancellors on August 1, 2016. This correspondence announced the launch of a joint Ohio State University–West Virginia University research project designed to create important information on the strengths, weaknesses, opportunities, and threats faced by institutions of higher learning as they attempted to fulfill their land-grant mission. The letter further noted that this empirical work would focus most specifically on how well the land-grant institutions were serving as regionalized institutions of learning in partnership with the communities to be served by those universities.

Two weeks later, an email was sent directly to these land-grant presidents and chancellors by Gavazzi with an invitation to participate in a telephone interview on this subject matter. A total of 27 presidents and chancellors from the 1862 land-grant institutions agreed to participate in the research project, and these representatives were subsequently interviewed by Gavazzi between August 16, 2016, and January 31, 2017. It is important to note that the respondents only included senior administrators representing the 1862 land-grant universities within the continental United States. Therefore, Alaska, Hawaii, Puerto Rico, the Virgin Islands, and the four land-grant institutions of the Pacific Basin were not represented in this sample, nor was the University of the District of Columbia. Additionally, two presidents from the 1890 land-grant institutions agreed to participate in the research project, and these senior administrators were interviewed by telephone as well. The extremely small sample size prohibited the use of data from the latter interviews in the study reported in this book.

The interview data from the 27 presidents and chancellors included in the present study thus represented just over half (56%) of the 1862 land-grant institutions in the continental United States. There was comparatively uniform distribution of these senior administrators across the country. Using US Census Region and Division categories, the greatest proportional representation of geographic areas was found in the 6 out of 9 states (67%) contained in the Northeast Region (New England and Middle Atlantic), followed by the 7 out of 11 (64%) West Region states (Mountain and Pacific), then the 7 out of 12 (58%) states from the Midwest Region (East North Central and West North Central), and finally the 7 out of 16 (44%) states contained in the South Region (South Atlantic, East South Central, and West South Central).

The presidents and chancellors who participated in our interviews were presented with four basic questions that followed the SWOT analysis format:

1. When it comes to the land-grant mission of serving the needs of communities, what do you believe are the areas in which land-grant universities currently are displaying the greatest strengths?
2. When it comes to the land-grant mission of serving the needs of communities, what do you believe are the areas in which land-grant universities currently are displaying the greatest weaknesses?
3. When you think about the land-grant mission of the future, what do you believe are the most important new opportunities for land-grant universities to meet the needs of communities?
4. When you think about the land-grant mission of the future, what do you believe are the most important new threats faced by land-grant universities as they attempt to meet the needs of communities?

In addition, the presidents were asked to comment on the impact that governing board members have on how well land-grant universities meet the needs of communities as part of the land-grant mission, to offer their thoughts on the impact that faculty members have on how well land-grant universities meet the needs of communities as part of the land-grant mission, and to express their opinions regarding the impact that students have on how well land-grant universities meet the needs of communities as part of the land-grant mission. These last three questions form the basis for the fourth, fifth, and sixth chapters of this book.

## The Context of the 2016 US Presidential Election

The fact that the interviews for this study took place between August 2016 and January 2017 meant that we were in contact with land-grant presidents and chancellors just prior to and in the immediate aftermath of the 2016 US presidential election. A total of 14 interviews (52%) were conducted before November 8, 2016, and those senior administrators typically made comments about the potential consequences of the looming Election Day as small talk either before or following the semi-structured interview questions. In the remaining 13 interviews (48%) that were conducted after the vote, however, the presidents and chancellors were embedding commentary about the electoral results directly into their responses to the SWOT questions. A few of those reactions were rather pessimistic and anxious about the results bringing potential harm to the country more generally and/or institutions of higher education more specifically. Most of the other comments were more circum-spect, however, and hinted at the possible role that land-grant universities might play in sorting out the aftermath. Here is an example:

> One of our greatest challenges right now is helping society deal with the am-biguity that emerged as a function of the last election. This concerns the val-ues and ethics and related behaviors displayed by both candidates from both parties. I think we have a role to play in helping society deal with the after-math of this election. Things were so opaque and agendas so hidden, and so much confusion was generated from the enormous range of behaviors dis-played by the candidates. And then to see how people were put into boxes because of their geographic location led to even more confusion. And yet people don't really fit so neatly into those kinds of boxes. Certainly, land-grant institutions have a role to play in disentangling this confusion. (presi-dent/chancellor pers. comm.)

At first glance, it might seem perfectly natural for universities—land-grant and otherwise—to seize on the opportunity to serve as "neutral ground" in discussions surrounding the politics of the day. In fact, as we shall see in the next chapter, one of the key indicators used to evaluate the public university's contribution to the greater good of communities is the provision of a nonjudg-mental context for debates about pressing social, economic, and political issues.[2] Alas, contemporary perceptions of college and university cam-puses painted a stereotypical portrait of faculty, students, and administra-tors which depicted them as left-leaning at best and, at worst, so invested in political correctness that they were in danger of failing to uphold their own treasured "academic freedom" in conversations among themselves. In the lat-ter case, it would be difficult to imagine a situation where the land-grant university would be able to facilitate even-handed debates about politically charged issues among members of the public at large who find themselves on radically different sides of various issues. Our great concern about these per-ceptions and their ramifications drove us to examine the political context of our interviews in more detail.

## The Great Divide, Middle America, Flyover Country, etc.

A recent op-ed article penned by Michael Barone provided us with an inter-esting framework in which to consider the highly charged politics that have created such sharp divisions among American citizens as of late.[3] The two sides depicted by Barone—the capital versus the countryside—approximate the voting blocs for the Democratic and Republican candidates, respectively. One the one hand, the "capital" is associated with metropolitan areas, with the coasts, with cultural elites, with greater educational levels, and with immigrants and minorities. The "countryside," in contrast, represents the heartland of the country, which is decidedly more rural, less educated, and less culturally and ethnically diverse.

Geographically, the divide fits neatly into a rural versus urban distinction. In strictly political terms, this might be described in "red" versus "blue" terminology. Regardless of the words we use to label these opposite ends of the spectrum, this polarization is real and has had unquestionable consequences for America. As but one example, the 2016 presidential election has been described as "the year that the white rural voter roared."[4] These are not times for the faint of heart.

We believe that the mentality and thus the political leanings of the majority of those who inhabit our nation's college campuses are thought to be associated with the "capital" variety of voters, a long-standing belief that has contributed to suspicion and angst about the left-slanted viewpoints being used to teach students inside of our American institutions of higher learning. In general, this perception serves to underscore the notion that institutions of higher learning are not seen as being in alignment with the "countryside" point of view. In Middle America, or Flyover Country, or whatever your favorite euphemism is for folks on the "other side" of the Great Divide, universities have come to be portrayed as "that's not me" by those individuals—so much so, in fact, that one 2017 Pew Research Center poll indicated sharpening divisions among Americans regarding the value of our colleges and universities, with Republicans expressing decidedly more negative views in comparison to their Democratic counterparts.[5]

Anything that contributes to the solidification of an "us versus them" mentality is bad enough. By early 2017, however, things seemed to get much worse than that. A series of protests on college campuses as widely varied geographically as the University of California at Berkeley and Middlebury College in Vermont led to riots and the eventual cancellation of speeches that were to be given by high-profile speakers thought to represent contrarian (one might more accurately label "countryside") viewpoints. Further fanning the flames was an op-ed article in the *New York Times* penned around the same time by a sitting provost from New York University, who asserted that the protests behind the canceled speeches were part of a "public good" being rendered by university students.[6] Said differently, these students were thought to be saving people the trouble of having to listen to inferior points of view.

Swiftly and predictably, condemnation of these restrictions on free speech followed. Blame was laid squarely at the feet of university leaders, who were portrayed as being incapable of upholding the First Amendment on their own campuses. The consternation was so great that, to cite but one example, calls were made to provide court-enforced penalties for this failure, which would include the loss of federal research dollars and other sources of government funding.[7] Additional legislation was being introduced in some states to create free speech zones and punish students who disrupt campus speakers, among other actions under consideration.[8]

The tragic events of August 9, 2017, on the Charlottesville campus of the University of Virginia further complicated these issues. A series of violent confrontations between white nationalist demonstrators and counterprotesters were followed by the death of one woman and the injury of scores of others when a car was intentionally driven into the crowd that had gathered.[9] As a result, questions about free speech now had to be balanced against issues concerning the safety and well-being of campus and community residents alike. Numerous senior administrators—including those at some of the nation's prominent land-grant universities—took preemptive steps to avoid the possibility of future clashes occurring at their universities by canceling upcoming events, actions that triggered another round of denunciations about the restriction of free speech on college campuses.[10]

Our point here is straightforward. This is a difficult balancing act at best. And yet, we wish to note that colleges and universities are doing themselves no favors by taking actions (and, in other cases, failing to act) that unwittingly (or otherwise) alienate portions of the US population. While we would agree with the general sentiment that university leaders often are placed in difficult situations when issues of free speech emerge on campuses,[11] we would argue simultaneously that not enough is being done proactively to address the communal need for "neutral ground," or what has been described by the Kellogg Commission (discussed in more detail in our second chapter) as "academic neutrality" in our engagement efforts with community members.[12]

This leads directly to our initial declaration of what we mean by "community" when we discuss the land-grant mission of meeting the needs of communities. Simply put, we do not believe that there are many instances where an effort—any effort—undertaken by a social institution fully resonates with a single unified community in America right now. Instead, we believe that we live in a multiverse of communities, albeit ones that tend to cluster around one of two lodestars: capital and countryside. We had the opportunity to discuss the ramifications of this situation with Michael Barone himself, who began by pointing us to some cartographical work done by Ryne Rohla, a land-grant graduate student at Washington State University.[13] Discussing Rohla's work, Barone stated,

> He produced precinct maps for every state across the country, indicating whether the precinct went for Hillary Clinton or Donald Trump. And what that map shows is that universities are little islands of Clinton supporters, surrounded by virtual seas of Trump supporters. (pers. comm., May 8, 2017)

Barone went on to indicate that this sort of mapping displays the enormous challenges faced by colleges and universities in today's political climate. It would be economic suicide, Barone noted, for universities to continue to be seen by the public at large as politically slanted so heavily toward the left (capital), especially in states where so many of their prospective students hail from vicinities that lean rightward (countryside).

In addition to providing information about general tendencies of voters, Rohla also had disaggregated the 2016 presidential election data to more specifically examine the liberal and conservative tendencies of college and university neighborhoods.[14] In general, this work indicated that those communities immediately surrounding college campuses (within a one-mile radius) displayed a strong tendency to have voted Democratic. One important point here, however, is that not all campuses and their host communities "leaned left." Religiously oriented institutions of higher learning and those located in the South and the Midwest tended to display more conservative allegiances, for instance. Furthermore, those campuses that did skew leftward as often as not existed in a "bubble" within their home county, that is, while the campus voted heavily Democratic, the remainder of the county displayed either more balanced or even rightward tendencies.

We were curious about the specific voting patterns of land-grant institutions and their host communities, so we requested assistance from Rohla, who was kind enough to oblige and constructed a database for our use. Table 1 provides readers with the precinct data of voters within a one-mile radius of the main campuses of each of the 1862 land-grant universities except for the University of California (dealt with separately below). Rohla defined liberal voters as those who voted for either Clinton or Stein and conservative voters as those who voted for Trump, Johnson, McMullin, or Castle. Similar to Rohla's earlier findings on colleges and universities in general, the majority (36, or 77%) of the 47 land-grant campuses skewed leftward by double-digit percentages. In contrast, eight universities (Auburn, Clemson, Mississippi State, North Dakota State, Oklahoma State, South Dakota State, Texas A&M, and Utah State) skewed rightward, and three universities (Idaho, Wyoming, and West Virginia) all leaned leftward by only single-digit percentages. For comparison purposes, we calculated the average left-right (L-R) skew for the entire group to be 30.8%.

Table 2 allows readers to zoom out to the countywide election results. The counties of all eight of the universities that skewed right in the one-mile radius discussed in the preceding paragraphs skewed Republican as well, although in three cases (Auburn, Mississippi State, South Dakota State) it was a lower-percentage skew to the right. The three universities that leaned Democratic by single digits in the one-mile radius all skewed rightward at the county level, although in the case of the county containing the University of Idaho it was only a single-digit skew. Further, there were 10 additional counties containing land-grant universities which skewed rightward. Three of these counties skewed Republican in double digits (the home counties of Purdue, Maine, and Tennessee), while the remaining seven skewed rightward by single digits (the home counties of Colorado State, Kansas State, Montana, Nebraska, Nevada, Virginia Tech, and Washington State). We calculated the average L-R skew for the entire group to be only 4.0%, a reduction of 26.8% from the one-mile radius average reported above.

This brings us to the University of California system, which does not have a defined "main campus." Instead, there are 10 campuses throughout the state which maintain separate but equal status as comprehensive land-grant universities. Rohla was able to access voter precinct data from eight of the California campuses (Berkeley, Davis, Irvine, UCLA, Riverside, San Diego, Santa Barbara, and Santa Cruz) and their host communities (the UC Merced and UC San Francisco data were not accessible). As readers might expect, these California campuses trended strongly leftward in the 2016 presidential election. We calculated the average L-R skew for the eight universities to be 64.3%, more than double the skew of the other 47 land-grant universities. However, even in the California system we see a major reduction in skew when we compare the one-mile radius data with the countywide results. We calculated the host county skew to average 32.8%, or roughly half of the

TABLE 1
*Precinct data of election results within one mile of campus (in percentages)*

| University | Trump | Clinton | Johnson | McMullin | Stein | Castle | L-R |
|---|---|---|---|---|---|---|---|
| Auburn University | 68.8 | 27.7 | 2.4 | 0.0 | 0.5 | 0.0 | −43.0 |
| Clemson University | 47.7 | 42.2 | 4.7 | 2.1 | 1.1 | 0.3 | −11.4 |
| Colorado State University | 19.5 | 69.5 | 6.5 | 0.8 | 3.0 | 0.0 | 45.4 |
| Cornell University | 9.1 | 84.0 | 2.4 | 0.0 | 2.8 | 0.0 | 75.3 |
| Iowa State University | 31.0 | 57.5 | 6.4 | 2.0 | 1.2 | 0.2 | 19.2 |
| Kansas State University | 32.9 | 55.6 | 7.9 | 1.1 | 2.5 | 0.1 | 16.1 |
| Louisiana State University | 24.5 | 67.1 | 4.6 | 1.0 | 2.3 | 0.1 | 39.2 |
| Michigan State University | 24.1 | 69.5 | 3.7 | 0.0 | 1.4 | 0.2 | 42.9 |
| Mississippi State University | 47.5 | 47.7 | 3.2 | 0.0 | 0.7 | 0.7 | −3.0 |
| Montana State University | 29.8 | 58.9 | 8.3 | 0.0 | 2.7 | 0.0 | 23.6 |
| New Mexico State University | 29.8 | 55.3 | 10.9 | 1.0 | 2.2 | 0.4 | 15.5 |
| North Carolina State University | 20.8 | 72.7 | 4.6 | 0.0 | 0.0 | 0.0 | 47.3 |
| North Dakota State University | 42.4 | 43.9 | 8.3 | 0.0 | 2.2 | 0.5 | −5.0 |
| Ohio State University | 18.2 | 75.2 | 4.6 | 0.0 | 1.8 | 0.0 | 54.3 |
| Oklahoma State University | 43.9 | 45.0 | 11.1 | 0.0 | 0.0 | 0.0 | −10.1 |
| Oregon State University | 15.9 | 71.7 | 5.8 | 0.0 | 3.5 | 0.0 | 53.5 |
| Pennsylvania State University | 29.1 | 63.9 | 4.2 | 0.0 | 1.3 | 0.2 | 31.6 |
| Purdue University | 34.0 | 56.3 | 7.2 | 0.0 | 0.0 | 0.0 | 15.2 |
| Rutgers University– New Brunswick | 14.8 | 80.7 | 1.5 | 0.0 | 1.8 | 0.1 | 66.2 |
| South Dakota State University | 50.9 | 38.2 | 9.6 | 0.0 | 0.0 | 1.3 | −23.5 |
| Texas A&M–College Station | 45.0 | 43.8 | 8.2 | 0.0 | 1.2 | 0.0 | −8.2 |
| University of Arizona | 15.4 | 77.2 | 3.4 | 0.0 | 2.7 | 0.0 | 61.1 |
| University of Connecticut | 19.3 | 74.3 | 4.1 | 0.2 | 2.1 | 0.0 | 52.8 |
| University of Delaware | 31.3 | 61.7 | 4.7 | 0.0 | 2.3 | 0.0 | 28.0 |
| University of Florida | 23.2 | 69.7 | 4.1 | 0.0 | 1.5 | 0.2 | 43.6 |
| University of Georgia | 27.8 | 66.5 | 5.8 | 0.0 | 0.0 | 0.0 | 32.9 |
| University of Idaho | 26.8 | 49.3 | 9.1 | 4.8 | 3.6 | 2.4 | 9.8 |
| University of Illinois at Urbana–Champaign | 13.4 | 79.0 | 5.0 | 0.0 | 2.6 | 0.0 | 63.2 |
| University of Kentucky | 29.0 | 62.2 | 0.0 | 0.0 | 0.0 | 0.0 | 33.2 |
| University of Maine | 32.0 | 58.9 | 6.6 | 0.3 | 2.2 | 0.0 | 22.2 |
| University of Maryland | 12.6 | 80.1 | 2.9 | 0.7 | 2.1 | 0.0 | 66.0 |
| University of Massachusetts–Amherst | 13.5 | 77.6 | 3.4 | 0.1 | 3.9 | 0.0 | 64.6 |
| University of Minnesota | 13.5 | 77.4 | 3.6 | 1.6 | 2.3 | 0.1 | 60.9 |
| University of Missouri | 27.2 | 64.6 | 5.5 | 0.0 | 2.3 | 0.4 | 33.8 |
| University of Nebraska at Lincoln | 30.3 | 60.8 | 6.0 | 0.0 | 2.9 | 0.0 | 27.5 |
| University of Nevada–Reno | 28.5 | 61.8 | 5.8 | 0.0 | 0.0 | 0.4 | 27.1 |
| University of New Hampshire | 25.4 | 67.5 | 4.7 | 0.0 | 1.2 | 0.0 | 38.6 |
| University of Rhode Island | 33.6 | 57.3 | 3.8 | 0.0 | 2.2 | 0.0 | 22.1 |
| University of Tennessee | 35.1 | 56.0 | 5.5 | 0.8 | 1.7 | 0.1 | 16.3 |
| University of Vermont | 17.7 | 70.6 | 2.6 | 0.0 | 2.8 | 0.0 | 53.0 |
| University of Wisconsin–Madison | 14.9 | 77.0 | 4.7 | 0.0 | 1.5 | 0.2 | 58.7 |
| University of Wyoming | 37.4 | 46.1 | 8.9 | 0.0 | 2.3 | 0.8 | 1.2 |
| Utah State University | 33.6 | 27.7 | 4.2 | 31.0 | 1.1 | 1.0 | −40.9 |
| Virginia Polytechnic University | 26.6 | 63.5 | 6.4 | 2.2 | 1.3 | 0.0 | 29.7 |
| Washington State University | 18.4 | 69.5 | 7.7 | 0.0 | 3.1 | 0.7 | 45.7 |
| West Virginia University | 39.2 | 51.3 | 5.6 | 0.0 | 3.2 | 0.7 | 8.9 |

*Note:* For the L-R column, positive values represent "left-leaning," whereas negative values represent "right-leaning."

## TABLE 2
### Precinct data of countywide election results (in percentages)

| University | Trump | Clinton | Johnson | McMullin | Stein | Castle | L-R | L-R Diff. |
|---|---|---|---|---|---|---|---|---|
| Auburn University | 58.5 | 35.9 | 3.4 | 0.0 | 0.6 | 0.0 | −25.4 | −17.60 |
| Clemson University | 73.9 | 21.1 | 2.4 | 1.1 | 0.7 | 0.3 | −56.0 | 44.50 |
| Colorado State University | 42.6 | 47.5 | 5.9 | 1.4 | 1.6 | 0.5 | −1.2 | 46.60 |
| Cornell University | 24.3 | 67.7 | 3.3 | 0.0 | 3.2 | 0.0 | 43.4 | 31.90 |
| Iowa State University | 38.4 | 50.7 | 6.0 | 2.1 | 1.0 | 0.3 | 5.0 | 14.20 |
| Kansas State University | 46.0 | 42.5 | 6.7 | 1.0 | 1.8 | 0.0 | −9.3 | 25.40 |
| Louisiana State University | 43.1 | 52.3 | 2.5 | 0.7 | 0.8 | 0.2 | 6.7 | 32.50 |
| Michigan State University | 33.2 | 59.9 | 4.0 | 0.0 | 1.4 | 0.4 | 23.7 | 19.20 |
| Mississippi State University | 47.3 | 48.9 | 2.6 | 0.0 | 0.6 | 0.6 | −1.0 | −2.00 |
| Montana State University | 44.2 | 45.1 | 7.5 | 0.0 | 2.0 | 0.0 | −4.7 | 28.20 |
| New Mexico State University | 35.9 | 53.7 | 7.7 | 0.8 | 1.4 | 0.2 | 10.4 | 5.10 |
| North Carolina State University | 37.2 | 57.4 | 3.7 | 0.0 | 0.0 | 0.0 | 16.5 | 30.70 |
| North Dakota State University | 49.3 | 38.8 | 7.5 | 0.0 | 1.5 | 0.5 | −17.0 | 12.00 |
| Ohio State University | 33.9 | 59.8 | 3.6 | 0.0 | 1.0 | 0.0 | 23.3 | 31.00 |
| Oklahoma State University | 60.0 | 31.7 | 8.4 | 0.0 | 0.0 | 0.0 | −36.7 | 26.60 |
| Oregon State University | 27.6 | 59.9 | 5.5 | 0.0 | 3.3 | 0.0 | 30.1 | 23.50 |
| Pennsylvania State University | 45.6 | 48.0 | 3.4 | 0.0 | 1.0 | 0.4 | −0.5 | 32.10 |
| Purdue University | 48.6 | 43.1 | 6.3 | 0.0 | 0.0 | 0.0 | −11.8 | 27.00 |
| Rutgers University–New Brunswick | 37.4 | 58.8 | 1.7 | 0.0 | 1.1 | 0.0 | 20.7 | 45.40 |
| South Dakota State University | 53.2 | 38.5 | 7.0 | 0.0 | 0.0 | 1.4 | −23.1 | −0.50 |
| Texas A&M–College Station | 57.6 | 34.4 | 5.7 | 0.0 | 0.8 | 0.0 | −28.1 | 19.90 |
| University of Arizona | 39.7 | 53.3 | 3.7 | 0.0 | 1.5 | 0.0 | 11.3 | 49.70 |
| University of Connecticut | 44.2 | 49.7 | 4.1 | 0.0 | 1.8 | 0.0 | 3.2 | 49.60 |
| University of Delaware | 32.5 | 62.0 | 3.5 | 0.0 | 1.5 | 0.0 | 27.5 | 0.50 |
| University of Florida | 36.0 | 58.3 | 3.1 | 0.0 | 1.2 | 0.2 | 20.1 | 23.50 |
| University of Georgia | 28.0 | 65.1 | 4.4 | 0.0 | 0.0 | 0.0 | 32.7 | 0.20 |
| University of Idaho | 40.0 | 44.5 | 6.6 | 3.8 | 2.6 | 1.8 | −5.1 | 14.80 |
| University of Illinois at Urbana–Champaign | 36.4 | 54.7 | 5.0 | 0.0 | 2.0 | 0.0 | 15.3 | 47.90 |
| University of Kentucky | 41.7 | 51.2 | 3.8 | 1.9 | 1.2 | 0.0 | 4.8 | 28.30 |
| University of Maine | 51.7 | 40.8 | 5.4 | 0.3 | 1.8 | 0.0 | −14.9 | 37.10 |
| University of Maryland | 8.4 | 88.1 | 1.2 | 0.0 | 1.2 | 0.0 | 79.8 | −13.80 |
| University of Massachusetts–Amherst | 25.9 | 65.8 | 3.7 | 0.0 | 3.1 | 0.0 | 39.3 | 25.30 |
| University of Minnesota | 28.2 | 63.1 | 3.6 | 1.8 | 1.5 | 0.2 | 30.8 | 30.00 |
| University of Missouri | 43.2 | 49.0 | 5.1 | 0.0 | 1.5 | 0.7 | 1.7 | 32.10 |
| University of Nebraska at Lincoln | 45.2 | 45.4 | 5.2 | 0.0 | 1.5 | 0.0 | −3.5 | 31.00 |
| University of Nevada–Reno | 45.1 | 46.4 | 4.4 | 0.0 | 0.0 | 0.5 | −3.6 | 30.70 |
| University of New Hampshire | 42.1 | 50.6 | 4.7 | 0.0 | 1.0 | 0.0 | 4.7 | 33.90 |
| University of Rhode Island | 41.0 | 50.8 | 3.8 | 0.0 | 1.6 | 0.0 | 7.6 | 14.50 |
| University of Tennessee | 58.5 | 34.8 | 4.1 | 0.7 | 0.9 | 0.1 | −27.7 | 44.00 |
| University of Vermont | 22.3 | 65.7 | 3.0 | 0.0 | 2.2 | 0.0 | 42.6 | 10.40 |
| University of Wisconsin–Madison | 23.0 | 70.4 | 3.4 | 0.0 | 1.4 | 0.3 | 45.1 | 13.60 |
| University of Wyoming | 44.6 | 40.4 | 8.2 | 0.0 | 2.0 | 0.8 | −11.1 | 12.30 |
| Utah State University | 45.3 | 18.3 | 3.5 | 29.3 | 0.7 | 1.4 | −60.4 | 19.50 |
| Virginia Polytechnic University | 45.2 | 46.5 | 4.7 | 1.9 | 0.9 | 0.0 | −4.3 | 34.00 |
| Washington State University | 41.1 | 45.2 | 6.8 | 0.0 | 1.8 | 0.9 | −1.8 | 47.50 |
| West Virginia University | 50.1 | 40.0 | 5.0 | 0.0 | 2.2 | 0.8 | −13.7 | 22.50 |

Note: For the L-R column, positive values represent "left-leaning," whereas negative values represent "right-leaning."

campus leanings, and in two cases (UC Irvine and UC Riverside) the left-ward skew was only in single digits.

We had the opportunity to discuss these additional voting patterns with Ryne Rohla. Importantly, he shared with us the further finding that, among all schools in his database with enrollments of at least 10,000 students, the average one-mile L-R skew was 28.0% (vs. the 30.8% L-R skew for land-grant universities). In addition, Rohla noted that the overall average "bubble" difference was 21.7% (vs. the 25.1% difference in the counties containing the land-grant institutions). Reflecting on these differences, he stated,

> It definitely seems to me that land-grant universities are more liberal-leaning than your average university, but I suspect that's partially due to the lack of private and religious universities among their ranks. Interestingly, land-grant "bubble" values don't usually benefit from being located in heavily black or Hispanic pockets like most of the top non-land-grant "bubble" schools like Wichita State, Lamar, Youngstown State, Hofstra, or Syracuse, meaning that their "bubble" scores are probably more reflective of actually being in a liberal bubble than is typical. While they seem to be pretty successful in transplanting capital attitudes into the countryside, the effects do not seem to extend very far beyond their own borders. (pers. comm.)

In viewing these voting patterns, we are left with the belief that there is some credible evidence that a "bubble" of left-leaning politics exists on many (but not all) land-grant campuses. Seen in this light, we believe that the leaders of our land-grant (and other public) universities should be taking actions that clearly and unequivocally provide reassurance to the public at large that a fair and balanced approach will be taken by their campuses regarding any number of issues held dear by campus representatives and their host community brethren. For the purposes of our study, therefore, we have calibrated our observational capabilities to detect signals that certain activities undertaken by colleges and universities might play better to the "capital" crowd, whereas other actions may reverberate more clearly with the "countryside" audience. In the ensuing chapters, we will evaluate the accumulated evidence from our investigative efforts to see whether we can reject the null hypothesis that no imbalance exists between efforts to address the needs of these two distinct communities.

Let us be crystal clear here in our attitude about this issue. We believe that there is nothing quite as uniquely American as its land-grant universities. Forged during a time of great civil strife, these institutions of higher learning were instrumental in training those scientists, politicians, artists, and other community leaders who helped heal the nation and move it forward on the path to greatness. So, our expectation is that the representatives of land-grant institutions will continue to stand as neutral ground during those times in which our citizens find themselves a "house divided," with the firm conviction that the American people will best work these issues out in debates that allow all sides to be respectfully heard, fairly judged, and ultimately decided on their full merits. If we are to retain our standing as the "people's universities," we had best be perceived as being an open and inclusive place for all those people.

## The Marriage Metaphor

Gavazzi has spearheaded an emerging body of work that utilizes a marriage metaphor to describe and measure the quality of relationships between campuses and communities.[15] Borrowing from early marital research,[16] a typology was created based on the notion that the quality of the campus–community (i.e., town–gown) relationship is a function of two dimensions—effort and comfort—that together yield four town–gown relationship types: harmonious, traditional, conflicted, and devitalized. The first two types—harmonious and traditional—tend to be associated with higher satisfaction levels, albeit for very different reasons. The remaining two types—conflicted and devitalized—are connected to lower satisfaction levels, and again with divergent explanations about how they came to be that way.

The most desirable relationship is the harmonious type, which consists of both higher effort and higher comfort levels. Harmonious marriages exist between partners who report elevated satisfaction levels amid engaging in a lot of shared activities with one another. In a similar way, harmonious town–gown relationships are created when a given campus and community are portrayed as "getting along" well when they interact with one another. This perception is generated because the town and gown partners are successful in working together across a wide range of undertakings.

We wish to invoke the harmonious relationship type at key points throughout this book to illustrate all the best qualities that go into community engagement efforts. Campus and community partners that are putting relatively equal efforts into building and maintaining their relationships with one another, and by association are experiencing those interactions at similarly comfortable levels, are more likely to be committed to each other's well-being and future. As we will see in the second chapter, frameworks have been created that define high-quality community engagement as a function of the degree to which university and community partners are collaborating in ways that are interdependent and mutually beneficial. To be sure, this is the very definition of the harmonious campus–community relationship we seek to promote in this book.

At the same time, we wish also to utilize the marriage metaphor and its three lesser types (traditional, conflicted, and devitalized) in our discussions about how and where things become decidedly more negative in terms of the relationship between higher education and the public at large. The traditional relationship type (lower effort and higher comfort levels) is reflective of partners that seem to be agreeably disconnected from one another as they lead separate lives and work toward goals in isolation from one another. The conflicted relationship type (higher effort and lower comfort) represents partners who spend rather copious amounts of energy on persistent quarrels that remain unresolved. The devitalized relationship type (low effort and low comfort levels) contains partners who are the least satisfied with one another, largely because they have given up on each other for all intents and purposes.

We believe that the interaction of campuses and communities at different points in time has resembled each of the three suboptimal relationship types, as well as more closely approximating harmonious relationships in other periods. Relationship quality at any single moment also might well vary as a function of the specific community being directly engaged by the university. In the third chapter, for example, we will listen to presidents and chancellors discussing the dynamic tension that exists between meeting the needs of more rural communities and addressing the issues and concerns of more urbanized communities. It will have the feel of a zero-sum game, one where resources directed toward a singular constituency will be perceived (real or otherwise) as a defeat for others. Other issues might seem to retain a similar veneer, provoking imagery of a second civil war, or at the very least the march toward a nasty divorce.[17]

## Creating Harmonious Relationships with Multiple Constituencies

Harkening back to the political divide discussed in the previous section of this chapter, we see reason to believe that attempts to create and maintain harmonious relationships with a more capital-oriented audience will coincide with decidedly less symphonic (i.e., traditional, conflicted, and/or devitalized) relationships with a countryside audience, and vice versa. In other words, comfort levels inside of campus–community relationships will fluctuate as a direct result of how university activities are interpreted as being in alignment with or against the core values of its multiple audiences. And the operative word in that last sentence was "multiple." The capital-countryside distinction is merely a heuristic device, not a definitive statement about there being only two types of audiences to whom institutions of higher learning must attend. There are any number of variations on this theme. Ask any politician who represents a "purple" district or state these days.

This exemplifies a fundamental communication challenge for institutions of higher learning, especially for those leaders who are used to speaking as if there is one unified audience (something that, in our opinion, does not exist). And the complexity does not stop there, we believe. In the next chapter of this book, we will introduce the concept of a "covenant" that is thought to have been struck between the public and its colleges and universities at the outset, an agreement that has been presumed to have created mutually beneficial outcomes for American society and its institutions of higher learning.[18] Throughout this book, we will discuss how we see the reciprocal nature of this special relationship being questioned, if not altogether threatened, in the highly charged political climate we see today.

For now, let us simply acknowledge that public support for higher education has been on the decline—and not just fiscally, but calling into question the very value of a college degree—at the very same time that campuses have been engaged in certain activities that seem more difficult to explain in terms of their contribution to the public good. We wish to frame this erosion of support as a symptom of an imbalanced (i.e., nonreciprocal) partnership between campuses and communities. Institutions of higher learning would be evaluated much more favorably by the public at large, we believe, if university activities were perceived to be performed in close partnerships with community partners. In contrast, efforts will be much less positively evaluated—or worse yet, simply ignored—when the "services rendered" are decided, acted on, or otherwise portrayed as being managed unilaterally by institutions of higher learning and their representatives. Without collaboration, universities give the public far too little experience with and insight into the amazing work that faculty, staff, and students of land-grant and other public institutions conduct every day and, as a result, provide far too much leeway to interpret our activities as simply self-serving (and therefore not a public good).

At the end of the day, this is a leadership issue, plain and simple, which is why we built this book around the viewpoints of land-grant university presidents and chancellors. Of course, senior administrators will only last as long as their governing board members are supportive of their actions, and of course we respect and value faculty governance within the academy. We believe that we provide ample platforms for those voices to be heard in the fourth and fifth chapters, respectively. And the most important people of all—the students of these land-grant universities—are given our full attention in the sixth chapter of this book. That said, we are living in an era that demands visionary and transformational leadership from the top. Land-grant universities cannot be led from behind.

So, what's a land-grant university president or chancellor supposed to do with all of this? Certainly not duck for cover, or otherwise try to conduct business as usual. Instead, this is precisely the time for university leaders to take bold action aimed at restoring the American citizenry's confidence in its public institutions of higher learning. We believe that this will be accomplished most effectively through the establishment and maintenance of more active and (hopefully, with enough determination) harmonious relationships with community stakeholders who represent multiple audiences. This requires higher levels of effort undertaken by land-grant universities, contributing correspondingly to higher levels of comfort that can only be generated within partnerships reflecting both capital and countryside sensibilities.

In related fashion, presidents and chancellors also need to do a better job of helping the campus community—faculty, staff, and students alike—understand the obligations they have in terms of making significant and continuous contributions to the well-being of the various communities our land-grant universities were designed to serve. Concurrently, these leaders must work to incentivize these sorts of activities, which means that they must work collaboratively with faculty representative bodies and governing board members as they look to transform the way their institutions of higher learning conduct business. And finally, these senior administrators must be tireless in communicating to the families of students, alumni, state legislators, and other community stakeholders about the public good being created by our land-grant universities, with special emphasis on those activities that are being undertaken in mutually beneficial and co-created partnerships. Only then do we believe that the original covenant—really a form of harmonious relationship, after all—will be fully restored between the public and its universities. For that reason, we have written this book ecumenically, that is, for the full body of these campus and community representatives to read and deliberate.

## Confusion in the Ranks

Our next chapter is focused primarily on the genesis and evolution of the land-grant mission, and we would like to get a head start on that topic as we close this first chapter by raising three important points for further consideration. First, there is wide-ranging agreement among the senior administrators we interviewed that the public at large has little understanding of how universities contribute directly to the well-being of communities, let alone understanding the more specific definition of what it means to be a land-grant institution. In the words of one senior administrator,

> If you ask people what they know about the university's contributions to the community, and you ask them to set aside college sports and the medical center, I'm not sure they would know what to say. And if you asked those same people to tell you what it meant to be a land-grant institution, I believe they would simply shrug their shoulders. Providing citizens with a better understanding of the land-grant mission and the university's commitment to community prosperity is a critical issue for our future. (president/chancellor pers. comm.)

At present, when anyone tries to reference the land-grant mission in a conversation, the terminology typically does not resonate with their interlocutor. As we will see, this proves to be especially frustrating to land-grant university leaders who are attempting to communicate to the public about all the great things that are being done for the public good by their institutions. Simply put, the land-grant mission is not a well-known concept among American citizens.

In part, we hold the land-grant institutions directly responsible for this lack of public knowledge. After all, if land-grant institutions are bestowing college degrees to close to 1.2 million undergraduate students per year, and concurrently are educating 70% of the graduate students enrolled in America's research universities, we have only ourselves to blame for the public's land-grant illiteracy.[19] Why are students graduating from our universities in these large numbers every year without a basic understanding of their alma mater's mission? In our seventh chapter, we will tackle this issue in greater detail and, among other things, offer a course syllabus that seeks to remedy this error of omission.

Second, the public's lack of understanding about terms and concepts related to land-grant institutions and their activities also may be related to the different ways that the land-grant mission is described by the senior administrators we interviewed. Interestingly, some of these presidents and chancellors are aware of this lack of consistency and have expressed concerns that their peer group may not share a common understanding of the twenty-first-century land-grant mission. Certainly, when the Morrill Act and other founding premises of the land-grant institutions were mentioned in the interviews (we will explore these congressional activities more extensively in chap. 2), the presidents and chancellors typically recounted this portion of the historical mission as being grounded in the advancement of knowledge in areas like agriculture and engineering. At the same time, however, these same senior administrators displayed much less uniformity in describing the critical activities that set apart the twenty-first-century land-grant institutions from all other colleges and universities. This seemed to be especially true for presidents and chancellors in terms of their articulating the role that land-grant universities currently play in meeting the needs of the communities they were designed to serve through their outreach and engagement activities.

Third, and related to our previous two points, a few of the presidents and chancellors interviewed in this study believed that the root problem was the insular nature of universities themselves. One senior administrator put it this way:

The greatest weakness of land-grant institutions is the very issue of the way they seek to become engaged with their communities. I think that our universities unfortunately are isolated and arrogant institutions. Often as not the thought process is: what's good for the university is good for the community. The problem is that we don't often really understand what is good for the community beyond the notion that an educated population is an extremely helpful asset. So, we end up being university-centric instead of being community-centric. It ends up being about me instead of about us. (president/chancellor pers. comm.)

This sort of self-absorbed viewpoint presents some real challenges to the campus–community relationship, of course, and gets us back to the issue of nonreciprocal interactions between universities and their constituencies raised earlier in this chapter. After all, if you are not routinely asking your partner what they want you to do, how can you know for sure that you are providing what your partner needs in actuality? If you are offering only what you assume your partner needs, some serious errors in judgment can (and often do) occur. These miscalculations result in missed opportunities to develop meaningful partnerships with community stakeholders while concurrently raising the specter of creating real damage to campus–community relationships in ways that can be very difficult to mend.[20] Bottom line: this is a recipe for relationship disaster, not for the building of more harmonious interactions with the public.

## The Clarity of a Servant University Orientation

We are very concerned about what we perceive to be a long-standing effort to make colleges and universities more like one another in our country. In response, we wish to argue forcefully against such attempts at homogenization because of the great disservice that is being done to the American public educational system. In fact, we believe that the American system remains the best in the entire world precisely because there is difference and choice here. The minute we try to homogenize our universities, we become more like a federalized education system, and we lose our luster in the process. The German universities and the Japanese universities are organized at a national level, for instance, and as a result they are not as good as the American universities. This, we believe, is due to the lack of such diversity.

Interestingly, modern-day attempts by universities to remain distinctive at times seem to be met with disapproval, especially when religious affiliation is a part of the equation. The Mormon institution of Brigham Young University often gets criticized because it lives by its religious tenets, for instance. It is fiercely Mormon. Rather than cast aspersions, we applaud this stance. Similarly, instead of trying to be more like their university brethren, we believe that Catholic institutions should be more fiercely Catholic, Baptist institutions should be more fiercely Baptist, and so on.

In the same way, we have stated our belief that land-grant universities should become more fiercely land-grant in their orientation. And although there is no organized religion involved, nevertheless we wish to offer a transcendent framework for thinking about what distinguishes the land-grant model from all others. In so doing, we wish to employ a phrase—the *servant university*—to describe and celebrate the distinctiveness of Mr. Lincoln's institutions of higher learning and how they prioritize their activities based on the needs of the communities they were designed to serve.

What do we mean when we employ the term "servant university"? Here, we borrow extensively from Robert Greenleaf's discourse on servant leadership.[21] Interestingly, Greenleaf began his work on servant leadership in large part as a reaction to the turbulence of college campuses during the 1960s. In the introduction to the 25th-anniversary edition of his seminal book, he wrote, "It was a searing experience to watch distinguished institutions show their fragility and crumble, to search for an understanding of what happened to them (and never be satisfied that I knew), and to try to help heal their wounds."[22] In some very real ways, we believe that there is a déjà vu moment at hand here. College campuses again are in turmoil, as we have described earlier in this chapter, and university leaders are searching for answers to many questions being raised about the role of higher education in meeting the present needs of American society. It is our steadfast belief that land-grant universities are uniquely positioned to respond to these challenges, and we believe that servant leadership principles can and should serve as the keys to unlocking this potential.

Servant leaders, according to Greenleaf, place strong emphasis on the stewardship responsibilities that come from being entrusted with authority over public resources. As a result, servant leaders are committed to building community, in the process encouraging followers to identify with and make significant contributions to something that is greater than themselves.[23] Stephen Covey, best-selling author of *The Seven Habits of Highly Effective People*, wrote that the core of Greenleaf's conceptualization of servant leadership involved four dimensions of moral authority, or conscience: conscience through sacrifice, conscience through commitment, conscience through process (where ends and means are inseparable), and conscience as compassion.[24] In this framework, leaders are chosen based on their proven ability to be more interested in the well-being of others than in their own personal advancement.[25]

Research has further delineated five factors related to servant leadership: (1) an altruistic calling to a leadership position; (2) an orientation toward the emotional healing of those with whom you work; (3) persuasive mapping, a term meant to connote that the servant leader sets goals and objectives based on the "bigger picture" of what the organization and its constituents need; (4) wisdom; and (5) organizational stewardship.[26] Building on Greenleaf's focus on the role of institutions as servants, these empirically derived factors have been further fleshed out as the following 10 characteristics for practitioners, and consequently 10 principles for application specifically in higher education administration:

1. Service to others is the highest priority
2. Facilitate meeting the needs of others
3. Foster problem-solving and take responsibility at all levels
4. Promote emotional healing in people and the organization
5. Means are as important as ends
6. Keep one eye on the present and one eye on the future
7. Embrace paradoxes and dilemmas
8. Leave a legacy to society
9. Model servant leadership
10. Develop more servant leaders[27]

We had the opportunity to discuss the application of these principles to land-grant universities with their author, Daniel Wheeler. Auspiciously, Dr. Wheeler is professor emeritus of leadership studies at the land-grant institution of the University of Nebraska at Lincoln, so he was well versed in the connection between the servant leadership framework and the land-grant mission. When asked about that linkage, he stated the following:

> If we sincerely think we are a part of a larger community, and if we are dedicated to helping people get the things they need for a better quality of life, then we must have some sort of collaborative leadership model in place. Otherwise, it's not possible for people to distinguish between land-grant universities and other institutions of higher learning. We need to serve as models of the servant leadership principles as they are reflected in the land-grant mission. This is related to another important part of Greenleaf's work regarding methods, where he says that the way we do things is at least as important as what we do. So, how we address problems and issues says a lot to people about who we are as land-grant universities. (pers. comm.)

Wheeler went on to provide the hopeful note that servant leadership can flourish at any level of the university. Therefore, while it would be ideal for governing board members and university presidents and chancellors to set the tone in upholding these principles, it is possible for faculty, staff, and students to make a significant difference by adopting a servant leadership posture in their smaller spheres of influence.

That said, we assert here that servant universities are those institutions of higher learning that directly and unequivocally give primary emphasis to the stewardship responsibilities they have been given by society to provide for the development and well-being of its communities. That is, we believe that the original agreement struck between the public and its colleges and universities means that, at least for the land-grant universities, critical decisions made at all levels of leadership should be filtered first through the lens of what provides maximum benefit for the citizens of each state and for American society at large. To remain in alignment with this focus, we assert in the strongest terms that the main players within the land-grant university—its leaders, of course, but also its students, faculty, and governing board members—must be engaged in stewardship activities that generate benefit to the community.

This is not an esoteric exercise. Rather, we believe that a continuous quality improvement process should be put in place, requiring constant vigilance about the land-grant university's adherence to its servant university orientation. Of primary importance, this is a direction with which faculty members must be allied, one where the fruits of instruction and empirical work are most immediately identifiable as having a positive impact on the communities that land-grant universities were designed to serve. Likewise, students enrolled in institutions with a servant university orientation—or what we might alternatively call the "people's university"—should be immersed in activities that have the clear purpose of benefitting those communities immediately adjacent to the land-grant university and back in the hometowns and neighborhoods from which the students hail. In turn, all other individuals who come together in support of the land-grant university (governing board members, alumni, families of current students, legislators, etc.) would be able to do so much more effectively with the guidance and direction offered by the servant university orientation. We will have much more to say about all of this in the latter portions of this book.

## Summary

We began this chapter by sharing the details of our SWOT analysis efforts, including information about our recruitment and interviewing of land-grant presidents and chancellors across this nation. We then highlighted the political context of the interviews we conducted, framed by the coincidence of the 2016 presidential election, and familiarized our readers with the capital versus countryside dialectic that seems to capture the sharp divisions facing American society at present. The marriage metaphor was then introduced, with great emphasis placed on the creation and maintenance of more harmonious relationships between campuses and communities. An initial discussion of the general public's unfamiliarity with the land-grant label and inconsistencies in articulating the land-grant mission across senior university administrators was then followed by a brief introduction of the servant university as a framing concept for the land-grant mission of the twenty-first century.

# CHAPTER 2

# The Land-Grant Institution and Mission in Service to Communities

In this chapter, we provide a brief and concise narrative about how the land-grant universities were created, as well as how these institutions of higher learning developed over time to include a strong community engagement component in their mission profile. Three major initiatives—undertaken by the Kellogg Commission on the Future of State and Land-Grant Universities, the Carnegie Foundation for the Advancement of Teaching Classification for Community Engagement, and the Association of Public and Land-Grant Universities (APLU)—are reviewed as organized attempts to systematize those university activities designed to engage community members. All of this, we believe, underscores the notion that a vibrant platform exists for land-grant universities to be at the forefront of activities designed to build more harmonious partnerships with the communities they were designed to serve.

The centerpiece of our narrative is the notion of a covenant, a bilateral bond that exists between land-grant institutions and the communities they were designed to serve. Although not stated explicitly by the creators of the land-grant institutions, the main ideology undergirding this narrative imagines a university that is of the people, by the people, and for the people. With all due apologies to Mr. Lincoln, we argue that the mutually beneficial relationship between the land-grant institution and the greater public good—

seen explicitly in the terms of the array of benefits derived by community stakeholders and society itself—should guarantee that these precious resources, properly stewarded, will never be in danger of perishing from this earth.

## The Original Land-Grant Mission

To begin the task of unpacking the original mission of land-grant universities, we must start with the notion that the term "land grant" straightforwardly describes the federal government's funding mechanism by which public institutions of higher learning were to be created. That is, in 1862 the US House of Representatives granted 30,000 acres of federally owned land to each state for the express purpose of providing financial support for the development of public universities in those states. Here is the original wording about the federal land to be granted to states for this purpose from what has become known as the First Morrill Act of 1862:

> *And be it further enacted,* That all moneys derived from the sale of the lands aforesaid by the States to which the lands are apportioned, and from the sale of land scrip herein before provided for, shall be invested in stock of the United States, or of the States, or some other safe stocks, yielding not less than five per centum upon the par value of said stocks; and that the moneys so invested shall constitute a perpetual fund, the capital of which shall remain forever undiminished (except so far as may be provided in section fifth of this act), and the interest of which shall be inviolably appropriated, by each State which may take and claim the benefit of this act, to the endowment, support, and maintenance of at least one college where the leading object shall be, without excluding other scientific and classical studies, and including military tactics, to teach such branches of learning as are related to agriculture and the mechanic arts, in such manner as the legislatures of the States may respectively prescribe, in order to promote the liberal and practical education of the industrial classes in the several pursuits and professions in life.[1]

We can see that the proceeds from this granted land were designated for some very specific uses, including the provision of learning aimed at agriculture, the mechanical arts (what we now refer to as engineering), and military tactics (the precursor to the Reserve Officer Training Corps[2]). The intertwined history of the agricultural colleges and the Morrill Act has led to the common misunderstanding that land-grant colleges (as they were known at the time) were designated only to provide financial assistance for activities that involved working the land. More recent use of nomenclature related to the National Oceanic and Atmospheric Administration (NOAA) "sea grant colleges," the US Department of Agriculture (USDA) "sun grant colleges," and the National Aeronautics and Space and Administration (NASA) "space grant colleges" has only added to that confusion.[3] In these cases, there is in fact a more concentrated focus on efforts by institutions of higher learning to better understand bodies of water, bioenergy, and aeronautic and space issues, respectively.

That said, agriculture did play a dominant role in the development of the land-grant universities over time.[4] Many of the individuals credited as forefathers to the Morrill Act, including perhaps most notably Horace Greeley and Jonathan Turner, consistently identified farming as the "most indispensable" of all professions.[5] To be fair, these men also asserted that a solid liberal arts curriculum could safeguard our country's democratic ideals by providing for a more educated citizenry from among the "industrialized classes" of this country.[6]

The fact of the matter is that faculty and staff members within the land-grant institutions continue to be quite adept at responding to the needs of agriculture, and therefore they maintain a stellar reputation in that realm. As one senior administrator stated,

> Currently, land-grant universities are very, very good at carrying out their very traditional role in agriculture and the agricultural industry as defined by the land-grant mission of the nineteenth and twentieth centuries. And certainly in big agriculture—and therefore in the big agricultural states—land-grant universities are hugely important, not just to their own success, but to the world. In this respect they are central to the economy and food supply. They do that very, very well. (president/chancellor pers. comm.)

However, the continuous emphasis placed on the need for greater numbers of "educated farmers" over time has created very stereotypical ways of thinking about land-grant institutions and the activities of their faculty, staff, and students.[7] Literary examples of this typecasting abound, including perhaps most famously "Moo U," the satirical name of the midwestern (and we suppose land-grant) institution lampooned in Jane Smiley's 1995 novel.[8] In short, we believe that it has been difficult for the public at large (let alone colleagues inside of academia) to see beyond the agricultural component of the land-grant mission. We will discuss this issue in more depth and detail in the next chapter, where we discuss the dynamic tension that exists between meeting the needs of rural communities and meeting those of a more urbanized America.

On a broader scale it is important to note that, when the land-grant institutions of higher learning were founded in 1862, it was a time in which there were significant threats to the integrity and future of the United States. Amid those incredibly dark times in American history, national leaders passed three incredible acts in one year: the Morrill Act, which founded land-grant universities, the Pacific Railroad Act, which allowed our country to build a transcontinental railway system, and the Homestead Act, which provided immigrants with the opportunity to acquire land of their own.[9] While steeped in the acute crisis of civil war, these politicians nevertheless were able to focus simultaneously on the long-term interests of America. One of the senior administrators who participated in our interviews remarked wryly,

> And when you think about who passed those Acts, they were passed by people who likely had never been to college, most of them had never been outside of their state other than to travel to and from Washington, DC, and certainly had little idea what was out in the western reaches of our country. That is incredible foresight in leadership. And compare that to our present-day Congress, comprised of people who have difficulties passing a budget continuation bill. Really, there's no comparison. (president/chancellor pers. comm.)

Of course, the ability to think and act on behalf of future generations did not end in 1862, nor did the land-grant acts themselves. Subsequent governmental actions eventually created at least one land-grant institution in every state in America and in each of the US territories. In 1890, the second Morrill Act was passed to provide additional financial support for the land-grant colleges. This legislation created 17 additional land-grant institutions specifically designed to educate African American students as part of the "separate but equal" doctrine of the times. This congressional act gave rise to the institutions now labeled HBCUs, or historically black colleges and universities.[10] Further federal legislation bestowed land-grant status on the University of the District of Columbia in 1967; to universities in American Samoa, Guam, Micronesia, Northern Marianas, Puerto Rico, and the Virgin Islands in 1972; and to 29 tribal colleges and universities in 1994 (six more tribal institutions subsequently were added).[11] Finally, Central State University in Ohio was granted 1890 land-grant status in 2014. In all, there are now 110 institutions of higher learning that have land-grant status.[12]

Two additional congressional acts further shaped the mission and destiny of the land-grant institutions: the Hatch Act of 1887 and the Smith-Lever Act of 1914. The Hatch Act appropriated federal funds for the development of agricultural experiment stations that were connected to each land-grant institution. Although the empirical aims of these experimental stations focused exclusively on agricultural issues at the outset, the expansion of their activities over time into other disciplinary fields contributed to the rise of what eventually became the model of the American research university.[13] Many of the university presidents and chancellors we interviewed were steadfast in their belief that research is the land-grant university's greatest strength at present (and thus becomes one of the main themes emerging from our interviews as described in the third chapter). Here is a representative quote from one of the senior administrators whom we interviewed:

> The land-grant mission was meant for us to do two things, perhaps not so explicitly stated in the first Morrill Act but maybe a little bit better by the second Morrill Act. We were there to train the next generation of leaders for our communities, but also to train them in modern techniques and science, in modern agricultures, and the intellectual basis of the industrial revolution, and trying to take good ideas and bring them to fruition in our communities. And as that has moved forward it has evolved into the base of our research enterprise. So, I think we have done a great job, and I assume a better job than would have been imaginable in the mid-nineteenth century of becoming real powerhouses for research. (president/chancellor pers. comm.)

In turn, the Smith-Lever Act established the Cooperative Extension Services system, designed to take important findings from the research laboratories and apply them directly to farms, fields, family homes, and related subjects.[14] This federal legislation created the very first impetus for institutions of higher learning to engage with members of the community, incentivizing university personnel to leave the confines of their campuses (the proverbial "ivory towers") and work among the public at large.[15] Again, we witnessed most of the presidents and chancellors making some mention of the importance of Cooperative Extension in their interview remarks, including this example:

> Although I know that it's gone through many struggles over the past few decades, I still think that Cooperative Extension is one of the land-grant university's greatest strengths. I know various states have really diversified

Cooperative Extension and include many disciplines, while others remain very restricted to agriculture. But I think regardless where states are on this continuum, the fact that they have Extension centers located out across the state that are responsive to the concerns of communities is an incredible plus. It puts us out across the state with a presence in every region, and there are very few public institutions that have even come close to mimicking that kind of reach. (president/chancellor pers. comm.)

Taken together, the Morrill Act, the Hatch Act, and the Smith-Lever Act constitute the congressional actions that placed an indelible federal stamp on (and appropriated funds for) the three core activities of the land-grant university—teaching, research, and service—which were designed to meet the needs of community stakeholders and American society at large.

One last and yet very important historical point to make here is a cautionary note about where the ultimate authority of the land-grant mission resides. Various criticisms have been leveled against the all-too-romantic writings of historians who long have insisted on the existence of a singular and unifying "land-grant ideal."[16] Instead, newer chronologies regarding the genesis and evolution of our nation's public institutions of higher learning have insisted on more diverse interpretations that account for the dynamic friction of various stakeholder groups.[17] Essentially, this scholarship places challenges in front of what might be thought of as an almost mythological account of the land-grant university's mission over time, offering instead a much more complicated picture of competing interests and realities.

We had the opportunity to discuss this sort of historiographical take on the land-grant mission with Nathan Sorber, a West Virginia University professor of higher education administration and director of that university's Center for the Future of Land-Grant Education, who has written extensively on the history of land-grant colleges.[18] There is tremendous variation in how the land-grant mission is expressed across America, Sorber insisted, in large part owing to the idiosyncratic ways in which the citizens and elected officials of each state chose to interpret federal legislation. Sorber went on to say,

The real genius of the Morrill Act is that it created opportunities for states to participate in the development of their own colleges and universities. However, because of our country's long-standing reluctance to allow the federal government to get involved in education, it was left to all of these state governments to decipher the Act. Because of that, we don't have a land-grant system; we have a lot of land-grant systems. You have to look at local and regional social and economic conditions first, and then and only then can you get a sense of what the land-grant mission is for each state. (pers. comm.)

Interestingly, Sorber's newest book offers a historical account maintaining that state-derived financial resources were provided to institutions of higher learning only when a return on investment was demonstrated, and that such fiscal support varied significantly across time and across regions of the country.[19]

In accord with this historical evidence, we wish to exercise an abundance of caution here in order to avoid making any sort of overgeneralizations about the land-grant mission without accounting for this state-by-state variation. In fact, in many ways we believe that a state-level analysis of community needs is precisely the direction land-grant universities need to take to best fulfill their core responsibilities to the public. That said, we do believe that there are some canonical viewpoints about land-grant institutions and their missions which, wholly correct or not, are driving contemporary thinking about our public universities. We now turn our attention precisely to one of those uncontested certainties.

## The Covenant between the Public and Higher Education

Within higher education, there is widespread belief in the notion that a "covenant" exists between the public and its colleges and universities, yielding both individual and social outcomes resulting from activities surrounding teaching, research, and service.[20] The individually oriented outcomes are thought to include elements such as more prestigious careers, greater lifetime income, improved health, and increased life expectancy, which result from the acquirement of a college degree. These outcomes largely are thought to be "private goods" in that they primarily benefit the individual who obtains the diploma. In turn, the more socially based outcomes include such factors as increased civic involvement, greater charitable giving, and a better-informed electorate, to name but a few examples. Owing to their more broad-based impact on the community at large, these outcomes are thought of more as "public goods."[21]

Scholars have expressed their concerns about the various ways in which assessments of higher education's worth have been tilted toward the private valuation of its outcomes in more recent years. In tandem, there are data indicating that per-student funding is increasing at the private universities (through upsurges in both tuition and donations), while per-student funding among the land-grant and other public universities has remained relatively flat.[22] This shift in thinking and the concurrent imbalance of resources made available to educate students at public versus private institutions have been the result of numerous economic and political factors that have arisen over the past several decades. The ensuing policy decisions have placed enormous financial and ideological pressures on public institutions of higher learning, much of which will be discussed in our third chapter when we focus on declines in funding and the need to create efficiencies.

Public universities have attempted to adapt to this changing landscape, to be sure, although the paths taken have not received universal acclaim. Clark Kerr, the first chancellor of the University of California at Berkeley and former president of the University of California system, was among the first writers within the academy to bring widespread attention to the corporatization of universities as a function of the partnerships they were developing and maintaining with business and industry entities.[23] Similar sentiments about the commercialization of higher education were echoed in the work of Derek Bok, former president of Harvard.[24] A host of detrimental effects are thought to have resulted from this shift in orientation, including an overemphasis on competitiveness and efficiency by university leaders and governing board members; inordinate weight given to vocational concerns in the curriculum, which promotes careerist students; and a disenfranchisement of faculty members, whose contributions increasingly are assessed by the research dollars and other revenue they generate.[25]

## The Land-Grant Mission of the Twenty-First Century

Traditionally, the emphasis on the *public* good of higher education has been rooted in the idea that land-grant universities are the "social conscience" of American society and its educational system.[26] Such sentiment has been based on the historical understanding that, until the Morrill Act was passed in 1862, a college degree largely was attainable only by wealthy, white, urban males. The development of land-grant institutions, in contrast, created a "moral force" that opened the doors of higher education to all comers, with a basis on ability and effort instead of affluence and social networks. As a result, land-grant universities are thought to reflect a common set of values that include, but are not limited to, academic integrity and ethics, humility, mutual respect and dignity, courage, common sense, a can-do attitude, and the promotion of active citizenship and service activities that come to resemble the servant leadership principles we introduced in our first chapter.[27]

However, the explicit emphasis on meeting the needs of communities writ large is a more recent phenomenon, especially when attention turns to non-farming populations. Certainly, Earnest Boyer's work on the reconsideration of scholarship in academia—stressing the need for universities to become a "more vigorous partner" with the public through equal attention paid to discovery, integration, application, and teaching activities—highlighted the need to reconnect institutions of higher learning with the needs of the greater community.[28] Boyer has served as both chancellor of the State University of New York (SUNY) and president of the Carnegie Foundation for the Advancement of Teaching (discussed below). Importantly, his book has been described as a "clarion call" for greater involvement in the community and has been discussed as being particularly aimed at land-grant universities because of their historic investment in applied teaching and research.[29] According to one senior administrator interviewed in our study, however, this has been something intentionally embraced by land-grant universities only in more recent times:

> I believe if you go back to the founding documents of the land-grant institution they don't actually say anything about the communities we serve. Over the years, however, because the needs of the communities have changed with time, land-grants have focused their mission on being relevant to the needs of the people of the state and the communities they serve. So this is a mission that we have adopted because we have viewed the origination of the land-grants to be about relevant needs of the communities of the people we serve. Having said that, I do believe that land-grants have a unique responsibility to serve our communities. It simply needs to be pointed out that, over the years, we have self-imposed a mission on our institutions that wasn't assigned by the 30,000 acres of land we were given by the federal government to establish these colleges and universities. (president/chancellor pers. comm.)

Thus, the gradual evolution of thinking within land-grant circles had led to a critical mass of scholars, university leaders, and other higher education thought leaders recognizing the need for a more sustained and coordinated set of community engagement activities.[30] What was missing at the time, however, was the ability to define and organize these sorts of efforts. Because nature abhors a vacuum, numerous organizations began to move in the direction of codifying exactly what colleges and universities needed to do in order to create and sustain partnerships in the communities they were designed to serve.

## Institutionalizing Community Engagement

As higher education continued to evolve in the 1990s, it became increasingly clear that state legislators were looking to balance state budgets by providing less support for public institutions of higher education, a move that triggered substantial tuition increases. In response, leaders of public universities went on the offensive, making the case that a special set of visible and sustainable relationships were maintained between their campuses and the communities they were designed to serve. A number of prominent organizations dedicated to the advancement of public higher education began to encourage this work and to describe what engagement-oriented activities looked like in practice. This included, but was not limited to, the call for more "engaged institutions" by the Kellogg Commission on the Future of State and Land-Grant Universities, the Carnegie Foundation for the Advancement of Teaching Classification for Community Engagement, and the Innovation and Economic Prosperity (IEP) Universities Designation developed by the APLU.[31] Because the work of these three entities has had a significant impact on many of the activities discussed throughout this book, their efforts warrant more attention here.

### *The Kellogg Commission on the Future of State and Land-Grant Universities*

The Kellogg Commission on the Future of State and Land-Grant Universities consisted of a group of 25 university presidents, largely representing the 1862, 1890, and 1994 land-grant institutions. However, presidents and past presidents of other public universities also were included, as was a national advisory group composed of high-profile community stakeholders. This group of esteemed individuals was brought together by the National Association of State Universities and Land-Grant Colleges (NASULGC)—the precursor of the APLU—through funding from the Kellogg Foundation.

The president of NASULGC at that time was C. Peter Magrath, who previously had served as the president of Binghamton University, the University of Minnesota, and West Virginia University, as well as having been the president of the University of Missouri higher education system. Magrath wanted NASULGC to take the lead in conducting a thorough analysis of the strengths and limitations facing America's public universities, land-grant and otherwise. Because of Magrath's interest in research-related issues, the Association of American Universities (AAU)—a small group of highly research-intensive universities—was invited to cosponsor the initiative, but that group declined to participate (largely, Magrath noted, because representatives of the private universities thought it would be political suicide to air higher education's dirty laundry in public).

Magrath pressed on nevertheless, standing firm on some very robust beliefs he maintained about the need for this work to be accomplished. He also felt very strongly about the need for the Kellogg name to be on the work, something he secured only after he led some "fairly intense" negotiations. What outdistanced all other convictions for Magrath, however, was the notion that community engagement was going to be the most important activity for university leaders to get behind as a part of the Kellogg Commission's work. In Magrath's words,

> Engagement was going to be the best seller, if you will, especially for the land-grant universities. It was going to be the key not only for universities to survive, but to thrive. Funding was on its way down, with no relief in sight. So, the question was: where was the money going to come from? And one of the most logical answers involved our need to engage with the community, and especially the business community. The very best business leaders have always recognized that connections with universities offered enormous competitive advantages. What they needed were university partners that were willing to engage and be more entrepreneurial. Of course, universities needed to establish partnerships with many other members of the community as well, and needed to do this in a way that was mutually beneficial. Not the university coming in and telling people how to do things like in the old days, but rather universities and their partners coming together and saying, "Hey, maybe we have things to learn from each other." (pers. comm.)

The first chair of the Kellogg Commission was E. Gordon Gee, who was handpicked by Magrath to lead the effort. In his role as president of The Ohio State University, Gee knew firsthand what the old "one-way" service model looked like, that is, universities providing information and other forms of assistance to constituents in ways that were designed to only benefit the receiver. Like Magrath, he yearned for something more for institutions of higher learning, a model that would forever change how partnerships developed between land-grant universities and the communities they were designed to serve. What Gee envisioned here was a set of activities that universities would design and implement with input from community stakeholders and, in return, would enhance and refine the university's teaching and research efforts.

With his subsequent move to become president of Brown University, however, Gee stepped down as the chairman of the Kellogg Commission and passed the formal leadership baton to Graham Spanier, the former president of Penn State. Gee remained an active member of the committee in the role of commissioner emeritus, however, and was instrumental in guiding and directing a series of reports over a four-year period (1996–2000) which sought to rethink and recast the role of higher education in American society. One of those reports focused intensively on renewing the covenant between land-grant universities and the public, with great emphasis on reestablishing responsibilities and activities on "both sides of the bargain," meaning that universities and the public at large equally had to recommit to the special relationship they had shared historically with one another.[32] Other Kellogg Commission reports included a focus on such topics as the student experience, student access, learning environments, campus culture, and of course the engaged institution.[33]

The reports were compiled in a very purposeful order, according to Richard Stoddard, who was an eyewitness to the proceedings in his role as both special assistant to the president and Ohio State's director of federal relations when the Kellogg Commission meetings were held. Student-oriented topics were dealt with first under the assumption that, no matter what senior leaders thought about the value of the research and service-related activities that their respective institutions of higher learning were involved in, the public believed that the prime responsibility of universities was to educate students. Stoddard noted,

> People wanted to talk about research, and others wanted to talk about costs, but we needed to make the case for who we were and what we did. It was the beginning of the time that people were saying college was too expensive, and not enough students were graduating, and so on. There was a common belief that we had fallen, that universities were broken. So, the student experience was done first to start things off, to let folks know that we knew what was expected of us. (pers. comm.)

Essentially, senior leaders already were feeling quite a bit of heat by the mid-1990s regarding the worth of public higher education, so much so that Stoddard believed that the relationship between universities and the public at large was at an all-time "low ebb" status. And while the Kellogg Foundation leaders were genuinely committed to rethinking public education for the twenty-first century, the activities legitimately can be viewed also as a not-so-subtle attempt to sway public opinion and otherwise stabilize perceptions during a time of great criticism and uncertainty about the value of America's colleges and universities.

The Kellogg Commission report on engagement was issued third and was intended to create the blueprints for a university that was decidedly more involved in and committed to meeting the needs of communities. Of course, there already was a term available for the land-grant university's involvement in the community: Extension services. Regrettably, that term had come to be associated with a "Mr. Green Jeans" mentality (or "Green Acres" if you prefer a different classic television reference), a stereotypical way of restricting one's thinking about land-grant university activities to include only rural and agricultural connections. Extension services also were seen in unidirectional terms, whereby the university provided resources to the community but nothing of value was necessarily returned. What was needed, Stoddard said, was a way of capturing campus–community partnerships that were bidirectional and thus related to activities that were both mutually derived and mutually beneficial, as well as not being portrayed as applicable to rural locations only.

The use of the term "engagement" as a label for these sorts of activities was derived in part from some parallel work that was being conducted concurrently by the Danforth Forum, an effort that involved the collaborative efforts of both the Danforth Foundation and the Public Agenda Foundation. According to James Harvey, who was serving as a consultant to both the Danforth Foundation and the Kellogg Commission at that time, the Danforth Forum had started employing the term "public engagement" to describe various efforts that the group was undertaking to involve the public in policymaking issues.[34] Owing to widespread dissatisfaction with the term "service" in the Kellogg Commission planning group (combined with the aforesaid wariness about public perceptions of "Extension" as a label), Harvey's suggestion to employ the term "engagement" in the context of university collaborations with community partners was quickly adopted.

The use of the term "engagement" also allowed public universities that were not land-grant institutions to be included in the conversation, especially those that were more urban focused in their mission. The desire to include both land-grant institutions and other public universities was important to the viability of APLU as an organization in light of ever-present questions about why the land-grant institutions were in an organization with the non-land-grant institutions, and vice versa. Such qualms stemmed back historically to the 1963 merger of the two organizations—the American Association of Land-Grant Colleges and Universities (AALGCU) and the National Association of State Universities (NASU)—that formed NASULGC, APLU's forerunner.[35] Efforts to bridge this divide by focusing on what was common to all public universities, coupled with the desire to have a more clear and concise brand image to project to the public, eventually led to an organizational name change in 2009 (to APLU). One senior administrator whom we interviewed put it this way:

> What happened at APLU was interesting. It used to be NASULGC, which is a mouthful, the National Association of State and Land-Grant Universities and Colleges. We went through a name change about six to eight years ago, to try to broaden the base beyond land-grant universities to include public institutions. Given the pedigree, they have been trying to figure out how to move the land-grants and non-land-grants forward in a more unified way. One of the issues that APLU has developed in this regard is a focus on university activities that occur in more urban settings. If you are largely urban, then what does it mean to be a land-grant university in the twenty-first century? One of the things that APLU has promoted is that, to broaden the base of the organization, you need to speak to the needs of the urban universities. They call them the urban land-grants. It's kind of a misuse of terms. Land-grant had a very specific definition that had to do with grants of land from the federal government. But the notion here is that APLU wanted to include urban universities, land-grant and otherwise, in this sense of purpose not only to educate people for careers, but to promote civil engagement and social progress through hands-on involvement. (president/chancellor pers. comm.)

Employment of the term "engagement" was both new to and inclusive of both the land-grant institutions and the other public universities, and it also seemed to satisfy the need to make room for more urban-involved efforts. Stoddard noted that the introduction of one fresh term created the possibility of applying modernized labels for other more traditional university activities. Hence, the term "learning" began to be associated with teaching efforts, and "discovery" was used to describe research and other forms of scholarship. Taken together, all the newer language being employed as the result of the Kellogg Commission's work was purposeful, Stoddard indicated, and was designed to make the reports immediately relevant and impactful.

Despite those efforts and desires, the only Kellogg Commission product that seems to have enjoyed a formidable and lasting shelf life is the report on the engaged institution. According to eyewitnesses to the inception of this work such as James Harvey, it felt like the most powerful of the reports even when it was first formulated. Harvey noted,

> It was very clear that the engagement report resonated the most with the pub-
> lic university community. The ideas in that report recast the concept of ser-
> vice in ways that appealed to people. And the term "engagement" transcended
> any one constituency group. It worked just as well with inner-city communi-
> ties as it did with farmers and food systems, with transportation systems, and
> with business and industry leaders and concerns. And I think it reminded a
> lot of people—at least, I hope it reminded a lot of people—about what it meant
> to be at a land-grant university, and why they entered that world in the first
> place. (pers. comm.)

Among other things, this report included the assertion of the following seven guiding characteristics (dubbed a "seven-part test" by the authors), which together were used to define the quality of the university's engagement with the community:

1. Responsiveness: Are university personnel listening to community members and, as a result, providing education, research, and service-related activities that meet their specific needs?
2. Respect for partners: Is the relationship one-sided and dependency-oriented, or are university and community partners collaborating in ways that are interdependent and mutually beneficial?
3. Academic neutrality: Does the university provide a nonjudgmental context for debates about pressing social, economic, and political issues?
4. Accessibility: Can all members of the community equally access the resources of the university, and are these community stakeholders regularly informed about various opportunities to engage these university resources?
5. Integration: To what extent do the university's teaching and research efforts include components of community engagement (i.e., how much engaged teaching and engaged research occurs in actuality)?
6. Coordination: Do various academic departments and other units within the university know what each other is doing in ways that reduce fragmentation and duplication of services to the community?

7. Resource partnerships: Are the resources allocated to engagement efforts sufficiently funded in a manner that allows these activities to be sustainable over time?

Taken together, the Kellogg Commission's seven-part test centered this conceptualization of university engagement on a key phrase related to the overall covenant concept: "the irreducible idea is that we exist to advance the common good." Hence, we see here a decided emphasis on higher education's ultimate worth as a public good, especially in terms of how universities directly meet the needs of communities, in comparison to its more privately oriented outcomes that impact individual gains.

Importantly, although the titles of each of the Kellogg Commission reports began with the phrase *"Returning to Our Roots,"* the authors explicitly stated that they were "called upon to reshape Morrill's conception anew" for the needs of twenty-first-century America. This underscores a point made earlier in this chapter: the explicit emphasis on meeting the needs of communities is a more recent phenomenon. As such, the emphasis on university engagement efforts was not as much a historic *return* to the land-grant heritage as it was a future-forward *revision* of the basic land-grant mission.

The prominence of community engagement within the present-day land-grant mission was noted emphatically by many of the presidents and chancellors we interviewed, especially as related to the need to remain relevant in contemporary American society. According to one of these senior administrators,

> When I hear people expressing angst about what it means to be a land-grant university in the twenty-first century, my reaction is always this. The mission is still the same, but the circumstances are different. And to be effective in whatever locale you find yourself, it likely will mean you are going to have to do different things than what you traditionally have relied on to fulfill the land-grant mission. Our mission is to provide the educational preparation that people need to pursue careers, but they also have to contribute to the economic development and social progress of the communities in which they live. Every graduate needs to have a sense that they have an obligation to provide service to others. That a meaningful life and a life fulfilled is not just about you. It's about how you connect with the world and make a difference. That to me is a mission that is limitless in its relevance. That's what the land-grant mission really is. (president/chancellor pers. comm.)

We now have a sense of coming full circle regarding the Kellogg Commission work. As the compilation of interviews for this book was wrapping up, we had the opportunity to speak to Peter McPherson, current president of APLU and former president of Michigan State University, as well as having been a member of the original Kellogg Commission. McPherson indicated that APLU was in the midst of planning activities in 2017 that were going to result in his organization going back to the Kellogg Foundation with a request for funding to support a new commission. The reinitiation of this Kellogg-sponsored work was meant to focus attention on the contemporary issues facing land-grant and other public universities, which included the exploration of the scope of engagement and why there were not more engagement activities currently being undertaken by these institutions of higher learning. According to McPherson,

> The fact that the Kellogg Commission report on engagement continues to have such staying power is remarkable not just in the context of higher education, but for commissions in general. Rarely does one witness so many people and so many institutions being affected by a commission in such a manner. It was the right issue at the right time, expanding the notion of Extension so that it could become something much, much bigger. That said, I think of areas like social work, criminal justice, and education, for example. These are professional colleges that sometimes are not as engaged as they could be with those sectors for whom they are training students to become new employees. It's critically important that we need to work on strengthening ties with those constituencies. (pers. comm.)

McPherson went on to say how struck he was by the dramatically different levels of community engagement displayed by some public universities, despite the foundational work that had been done by the Kellogg Commission and the broad commitment to engagement he believes most public university leaders have made. He also stated that a new commission could tackle issues specifically designed to increase university engagement across the spectrum of land-grant and other public institutions, including perhaps most critically through an examination of the various ways in which engagement is incentivized or otherwise rewarded inside of academia. This is something we will be exploring ourselves in much greater detail in the fifth chapter of this book.

### The Carnegie Foundation's Classification
### for Community Engagement

Both within and beyond higher education circles, the Carnegie Foundation perhaps is most famous for its development of Carnegie Units, higher education's basic unit of measurement that is best well known to students and faculty alike as "credit hours."[36] These Carnegie Units, which are used to determine everything from graduation requirements and student financial aid to faculty teaching responsibilities, have a very interesting origin story. Until the early 1900s, university professors had no retirement system and therefore often worked until they died. There was widespread recognition within higher education circles that many of these academicians were working long past their productivity peak, and so a concerted effort was put together to create a retirement system.

Andrew Carnegie, a renowned industrialist and major philanthropist at the turn of the twentieth century, established the Carnegie Foundation for the Advancement of Teaching in 1905 in large part to create a pension system for professors. Access to this new system was predicated on colleges and universities adopting a set of criteria that standardized such things as admissions criteria, staffing levels, availability of facilities, and courses of instruction. With an initial gift of $10 million from Andrew Carnegie, the new pension program was formally put into place by 1918, allowing universities to begin refreshing their professorial ranks with some greater regularity. Eventually, all these activities were spun off into the independent nonprofit organization known today as TIAA-CREF (Teachers Insurance and Annuity Association–College Retirement Equities Fund).

The Carnegie Foundation for the Advancement of Teaching continued to have a substantial impact on higher education over the years. In 1970, the Carnegie Commission was created in order to compare and contrast institutions of higher learning for research and policy purposes.[37] Led by Clark Kerr, the former president of the University of California system mentioned earlier in this chapter, this commission developed categories (released in 1973) by which colleges and universities could be grouped: doctoral-granting institutions (with corresponding labels: heavy emphasis on research, moderate emphasis on research, moderate emphasis on doctoral programs, or limited emphasis on doctoral programs), comprehensive colleges (with two levels of master's degree program emphasis), liberal arts colleges (with two levels of selectivity), all two-year-degree-granting colleges and institutes, and professional schools and other specialized institutes. Although these categories and labels have been modified over the years (last updated in 2015), they remain the de facto classification system for institutions of higher learning in the United States.

The Carnegie Unit and Carnegie Classification efforts form the backdrop for the creation of the Classification for Community Engagement designation. This effort was initiated in 2010 by then president Lee Shulman as a voluntary taxonomy for those colleges and universities wishing to be recognized for their community engagement efforts, activities that were invisible in the original classification categories described above. The process for both receiving the initial designation and being reviewed for renewal purposes now occurs on a five-year cycle, with the next round scheduled for 2020. Administration of the Classification for Community Engagement designation review process is currently housed in the Brown University Swearer Center for Public Service, having moved there in January 2017 from the New England Resource Center for Higher Education.[38]

Colleges and universities submit applications for the Classification for Community Engagement which are based on self-assessment of how community engagement is built into the very fabric of the institution.[39] The application consists of two main sections: "foundational indicators" and "categories of engagement." The "foundational indicators" section is further divided into two component parts: the "institutional identity and culture" segment requires applicants to document how engagement is embedded in their mission statement, while the "institutional commitment" portion asks for evidence that budget, infrastructure, and strategic planning efforts all provide support for engagement efforts. Next, the "categories of engagement" section requires documentation of both "curricular engagement" and "outreach and partnerships." The "curricular engagement" segment asks for information about how teaching and learning activities are connected to the enhancement of community well-being. In turn, the "outreach and partnerships" segment requires applicants to provide evidence that institutional resources are being expended on activities that are mutually beneficial to both campus and community and that the scholarship and other outputs generated from the engagement activities involve a beneficial exchange of information and application of knowledge between the university and community collaborators.

We had the opportunity to speak with Paul LeMahieu, senior vice president of programs and operations at the Carnegie Foundation for the Advancement of Teaching, about the Classification for Community Engagement designation. LeMahieu emphasized that the voluntary engagement designation was meant to be part of a categorization system about institutional thrust or emphasis on community engagement, not a ranking system per se, nested inside the larger "involuntary" (in that institutions are categorized regardless of their input) Carnegie Classification system, which also was meant to be a nonjudgmental way to organize information about colleges and universities. He went on to say this:

> In both instances, the purpose was to give researchers a reasonably coherent and independent taxonomy by which to describe the nature of the institutions of higher education. Human nature being what it is, however, there sometimes is an implied hierarchy, where highly research-active universities are seen as better than non-research-active universities, for example. And so those universities with the community engagement designation might also be viewed as being better than those without the designation. This was never the intention of Carnegie's efforts. Our organization did not wish these categorizations to be viewed in the same light as the *U.S. News and World Report* rankings of colleges and universities. (pers. comm.)

Members of the academy who are involved more intensively in engagement efforts in fact have begun to weigh in on the merits and implications of the Carnegie Classification for Community Engagement. Among other notable compilation efforts, this includes a special issue of the journal *New Directions for Higher Education* which was published in 2009. Entitled "Institutionalizing Community Engagement in Higher Education: The First Wave of Carnegie Classified Institutions," this collection of articles covered a range of topic areas, including, but not limited to, rewards associated with engagement scholarship, innovative service-learning practices, benchmarking issues, fundraising, and leadership.[40] Reflecting on the contents of these contributions, the editors of this special issue were particularly struck with how the process for receiving this designation most often "served as the tool that forced an institution to change direction" toward more rigorous and impactful engagement efforts.[41]

## APLU's Innovation and Economic Prosperity Universities Designation

At the same time that land-grant and other public universities were attempting to more rigorously document their community engagement efforts across a broad spectrum of impact factors, these institutions were facing more specific questions about the degree to which they were directly impacting the economic well-being of the communities they are designed to serve. What became known as the Commission on Innovation, Competitiveness, and Economic Prosperity (CICEP) was formed within APLU for the express purpose of providing direction and guidance to members on university engagement activities that directly impact economic development in all its forms.[42]

The efforts of CICEP served to heighten awareness of the economic value that universities bring to communities through such activities as technology transfer, entrepreneurship, intellectual property development, and collaboration with business and industry partners.[43] It is important to note that the taxonomy put forward by CICEP to describe the economic engagement efforts of universities included all three components of the tripartite land-grant mission. Hence, it is believed that economic activities that are the direct result of teaching (described as the development of "talent"), research (dubbed "innovation"), and service (discussed as "stewardship of place") together can create the conditions for a more prosperous society.[44]

Out of these CICEP efforts, the IEP Universities Designation was developed by APLU to recognize colleges and universities that are leading the way in these sorts of economic development efforts. At present, institutions of higher learning undergo a rather intensive assessment process (including both self-study and external stakeholder input components) that leads to the IEP designation following a positive review from a program review panel.[45] Awards also are given out every year in four categories—Economic Prosperity Connections, Talent, Innovation, and Place—which serve to further underscore how various campuses are making a critical difference in the economic development of their host communities.

The IEP designation and the annual awards are based on a set of metrics that perhaps can be best understood through the set of assessment tools developed by CICEP for the express purpose of helping universities document their economic engagement efforts.[46] These tools are based on what has been described as "four simple ideas": know, measure, tell, and engage. That is, economic engagement activities are thought to have meaningful impact when universities *know* what they do well and what they need to improve on, when they *measure* their engagement levels, and when they are able to *tell* the story of their economic contributions.

More specifically, surveys are offered by CICEP that pose approximately 40 questions to both internal and external stakeholders on a variety of characteristics thought to be reflective of economic engagement activities undertaken by institutions of higher learning. These items fall into categories related to the assertion of leadership; the creation of a supportive culture; ensuring that university activities benefit the public; making contributions to an innovation economy; providing relevant educational opportunities and programs; promoting the core values of openness, accessibility, and responsiveness; and communicating effectively about university contributions, successes, and achievements that benefit the region. Interestingly, each of the items is rated twice, first in terms of how important the characteristic is to the institution's role in economic development, and second in terms of how well the university is performing that characteristic in actuality.

We were able to discuss a range of issues related to these assessment strategies and CICEP's economic engagement documentation efforts as a whole with James Woodell, APLU's vice president for economic development and community engagement. Woodell asserted,

> We need to take all the spirit of what was laid out in the Kellogg Commission and we need to ramp it up. We need to say we weren't kidding. We weren't simply saying you need to change the name of outreach to engagement and everything's good. We need to continue to advance the idea that community-university engagement should be reciprocal and mutually beneficial. We need to make engagement about community *and* economic development in all their forms. And we need to get beyond an atomistic view that creates pockets of engagement interest within universities. We need to create a more holistic, institution-wide approach to engagement, and I think that is what we are helping to build through the IEP Universities program. (pers. comm.)

Woodell went on to state that one of the most important by-products of the CICEP work to date has been the development of a comprehensive qualitative database of rich descriptive information about what university economic engagement looks like from the standpoint of the 55 universities that have received the IEP designation (including 23 land-grant universities). As researchers begin to access and analyze this database in the near future, campuses and communities stand to benefit from a comparison and contrast of how universities are attempting to meet the economic needs of the communities they were designed to serve.

## Summary

We began at the beginning of the land-grant institution's history, which was the 1862 Morrill Act. From there, we covered subsequent federal legislation that included the Hatch Act of 1887, the 1890 Morrill Act, and the Smith-Lever

Act of 1914, which together created the land-grant university's tripartite mission of teaching, research, and service. Next, we discussed the idea of a covenant that exists between the public and its institutions of higher learning, with special attention paid to the private versus public good that accrues from activities undertaken by colleges and universities. This chapter also noted that the emphasis on the public good generated by land-grant institutions helped spur recognition for more sustained and coordinated engagement efforts with various community stakeholders, which in turn created a need for ways to organize and recognize these community engagement activities. Finally, we reviewed the work of three main entities in this regard—the Kellogg Commission on the Future of State and Land-Grant Universities, the Carnegie Foundation for the Advancement of Teaching Classification for Community Engagement, and APLU's IEP Universities Designation—with special emphasis on how each of these efforts has contributed to the codification of building relationships with community stakeholders.

# CHAPTER 3

# Land-Grant Strengths, Weaknesses, Opportunities, and Threats

Building on our discussion of the evolving nature of the land-grant institution and mission, in this chapter we present the main findings of our SWOT analysis. The 27 presidents and chancellors of the 1862 US land-grant universities interviewed for our study answered questions about the various strengths, weaknesses, opportunities, and threats faced by land-grant institutions as their representatives attempted to meet the needs of community stakeholders. As noted in the first chapter, the presidents and chancellors were presented with four basic questions regarding the land-grant mission of serving the needs of communities: (1) areas in which land-grant universities currently are displaying the greatest strengths, (2) areas in which land-grant universities currently are displaying the greatest weaknesses, (3) the most important new opportunities for land-grant universities to meet the needs of communities, and (4) the most important new threats faced by land-grant universities as they attempt to meet the needs of communities.

Seven main themes emerged from our analysis of the qualitative data generated from the presidents' and chancellors' responses to these four interview questions:

1. Concerns about funding declines versus the need to create efficiencies
2. Research prowess versus teaching and service excellence

3. Knowledge for knowledge's sake versus a more applied focus
4. The focus on rankings versus an emphasis on access and affordability
5. Meeting the needs of rural communities versus the needs of a more urbanized America
6. Global reach versus closer-to-home impact
7. The benefits of higher education versus the devaluation of a college diploma

The remainder of this chapter focuses attention on these dialectically situated themes. These themes will be presented in a relatively straightforward manner, factually and unembellished, with direct quotations from the land-grant presidents and chancellors used as anchor points for our discussion. Where relevant, the responses of these senior administrators will be compared and contrasted with pertinent literature on these topic areas.

## Concerns about Funding Declines versus the Need to Create Efficiencies

The first theme emerging from our interviews of presidents and chancellors centers on their concerns about declines in funding for public institutions of higher learning in juxtaposition to their acknowledgments about the need to create more efficient ways of running land-grant universities as a business. In general, there are four main sources of support for colleges and universities: tuition and fees from student enrollment, government appropriations (including both state subsidies and federal support), sponsored research, and philanthropic giving.[1] From a residential campus perspective, student housing and meal plans (room and board) generate significant additional revenue dollars. Taken together, these funding streams combine to create budgets for many land-grant (and other major public) universities which typically exceed $1 billion. The sheer size of these expenditures is thought to have created skepticism (if not outright cynicism) among funders and the general public about the need for such large allocations of money, something that has made life quite difficult for university leaders who attempt to make the case for continued fiscal support from the public's coffers.[2]

A recent report issued by the American Council on Education (ACE) focused on a variety of issues and concerns facing current college and university presidents.[3] By far, finances were the primary focal point of the senior administrators participating in the ACE study, with more than half of the sample expecting reductions in state support over the next five years, and another quarter expecting no more than flat funding over that same period. In response, roughly two-thirds of these presidents forecasted that fiscal management and fundraising were going to be their two most time-consuming activities.

Sounding a similar note, the most frequently mentioned topic in the interviews we conducted with the land-grant presidents and chancellors concerned the significant funding pressures being felt by these higher education leaders at present. The following quote is representative of the most pervasive comments made by the senior administrators who took part in our interviews:

> I'm not going to surprise anyone if I say that funding is one of the most important future threats faced by land-grant universities. It's kind of ridiculous that one of the greatest contributions that the United States has made to the world is its land-grant universities, and we can't find the funding necessary to sustain these institutions? To continue to cut funding and not embrace and support the land-grants is a huge, huge risk. (president/chancellor pers. comm.)

Almost to a person, these senior administrators centered their remarks on fiscal concerns as the most dominant issue their land-grant institutions are facing at present, especially when asked about the present weaknesses and future threats faced by land-grant universities as they attempted to meet the needs of communities.

There is no doubt that the degeneration of fiscal support for higher education has been real, impactful, and well documented in the higher education literature. As but one example, the *Chronicle of Higher Education* published a series of articles in 2014 which examined the decline in financial support for public higher education. This included statistics that provided readers with a 25-year look (from 1987 to 2012) at the falloff of state and federal support as a share of overall revenue, which ranged from −3.7% to −35.9%.[4] A companion article described this "era of neglect" not as the result of one easily defined issue, ideology, or moment in time, but rather as a series of many decisions made and directions taken over time by a variety of actors—including but not limited to lobbyists, governors, local and state government representatives, and policymakers—whose interests and activities were in direct competition for funding support.[5]

The land-grant university presidents and chancellors interviewed for this study seem to be all too familiar with the fiscal predicaments generated by the environment of rivalry being created within state budgets. Said one,

As Medicaid, Medicare, other health care needs, and the prison system take a larger and larger percentage of the discretionary budget of the states, higher education really is vulnerable because it is seen as a luxury item instead of a necessity, especially in comparison to these other elements. (president/chancellor pers. comm.)

Rising health care costs most specifically have been thought to have had a deleterious impact on higher education budgets over the years. More recent political events seem to have exacerbated this situation. For instance, congressional attempts to repeal the Patient Protection and Affordable Care Act in early 2017 intensified the warning that higher Medicaid costs for states would translate into even more significant cuts to colleges and universities as states assumed more of the financial responsibilities for health care originally taken on by the federal government.[6]

One of the articles in the 2014 *Chronicle of Higher Education* series mentioned above described a "tipping point" that our country has reached regarding the transformation of public higher education into a private good, where students and their families increasingly are expected to foot the bill for a college diploma.[7] This too is something on the minds of the land-grant presidents and chancellors we interviewed. As one stated,

It seems as if state legislators think much less of us at present. Higher education has always been on the more discretionary side of the budget, of course. But now we are witnessing situations where the funding for public universities, including land-grant universities, is being drastically reduced. As a result, families are being asked to shoulder more and more of the burden for financing their children's college education. And so questions arise about the degree to which land-grant institutions can continue to provide all of the services and resources that they once did, alongside questions about how much more these families should be asked to provide financially. There are significant ethical issues that arise alongside these questions that all surround the balance of burden associated with the costs and rewards of higher education. (president/chancellor pers. comm.)

As discussed in the previous chapter, the notion that a covenant exists between the public and its colleges and universities is firmly rooted in higher education circles. From such a vantage point, the decline in funding for public higher education was portrayed by some of the presidents and chancellors interviewed for this study as a betrayal of that covenant. Left to their own devices, what we witnessed were senior administrators explaining that they were being forced to become more innovative and tactical in their orientation to budget-related issues. For some of these individuals, the answer involved the diversification of revenue streams. This sentiment was expressed explicitly by one of the senior administrators we interviewed:

> We need some kind of funding model that allows us to conduct our research as well as to educate the students. And at the same time, we have to put on top of all that the duties and obligations associated with outreach and engagement that we do as part of the land-grant mission. It's really an issue because there's a lot of pressure to not raise tuition. We are at a tipping point, having recruited out-of-state students because they produce more revenue. But that revenue is starting to level off and plateau. So we need to find other ways to fund the activities of the university that are not connected to tuition increases, and most prominently that involves development dollars. Unfortunately, often as not those development dollars are not given by donors to support community engagement efforts. (president/chancellor pers. comm.)

Those individuals in charge of state purse strings—governors and legislators—reportedly are troubled by what they perceive to be higher education's lack of concern for and failure to address real-life issues faced by the state and its citizens.[8] Ironically, the uncertainty of state support for higher education has propelled public institutions toward more entrepreneurial activities and for-profit ventures, efforts that paradoxically can move them ever farther away from a concentrated focus on the public good of universities.[9] Essentially, these institutions shift their focus to building up the administrative infrastructure that supports the solicitation and processing of funds from these alternative sources, including but not limited to donor relations and industry partnerships that revolve around tech transfer and business incubation activities.

On the other side of the coin were those presidents and chancellors whose remarks underscored a belief that higher education must be "reengineered" in some manner to create cost efficiencies.[10] These senior administrators had determined that colleges and universities were long overdue in examining their expenditures:

> There is a statistic within our current fiscal scenario that none of my colleagues like to talk about. And that's this: the cost of education is constant, within about $300 over a 20-year period of time. Which is pretty interesting, because

that usually suggests a very inefficiently run industry. Because to not have had an efficiency gain over a 20-year period, well, that industry typically would have been out of business. That's the part of the story that presidents rarely point out. So I actually think we have lots of challenges around the support that we should expect to be receiving. I think we owe it to ourselves and the nation to simultaneously improve the efficiency and the quality of the education we are providing. And that's a tough challenge. (president/chancellor pers. comm.)

The most commonly selected target for further scrutiny by presidents and chancellors was administrative bloat in its many forms. This should not be surprising, especially in light of the expansion of infrastructure designed to capture the diversified external funds we noted above. And yet, there also was a palpable sense among some senior leaders that universities increased in size over the course of many years simply because there was no prior demand for efficiency. Here is what one president shared with us:

Our greatest weakness is seen presently in our efforts to transform our universities into a sustainable enterprise. Most of us have developed into comprehensive universities that are the envy of the world. But we also developed bad habits along the way. We have developed business practices that are unsustainable. I'm now going through my university, unit by unit, and we are limiting our levels of management and increasing our static control. We had a static control here of one to three, or three to one if you prefer, which equates to one manager and three employees. Yet standard business practices put desirable static control levels at eight to one or twelve to one. So, we developed bad habits as part of our historical tradition, and because this is unsustainable we have to make these changes, and quickly. (president/chancellor pers. comm.)

One further point of discussion for those presidents and chancellors contemplating efficiencies involved the increased use of distance education technology. Although these senior administrators noted that it may have been the case that the land-grant institutions had been a little slow in warming to distance education in the past, to them it now seems to be the case that market demands (especially students wishing to have more flexible access to courses) have forced these institutions of higher learning to more aggressively develop online courses and, at least in some cases, offer entire degree-granting programs online. There was a demonstrable awareness among some administrators that further disruptive technology on the near horizon would provide ever more efficient ways to pursue an education at dramatically lower costs and cut time to degree. One clear example provided in the interviews surrounded recent gains made in virtual reality technology, with several leaders' remarks pointing to the growing ability of universities to provide access to virtual reality classrooms from anywhere in the world.

An additional significant threat to the status quo and the attendant demand for efficiencies mentioned by a few presidents and chancellors taking part in our interviews involved alternative certification. The general idea here is that, over time, inadequate rigor in some disciplines had eroded trust in what university students were able to do upon graduation and entry into the workforce. In reaction, some companies have begun to develop alternative ways to verify that students know what they claim to know. While likely impacting schools other than land-grant universities in the near term (this seems especially the case for two-year technical colleges at present), all sorts of potential problems were seen in cases where individual businesses or entire industries decided that they were no longer going to accept a college diploma as "the price of admission" for employment. Hence, it was mentioned by some senior administrators that, if such a threat arises for these other schools in the near term, it might well be the case that eventually this would become a difficulty that land-grant universities would have to grapple with as well.

Yet another efficiency issue discussed in our interviews focused on how institutions of higher learning historically have scaled their innovation efforts, especially as university personnel interacted with community stakeholders around various economic development issues and concerns. In the words of one university president,

> If you look at the reports from Extension and the experiment stations, all of us want to be a bigger component of economic development. And that requires not just all of the projects we tend to focus on, but how we work on the scalability of those efforts. We also are not doing a very good job of transporting ideas from one part of the state to another, and from one state to another, and from one country to another. If you think about the way land-grants work, a lot of what we do is project-based at the county level. So what we need to do is to take that work and do a meta-analysis. Everybody thinks that their situation is unique. But in a meta-analysis, you begin to understand how to leverage what works in one situation and apply it to others. (president/chancellor pers. comm.)

Relatedly, because there does not seem to be enough funding to do everything in a way that is customized to individual community needs, it was suggested that land-grant universities had to invest more time and energy into training-the-trainer efforts that would build more generalizable skill sets for individuals involved in community-serving activities. Further, several presidents and chancellors mentioned the need for land-grant universities to get better at cooperating across colleges and institutions to create efficiencies that were both interdisciplinary and transinstitutional.

Some senior administrators believed that their institutions were at or near a breaking point, however, and thus thought that time had run out on efforts to create gradual and deliberate change through increased efficiency measures. Instead, there was a sense that dire financial situations were going to result in rather drastic action, including an immediate and significant decline in services provided to and connections maintained with communities. Those who did speak about making such cuts believed that it was a bad direction to take, and yet there was uniform agreement that the financing of teaching and research efforts was always going to take precedence over the funding of community engagement activities. As one administrator noted,

> With all the stresses related to costs, it's very easy to slip back into a mode where you have to prioritize, and that first priority is graduating that student. So, these activities where you extend yourself in service to society, some people will look at those things and say well, these things aren't primary anymore. Questions arise about being able to afford that kind of investment. It's why we have insisted that all our engagement efforts have to be a partnership with the community, so that our funds are amplified and leveraged by the community in order to be successful. Quite frankly, if I were to use a tuition dollar to make a new connection to the community, there would be a lot of unhappy people. As in, you're raising my tuition and you're doing what with my money in what community? (president/chancellor pers. comm.)

Decisions that involved cutting back on efforts to engage community partners in the name of efficiency were agonizing to some of the senior administrators we interviewed. They saw state support, especially for Cooperative Extension Services, as having been eroded at the very time that there has been a massive uptick in community needs. With much regret, however, they stated that they felt that their land-grant universities could no longer afford to be all things to all people, and that outreach and engagement activities were most likely to be cut in order to balance their budgets.

## Research Prowess versus Teaching and Service Excellence

The second theme emerging from our interviews of presidents and chancellors focuses attention on the celebration of the land-grant university's research contributions versus the need to bolster excellence in teaching and in outreach and engagement activities. As we noted in the second chapter, the Morrill Act, the Hatch Act, and the Smith-Lever Act together constituted the congressional actions that appropriated funds for the three core activities of the land-grant university: teaching, research, and service. After the Hatch Act was passed in 1887, our country witnessed a slow and steady rise in research prowess among the land-grant universities, right up to the advent of World War II. At that time, massive increases in federal funding for research—especially in areas concerning defense and public health—fueled a rapid expansion of university-based research programs, especially for those claiming a land-grant heritage.[11] As a direct result, we believe, research efforts have become the coin of the realm in today's land-grant university, far eclipsing teaching and service in terms of both what is highlighted and what is rewarded.

The most common response to the questions we posed to the presidents and chancellors we interviewed about land-grant strengths and opportunities surrounded the achievements these universities have accomplished through research efforts. Readers will remember that we first introduced this strong emphasis on research in our discussion of the Hatch Act in the previous chapter. Here is an illustrative quote from one of the senior administrators we interviewed:

> Clark Kerr said that knowledge makes the world go around, and the university is still the best place for ideas. I think that certainly has been true and is still true today. Many of the great things about our country right now, and our place as a leader in the world, have come from ideas that were created at universities through research activities. As a result, I think that universities have been central to our dominance in the health sciences, for instance, and in economics and manufacturing. Land-grant universities were founded to help us do a better job in agriculture and technical skills, so I think we have been a platform on which our country has grown in those areas as well. And if we are going to continue to stay out front, I think that our research efforts have to continue to be elevated. Our challenge is to stay ahead empirically, so that we

can continue to be at the center of the fabric of this country. (president/ chancellor pers. comm.)

The large increases in federal funding directed toward research as the Second World War ended certainly have laid the foundation for this dramatic uptick in empirical activities within land-grant universities. Two additional actions at the federal level also impacted the further development of this powerful emphasis on research within many of America's public universities. First, there was the 1945 release of a federal science policy guideline authored by Vannevar Bush, the director of the wartime Office of Scientific Research and Development. Entitled *Science—the Endless Frontier: A Report to the President for Postwar Scientific Research*, this document almost single-handedly formalized the relationship between the federal government and the institutions of higher learning it wished to use as its research laboratories. In large part, this was accomplished through the establishment of organizations such as the National Science Foundation (NSF) and the National Institutes of Health (NIH), federal agencies that were designed to administer over and direct research funding to universities. Second, the US Congress passed the Bayh-Dole Act in 1980. This congressional action granted universities the right to patent the results of this federally funded research. Almost instantaneously, this congressional action created huge economic incentives for universities to conduct studies in close collaboration with business and industry partners.

In combination, these two federal actions, taken over the course of 35 years, are thought to have placed American university researchers squarely at the center of the development of today's global knowledge economy.[12] Most specifically, land-grant universities have been at the forefront of many important discoveries and scientific advances within this period, creating both the pride of accomplishment and an enduring sense that research activities conducted by universities are an essential contribution to the nation's prosperity. But what about teaching and service, the other two core components of the land-grant university mission?

There was a clear sense among the presidents and chancellors that an emphasis on teaching excellence has lagged within the confines of land-grant universities. In the words of one senior administrator,

Our educational efforts, although outstanding, have not kept pace with our research. The reward systems for our faculty are uneven, emphasizing research prowess over teaching efforts. Having to say teaching is important to a university is like saying that hygiene is important to a hospital. I mean it should be a given, a basic premise. There are parallels between health care in the medical sphere and teaching efforts in higher education. The medical profession has done a pretty good job in the last generation moving from the nineteenth century to the twenty-first century by looking at outcomes— length of stay, for instance—things that we didn't look at routinely even 20 years ago. I think we've done a good job of moving toward objective and merit-based outcomes in the health sciences, and I would love to see us take those same steps in higher education as well. (president/chancellor pers. comm.)

We believe that the lack of emphasis on teaching excellence is troubling at many different levels, not the least of which is that this is precisely what the general public expects of universities. We are also in danger of forgetting our historical roots. After all, offering a practical education for the sons and daughters of toil was part of the original land-grant charter vis-à-vis the Morrill Acts. At minimum, then, we believe that this requires us to acknowledge that all empirical activities being undertaken within the land-grant university should be closely aligned with its teaching responsibilities, thus emphasizing the complementary relationship between excellence in teaching and excellence in research.[13]

Part of the problem here is the challenge of quantifying exactly what teaching excellence looks like. Compare this to the ease by which one can measure research prowess. One can count the number of citations that a refereed journal article receives, for instance, indicating how often a faculty member's peers are referring to her or his body of research work in their own scholarly pursuits. Another example might be the dollar amount of total grants received by a faculty member, indicating the level of support that one's research program can garner from external stakeholders such as federal agencies and industry partners.

As the old adage goes, administrators cannot read, but they can count. Regrettably, at present most of the data that "counts" with regard to teaching excellence is generated through students' evaluation of the instruction they receive. While it certainly is the case that the opinions of customers (in this case, students in the classroom) are invaluable, such measures as often as not can be reduced to little more than popularity contests among faculty members. We would argue strongly here that a well-liked instructor is hardly a viable criterion for excellence in teaching. While many land-grant universities are now developing centers of excellence that are beginning to address this issue, most presidents and chancellors were in agreement that we have a long way to go here.

There is then the even greater challenge of quantifying what excellence in service (or in outreach and engagement) looks like. Here again we turn to the words of a senior administrator whom we interviewed:

> As universities move toward resource allocation models that are based on certain performance metrics, the metric we have the poorest information on is engagement with the community. You can count most other things having to do with research, and at least with teaching you can count such things as courses offered and student opinions about instructor abilities. It gets much more difficult to account for community interaction. In an age that is becoming more and more data driven, that also can move us away from more engagement-oriented activity. (president/chancellor pers. comm.)

In our second chapter, we reviewed the efforts of the Carnegie Foundation for the Advancement of Teaching and CICEP (the latter formed within APLU), two organizations that have contributed to the progress of measuring excellence in engagement. The Engaged Scholarship Consortium (ESC) more recently has provided guidance and direction in this area as well, especially in terms of promoting an increased awareness of and valuation for empirical efforts aimed at this component of the land-grant mission.[14] We will have more to say about the efforts of ESC in our fifth chapter, which concerns the role of faculty. At present, however, we must recognize that there is much more work to be done in terms of understanding and coming to agreement within the academy on how to define equivalent levels of excellence in service, outreach, and engagement.

## Knowledge for Knowledge's Sake versus a More Applied Focus

There is another research-related topic that emerged as the third theme derived from the interviews we conducted with university presidents and chancellors: the relative balance of basic research versus applied research conducted by faculty, staff, and students in land-grant universities. Basic (or pure) research concerns those empirical efforts driven by intellectual curiosity, with the main motivation to make a contribution to the knowledge base of science (knowledge for knowledge's sake). Applied research, in contrast, concerns those empirical efforts that are designed to solve existing problems, with the main motivation to improve some condition of life.

Although there has been some recent debate about the distinctiveness of this terminology, we believe that the basic and applied research labels are useful heuristics in discussions about empirical work being conducted within institutions of higher learning.[15] This is especially so given that the historical mission of the land-grant universities largely has been defined by an emphasis on applied research activities. Here is how one senior administrator we interviewed expressed her take on this matter:

> I remember an old colleague once remarking to me that the general public had no understanding of the difference between a public university and a land-grant university. And he seemed to think that was a good thing. I thought it was kind of stupid. What separates land-grants from public universities and research universities writ large is that sense that you want to be tethered to the world in which you live. There's always the need for basic research in any type of university. But in land-grant universities there is the sense that your research needs to be applied, that it addresses contemporary or pending economic, social, or political problems, and is a part of the fabric of life in land-grant universities to a greater extent than in other public and research universities. (president/chancellor pers. comm.)

Most of the senior administrators taking part in our interviews expressed similar viewpoints. Researchers within land-grant universities, and especially those taking advantage of available federal research dollars described above, have been portrayed as contributing mightily to the development and well-being of our nation by taking theoretical work and bench science efforts and applying them directly to the needs of communities.

When it came to specific focal areas, these presidents and chancellors typically articulated the need for land-grant universities to conduct this applied research in ways that directly stimulated economic progress within their particular geographic regions. Here is what one senior administrator told us:

> This issue of basic and applied research will always be with us—what's the right mix—but in land-grants there will always be the sense that we need to be engaged in a healthy dose of applied research. A good contemporary example of this are university-industry partnerships, which is a very natural

relationship to develop if you are a land-grant researcher. At other public and private research universities, there may be some angst over whether or not those researchers should be engaged in those types of research partnerships, working in collaboration with industry in a significant way. This is not the case in land-grant universities, where such partnerships are celebrated. (president/chancellor pers. comm.)

As a rule, most of the presidents and chancellors highlighted the importance of their universities being centrally involved in the economic development of their communities. And they often noted with pride that their land-grant institutions were the best thing going for their regions in terms of economic impact.

More specifically, these senior administrators were quick to emphasize that the commercial power exhibited by their land-grant universities was not just reflected in the dollars that flowed through communities as the result of students living on or near campus, nor was their financial impact merely based on the fact that they were providing well-trained new employees for corporations upon graduation from any number of majors and programs. These sentiments were founded specifically on the applied focus of research being conducted within the confines of these land-grant universities. Here, the presidents and chancellors were highlighting the direct role their institutions of higher learning played in the attraction and recruitment of new businesses and investment opportunities, specifically because industry leaders knew that they could access researchers who were keenly interested in and adept at solving problems. Any corporation locating itself close to a land-grant university and its personnel, these senior administrators reasoned, did so because they knew they could access and leverage their applied research firepower to grow their businesses.

It should be noted here, however, that not all the university presidents and chancellors we interviewed believed that they currently were having this sort of significant economic impact, especially when it came to translating research findings into the marketplace. Here is what one senior administrator recounted:

> I think some land-grant universities still struggle to understand how they can impact the economic development of the state. How they can really help drive the economic engine. Now, some land-grants do this better than others. But I think as a whole, moving into the economic sector, and really trying to help by developing new economies and new technologies and new revenue streams,

we have really struggled. This is likely to be especially true in more rural states, where there isn't as much infrastructure to do these things. It's not that we don't want to do it. It's more the case that we don't know how to do it, especially when the tools to help are not immediately in our grasp. (president/chancellor pers. comm.)

Of course, the applied research efforts of land-grant universities are not limited to economic development and collaborations with business and industry partners. For many of these institutions of higher learning, there has been historical strength displayed in applied research efforts within the areas of agriculture, natural resources, human sciences, and the interface of the sciences that are usually held within an agricultural and life sciences college.

At the same time, many of the presidents and chancellors reported that any new opportunities for growth (or at the very least preventing even harsher budgetary cuts) were going to come from efforts that universities would undertake within the partnerships (through applied research and otherwise) that surround economic development. Essentially, they believed that a significant portion of the future of the land-grant university hinged on the development of better connections between the creation and seeding of entrepreneurism and economic development across the entire state. In large part, this pivot toward economic development is thought to be a strategy aimed at halting state subsidy declines. In the words of one senior administrator,

We haven't had a budget increase in over ten years, similar to what is happening in other states. So, I think a lot of universities are saying hey, we've got to prove our worth to the business community. We need the business community and other groups to put the pressure on state government to do something to better fund us. And there's nothing like success stories in stimulating the economy and economic development to show your worth. I think that's what a lot of universities are going to be focusing on right now in terms of research efforts, tech transfer, business incubators, and the like. (president/chancellor pers. comm.)

We also wish to point out that there was some undercurrent in our interviews to the effect that land-grant researchers should not lose sight of the role that they can and should play in basic research efforts. This belief was tied to the recognition that the relationship between public universities and state governments has been shifting in ways that extend beyond the financial declines we have been discussing to this point. Ironically, the drop in fiscal support has occurred in the face of significant increases in accountability demands from state legislators. It has been argued that while a portion of this answerability has to do with cost controls, there also has been a demand for more "utilitarian" (i.e., applied research) activities that directly benefit the economic development and workforce needs of the state.[16]

## The Focus on Rankings versus an Emphasis on Access and Affordability

The fourth theme that emerged from our interviews with presidents and chancellors concerned their concentration on moving their land-grant universities ever higher in national rankings as compared and contrasted to efforts that make their institutions of higher learning more affordable and accessible to students of modest means. In the previous chapter, we introduced the work of the Carnegie Foundation for the Advancement of Teaching, an organization that developed a classification system to compare and contrast institutions of higher learning for research and policy purposes. There also are much more media-driven rankings that invariably promise readers some insight into the relative value of attending colleges and universities on their lists. Although the *U.S. News and World Report* rankings perhaps are the most well known, in actuality there are over 30 systems currently in place that evaluate institutions of higher learning in one form or another.[17] Typically, these rankings include some attention paid to academic reputation (often the opinions of senior university administrators and/or high school counselors), student retention rates, faculty-related factors (class size, faculty-student ratio, faculty compensation), student-related factors (ACT/SAT average scores, high school ranking, admitted vs. applied ratio), average spending per student, alumni donations, and six-year graduation rates.[18]

The presidents and chancellors whom we interviewed uniformly did not believe that these ranking systems were of much intrinsic value, yet they considered it almost impossible not to pay them heed. Here is what one senior administrator said:

> In the academy, we all spend way too much time paying attention to rankings and survey results. Most of them have methodologies that are so flawed they aren't worth very much at all, but nevertheless we are inundated with this kind of stuff. And yet, I would make the observation that there is not one ranking, national or international, of land-grant institutions. And because there isn't any ranking—and I'm not suggesting that we should have such a ranking—but

because we have no ranking for land-grants, it undercuts the visibility of land-grant institutions. Nobody walks around saying hey we're the second-best land-grant university in the nation. Nobody says that. People would look at you and say, "What are you talking about?" But if you say you are the number two public research institution in the nation, then everybody knows what you are talking about. We simply don't talk about the land-grant institutions in a coherent way like that. The fact that we do not have a national focus on land-grant universities as major entities in and of themselves, separate from public and private research universities, means we have lost the opportunity for some coherence about who we are. (president/chancellor pers. comm.)

Many of these presidents and chancellors went on to argue that pursuits of better rankings within these evaluation systems were creating some unintended and rather significant negative consequences. Essentially, they believed that their institutions were moving farther away from the original mission of providing access to higher education to the "sons and daughters of toil," as indicated in the founding discussions and documents of the land-grant universities. A portion of this shift in emphasis was discussed as being related to the move toward a more selective admissions process, a strategy designed to impact the student-related factors mentioned above regarding the test scores and high school rankings of incoming students. And when you go after greater numbers of higher-achieving students, you are competing with other schools following the same admissions strategies, which translates into the necessity of offering ever more lucrative merit-based scholarships.

This is all well and good, until, of course, what you discover is the lack of any sort of backfilling of support in the way of needs-based scholarships. Some of the senior administrators we interviewed admitted that the latter issue has been more insidious than might first have been imagined. The result is that land-grant universities have become places where the needs of the middle and upper classes have been reinforced, and yet they have increasingly failed to provide opportunities for the very people who originally were intended to benefit from the land-grant university. One senior administrator put the current predicament and challenge this way:

> The number one opportunity is for us to do a better job of creating a pathway for brilliant students from the lower half of the income distribution to be educated at our most competitive and successful colleges. In my institution, we are probably four to one in terms of distribution between the upper and lower halves of the income distribution. It doesn't seem to me that intelligence or

human qualities like decency and integrity are split four times as much in the upper income distribution versus the lower half. And yet somehow it seems that there are many more opportunities for those children coming from the upper half. (president/chancellor pers. comm.)

While it should be obvious that maintaining the highest standards of academic excellence can and should coexist with efforts to maintain access and affordability, it is not at all clear that most land-grant universities are striking any sort of reasonable balance at this time.

Most poignantly, very few of the senior administrators we interviewed were of the belief that their institutions were capable of bragging about the ability to maintain a full commitment to educating students at the lower end of the income distribution scale. They stated that they may have been able to recount points of pride around attention given to issues of increasing diversity in areas associated with race and culture, for example, but not as much about how they have made significant impacts on the recruitment, retention, and graduation rates of lower-income and first-generation students more specifically. In the words of one senior administrator we interviewed,

> The educational divide in this country is appalling. The gap between the haves and the have-nots has been increasing exponentially in the last 40 to 50 years when it comes to educational access. We don't meet the needs of underserved populations very well. And we don't serve first-generation students very well either. Like many other land-grant institutions, we are the state's flagship university, and yet we don't recruit from some of the areas within our state at all. Instead, we have paid attention to the more affluent areas of the state. That's really quite a weakness here. (president/chancellor pers. comm.)

The one noteworthy exception to this shortcoming came from those schools that maintained branch or regional campuses, where often there was not as stark a difference in terms of the family income of admitted students. Senior leaders reported that significantly more students who were Pell Grant eligible (a form of federal financial aid that serves as a common marker of greater economic need) were enrolled on these branch and regional campuses, for example. Also, unlike the more selective admissions requirements of the main campuses, these branch and regional campuses operated in an open enrollment environment. Hence, those presidents and chancellors with multiple campuses spoke more definitively about these alternate locations as pathways to a college education for many more students from the lower half of the income distribution. Fundamentally, these administrators were admitting that the land-grant mission of serving the sons and daughters of toil largely was being kept alive on and by these branch and regional campuses.

## Meeting the Needs of Rural Communities versus the Needs of a More Urbanized America

In our first chapter, we introduced the terms "capital" and "countryside" to describe the American political divide at present, a polarization that geographically fits neatly into an urban versus rural distinction. In chapter 2, we highlighted the agrarian roots of the land-grant university, noting the dominant role that agriculture played in the development of these institutions of higher learning. All of this comes together quite handily as a lead-in to our discussion of the fifth theme emerging from the interviews we conducted with presidents and chancellors, which spotlights those activities undertaken by land-grant universities to meet the needs of rural communities in comparison to those efforts designed to address the concerns of stakeholders located in more urban areas.

There was uniform belief that land-grant universities have always served the needs of rural America through an emphasis on its agricultural roots. At the same time, there was a widespread sentiment that this was not only a propagation of historical strengths but also a focal point for new opportunities. Here is what one senior leader said about this:

> Like any large organization, I think it's easy for any university—and particularly land-grants because of their applied orientation—to become very comfortable in what they are doing and therefore not really looking for what the next big thing might be. That said, agriculture is a really good example of finding new opportunities for involvement. We have gone from a traditional orientation of looking for better, more efficient ways to plant and harvest crops to looking for better, more efficient ways to genetically and organically enhance the productivity of our agricultural activities. It's moved from planting and harvesting activities to plant science, and soil science, genomics, and genetics. Of course, the trick will still be figuring out what comes next. Most agriculturalists believe that we are going to have to expand genetic modification if we are going to feed the world. (president/chancellor pers. comm.)

Many of the senior administrators emphasized that land-grant university assistance to rural communities extended beyond agricultural help to include a focus on the specific needs of rural families. And while it was acknowledged that this sort of support originally began as helping farm families with everyday needs surrounding canning and other methods of food preservation and preparation, more recently these activities had moved toward the provision of direct assistance to families under stress, especially in smaller rural communities where other social support services had failed in some manner. Of course, this expanded work in the community is being undertaken at the same time that land-grant institutions continue to focus on agricultural production, perhaps most notably including the development and maintenance of community food systems.[19]

Regardless of the specific activity being referenced by the presidents and chancellors we interviewed, the presence of the land-grant university in rural communities invariably was considered in conjunction with the efforts of Cooperative Extension Services. As introduced in the discussion of the Smith-Lever Act of 1914 in the previous chapter, the Cooperative Extension Services system was designed specifically to take findings from research studies conducted by land-grant universities and apply them directly to the farms, fields, and homes of families. Axiomatically, the majority of those sorts of applications were directed toward rural stakeholders. Here is one example of what a senior administrator told us in an interview:

> My view is that, when it comes to the land-grant mission of serving the needs of the community, we continue to do a great job of serving the needs of rural communities, because of our historic strength in agriculture and Extension. But we also are unique within all public universities in terms of being connected to all parts of the state because of Extension. That has kept our view of our communities as more broad than just our rural constituents, at least at a conceptual level, so this is a strength of all land-grants. Of course, this is a fluctuating strength across the country because of the variation in how willing each state's Extension folks have been to get out of their rural comfort zone, as well as how much financial pressure has been placed on a given state's land-grant institution. (president/chancellor pers. comm.)

A number of senior administrators mentioned the fiscal struggles that Extension has faced over the past several decades, having been hurt not only by the general reduction in state support to public universities but also by declines in funding at the federal level. The variability of this decline in financial support was thought to be one contributing factor in how well some land-grant universities had diversified their Cooperative Extension Services to include issues and concerns of interest to a variety of academic disciplines which touch a wider range of geographical areas, while others remained very restricted to agriculture and a distinctly rural presence.

The majority of presidents and chancellors believed that land-grant universities in general and Cooperative Extension Services more specifically were obliged to become more involved and more impactful in urban locations. Here is an example of how one senior administrator viewed this issue:

> Clearly, land-grant universities need to become much more comfortable in working with more urban-based populations. That's where land-grant universities have fallen short, and haven't done as good a job. For many states that's critical, because that's where the majority of people live. They are going to have to become more effective in urban areas if they expect to be supported by the state. For more rural states, we have long been all things to all people. We are now going to have to learn how to prioritize. We will have to identify the greatest needs of the state and then place our outreach and engagement efforts there. (president/chancellor pers. comm.)

A few of the senior administrators we interviewed were quite critical of the lack of progress being made by Cooperative Extension Services in meeting the needs of a more urbanized nation. Here is an example of one leader's thoughts on the matter:

> When I look at what Extension is trying to do in population centers, even very small metropolitan areas, they seem to be very limited in the scope of their activities. They tend to take very few programs into these areas, oftentimes related to food, such as FNP [Family Nutrition Program] and SNAP [Supplemental Nutrition Assistance Program]. They'll take those programs into more urban areas and you will see that they are alive and functioning very well. And sometimes they will attempt to do some urban-based 4-H. If you go beyond food and 4-H, however, you don't see a whole lot of Extension involvement in those more urban environments. But then you go out into more rural and small town areas and you see all of these Extension programs thriving. (president/chancellor pers. comm.)

A variety of other criticisms were shared by these senior administrators during our interviews. Some were disturbed by what one leader termed the "rather myopic viewpoint" that outreach and engagement efforts are only seen through the lens of Cooperative Extension offices and agricultural colleges. There were a small but significant number of presidents and chancellors who were quite proud of the presence of faculty outside of these traditional backgrounds in meeting the needs of both rural and urban communities. Here is what one senior administrator said about this:

> Another big strength of the land-grant university is its outreach and engagement mission, especially when all disciplines are all hands on deck, and when they are meeting the needs of all kinds of communities. It's amazing to witness how many faculty members see connecting with communities as part of their fundamental job. To take their particular knowledge, their expertise, in whatever their academic area is, out to the people of the state. A lot of universities talk a good game when it comes to outreach and engagement, but the land-grants are living that mission on a daily basis. It's really engrained in the culture here. (president/chancellor pers. comm.)

Others were concerned about the fact that financial resources targeting community-based efforts often were not available outside of rural and agricultural areas. Relatedly, one senior administrator noted that colleges of agriculture were extremely protective of those resources aimed at community engagement efforts, suggesting that they "jealously guarded" them and "were loath to allow them to be used outside of their traditional areas." This last point perhaps is most interesting when one reads the criticisms that have been lobbed in the academic literature at deans of agriculture for their failure to more systematically integrate Cooperative Extension Services into both university life and the community at large.[20]

What all these critical comments have in common is an all-or-none viewpoint about working in rural and urban settings—as in, if you are active in rural communities, then there is no room or reason for you also to be working in urban areas. This dichotomous stance can be found in two additional sets of comments made by the presidents and chancellors we interviewed regarding rural and urban issues. One group of remarks centered on the "zero-sum" mind-set that these senior leaders believed was present in current thinking about working in rural and urban settings. That is, if resources were going to be applied to the development of new services in more urbanized locations, then that funding was going to be taken away from programming traditionally implemented in more rural locations. Of course, given the current state of funding for higher education and Cooperative Extension Services, this worry would seem to be well anchored in reality.

The second and last set of comments we wish to highlight in this section pertains to the way some presidents and chancellors discussed a "division of labor" that has been bandied about in an informal manner at professional meetings and other gatherings attended by leaders of public institutions of higher learning. Here, the basic premise is that land-grant universities should "own" community engagement as it pertains to rural communities, whereas the non-land-grant (and typically metropolitan-located) universities would maintain "proprietorship" of services rendered to urban communities. Not a single senior administrator thought this was an appropriate apportionment of responsibilities, it should be said, and one leader was sufficiently worked up to have shared the following statement:

> I think the idea that land-grant universities are supposed to meet the needs of rural communities while the other public universities serve the more urbanized communities is a stupid idea, and yet it seems to have taken hold with a vengeance. The urban-serving universities are deeply embedded in the neighborhoods that surround their campuses. And this creates a situation where that relationship has become critically important to both the non-land-grant public university and the urban communities it serves. In turn, it would be laughable to suggest that the land-grant university's work on food production in Africa had anything to do with the needs of those communities, for example. As a result, by and large the land-grants have not yet figured out how to engage communities in activities that would meet the needs of those more urbanized geographic areas. (president/chancellor pers. comm.)

While the land-grant model has been deliberately applied to urban issues before—see especially the "urban grant university" concept that has reappeared at various times throughout the past half century[21]—it seemingly has failed to take adequate root in fertile soil.

## Global Reach versus Closer-to-Home Impact

The last quotation in the previous section regarding the land-grant university's work on food production in Africa provides a solid segue to the sixth theme that emerged from our interviews of presidents and chancellors. The internationalization of the world economy has provided land-grant universities with strong motivation to expand their global reach, while the reality of being a state-sponsored public institution of higher learning has maintained the demand for closer-to-home impact. The call for a more international presence among land-grant universities has been made for at least three decades, often tied to reimagining and reinvigorating the land-grant mission in service to a more globally connected society.[22] Without question, the world has entered a period of intensive globalization, and higher education has been profoundly impacted as a result.[23] The question is, how do land-grant institutions best respond?

The "world-grant ideal" first offered by former Michigan State University president Lou Anna Simon provides a robust conceptual framework for discussion of this theme.[24] In brief, this viewpoint holds that the Morrill Act's stipulation for land-grant universities to be responsible for their "own backyard" can be extended to include a "worldwide backyard." The ensuing dynamic tension fostered between local and global priorities is portrayed as healthy in the abstract but can often lead to any number of counterproductive pressures as well, including perhaps most poignantly here the viewpoint that global engagement is an "either/or" or zero-sum proposition.[25]

Two successive quotes from the presidents and chancellors we interviewed put this dynamic tension into sharp relief. Here is one senior administrator discussing the need to think and act more globally:

> One of the major threats facing land-grant universities is not being able to meet people where they are, not engage them and ignore what they need. So, we need to be able to engage in problem-solving activities for the communities we serve, and that isn't limited to just the people in our state, or even our nation. There is a very strong current of thought that we need to be globally and internationally connected. Land-grant institutions ignore this at their peril. (president/chancellor pers. comm.)

And here is a quote we believe captures the other end of this spectrum:

> I'm a little bit cautious about this push to be more global. Everyone seems to want to be global these days. I want our students to be able to navigate this interconnected world, of course. But the people who are paying for this place are the citizens of our state. So, when I think about mission I am thinking first and foremost about them. (president/chancellor pers. comm.)

Just as there is a continuum of thought about how far land-grant universities should extend their efforts internationally, so too is there a recognition that place matters more locally. For example, a given institution's location within the state also plays a major role in determining impact. Here, many of the presidents and chancellors made pointed comments about the fact that geography matters. Some universities are located in the center of the state, for example, and it is relatively easy for everyone to get there. As a result, these senior administrators noted, the people of that state recognize the land-grant university as a flagship institution, but one that is not elitist. Other universities are situated in less accessible places, or in areas that are viewed as orthogonal to the profile of the state as a whole. In these cases, it creates a dynamic tension politically with other areas of the state. What happens here is that, rather than having the citizens look at the land-grant university as an accessible and useful resource, many people will come to view that university as elitist and not as connected to the state in its entirety.

Part of being accessible has to do with closeness to main population centers, of course, and this is where the rural versus urban distinction again comes into play. However, in the present context we are talking about where the university's campus is located, not only where it seeks to engage the public. One senior administrator put it this way:

> When land-grant universities exist in larger metropolitan areas, you see greater "closer-to-home" impact of the universities on economic development. In essence, the university is a central part of growth in urban areas, and therefore it has to attack issues at the urban level. When those land-grant universities are situated in smaller municipalities, the impact on economic development by definition must have a greater emphasis across the state. (president/chancellor pers. comm.)

And finally, some of the presidents and chancellors we interviewed also indicated that geographic location across the nation mattered as well, especially in terms of the reputational impact of the land-grant university. Here is what one senior administrator with presidential experience in multiple institutions of higher learning said about this issue:

> I have experience leading two land-grant universities, and each of them was very different. Clearly in the Midwest agriculture continues to play a significant role, and as a result the land-grant universities have a tremendous impact on the needs of the state in which they are located. On the East coast, in contrast, and especially in the Northeast region of the country, agriculture does not play as prominent a role in the local economy for many decades at this point. In an interesting way, the adjustment to a non-agriculturally based involvement with the community has occurred gradually and naturally, with a greater emphasis on manufacturing and related sectors of the economy. Of course, more recently there has been an upsurge of interest in local sourcing of food, so there is a bit of a comeback for agricultural connections again. (president/chancellor pers. comm.)

## The Benefits of Higher Education versus the Devaluation of a College Diploma

The seventh and final theme that emerged from our interviews with presidents and chancellors concerned the general public's perceptions regarding the return on investment of a college degree. Clearly, one of the most consistent responses to the question we posed about current risks and future threats surrounded the concern that increasing numbers of American citizens are questioning whether a university education is worth the time, energy, and cost. Many of the senior administrators we interviewed were quick to point out how higher education had significantly changed their lives personally, as well as recounting narratives about recently graduated students and long-term alumni alike who reported much the same story. All told, these leaders were steadfast in their belief that their institutions displayed their greatest strengths by creating opportunities for students to gain access to outstanding educational opportunities. Simply put, they stated unequivocally that land-grant universities were still the front door to the American Dream.

However, these leaders expressed a great deal of worry about another group of citizens who say that college is not really worth the time or money. Perhaps most frustrating of all to these presidents and chancellors is that these dissenting voices seem to be getting louder, not quieter, with the passage of time. Here is how one senior leader put it:

> I'm sensing that we are losing the culture of education in this country. It appears to me that young people are less and less likely to be taking up higher education pursuits than they have in the past. When I grew up, there was the expectation that everyone in my family was going to have a college degree. Because it was an expectation, we did it. I'm not sensing there is that same kind of expectation now in families. And I'm not seeing a sense of urgency about getting a college education. I'm a little discouraged, and I'm wondering what land-grant universities can do to better promote what I would call a culture of education. We don't seem comfortable suggesting to people that we have a good product that will improve their quality of life forever. (president/chancellor pers. comm.)

A related threat is associated with the issue of what students choose to study when they attend a land-grant university, a concern raised prominently by those in state government connected to the funding of these institutions of higher learning. The senior administrators we interviewed wondered out loud, should students be enrolled only in vocationally oriented majors—engineering, agriculture, and business, for instance—or is it okay to choose English, history, psychology and other kinds of undergraduate majors that are not as immediately career focused? When this issue arose in our discussions, many of the presidents and chancellors emphasized their belief that a land-grant university education was something that prepared you more generally for life itself than for any one career specifically. Their comments on this topic surrounded the idea that students should be able to learn, adapt, and innovate in the face of change. Here is what one senior administrator said about this matter:

> You find people from all types of majors doing all types of jobs, so we aren't really a career school, we aren't really a vocational school. There's nothing wrong with those types of schools, but our job is to prepare you to deal with life and life's changes, and to be a lifelong learner. But we have legislators throughout the country who wonder if states should subsidize students who are majoring in business and engineering and penalize students who are majoring in any of the arts and humanities. I don't think that's a very enlightened philosophy but it's certainly something that's getting a lot of attention. (president/chancellor pers. comm.)

Pressures from state lawmakers on universities to become engaged in more practical activities were initially discussed in the earlier section on basic versus applied research, and we will again deal directly with the intersection of higher education and policymaking in our next chapter when we discuss the impact of governing boards.

Another threat raised in this thematic area surrounded the question of student debt taken on as the result of the pursuit of a college degree. Presidents and chancellors were quick to point to statistics that indicated the relatively sizable number of students who graduated with no debt at all, while many others received their degree with only limited amounts of loans to repay (one senior leader equated that amount to "the price of a modestly priced new car"). At the same time, these administrators also were quick to point out the irresponsibility related to encouraging students to take on debt they cannot manage, especially if they are not able to complete their degree program and receive the diploma they were seeking. Of course, all of this harkens back to the conversation raised in the section above regarding the need to emphasize access and affordability for the sons and daughters of toil originally targeted in the land-grant mission. Simply put, more needs-based scholarships must be put into place, according to many of these senior administrators, and not only when students matriculate into programs, but also if and when students are struggling to pay for the final semester or two of their studies.

While we have indicated that presidents and chancellors expressed some exasperation at the present fiscal and existential circumstances facing higher education in general and land-grant institutions more specifically, many of these same individuals did not shirk from holding themselves accountable for the situation they now find themselves in as leaders. One specific quote serves to represent well the honest self-appraisal of these senior leaders:

> Our greatest weakness is our inability to communicate persuasively about how we bring value to communities through our research efforts. I don't think that our constituents understand the nature of our Extension offices, either. And it's our fault. We do a poor job—we think we don't, but when you look at the results, we do a poor job of communicating the critical importance of our efforts. No matter what you are looking at, whether it's the newest techniques in organic farming, or any other product or commodity, it probably came from a land-grant university. Yet we clearly don't do a good job of communicating how much of an impact we are having on helping local communities through our research efforts. (president/chancellor pers. comm.)

As a whole, the group of presidents and chancellors we interviewed had adopted this "buck stops here" mentality. This stance will serve us well when considering these seven themes as a whole, especially as leaders are implored to deliberate their full effect on the mission of the land-grant university in the twenty-first century.

## Summary

We began this chapter by presenting the main findings from the interviews we conducted with 27 presidents and chancellors of the 1862 US land-grant universities. The responses to our questions about the various strengths, weaknesses, opportunities, and threats faced by land-grant institutions generated seven main themes, including concerns about funding declines versus the need to create efficiencies, research prowess versus teaching and service excellence, knowledge for knowledge's sake versus a more applied focus, the focus on rankings versus an emphasis on access and affordability, meeting the needs of rural communities versus the needs of a more urbanized America, global reach versus closer-to-home impact, and the benefits of higher education versus the devaluation of a college diploma. We presented these themes alongside direct quotations from land-grant presidents and chancellors and compared and contrasted their viewpoints with relevant literature where applicable.

# CHAPTER 4

# The Impact of Governing Boards, Elected Officials, and Accrediting Bodies

In addition to the four basic questions surrounding the strengths, weaknesses, opportunities, and threats faced by land-grant universities covered in the third chapter, the land-grant presidents and chancellors we interviewed also were asked to comment on the impact that governing board members, faculty members, and students had on how well these universities were meeting the needs of communities as part of the land-grant mission. The present chapter covers the responses of these senior administrators to the question of governing board member impact. We again use direct quotations as exemplars of the main issues generated by the land-grant presidents and chancellors, augmented where appropriate with referential material from literature available on this topic.

Following a brief description of governing board members, their core responsibilities, and variation in their duties across different institutions of higher learning, we discuss the viewpoints of presidents and chancellors from the vantage point of several themes we introduced in chapter 3. What we present here is an overall portrait of governing board members who typically were viewed by senior administrators as, at least at times, struggling to understand the value of higher education in the context of the land-grant mission. Additionally, these individuals were described as being intricately bound up in financial issues and most heavily invested in research activities. Finally, when board members were perceived as being more knowledgeable about rural and agricultural issues, they were deemed to be more attuned to the needs of communities.

Land-grant president and chancellor perceptions of governing board members are placed in a broader context of understanding how other institutions and organizations that have a say in university governance are responding to present-day issues and concerns. Because elements related to the parallel impact of governors and state legislators were raised so consistently in this portion of the interviews, we address the impact of state-level politicians in this chapter. In addition, we believe that higher education accreditation bodies also can and, at least at times, do play a role in providing guidance and feedback that relate both directly and indirectly to the land-grant mission. For those reasons, we also cover the influence of the regional institutional accreditors that review degree-granting postsecondary institutions in the United States.

Before moving forward, we must acknowledge the fact that any healthy governance structure inside of a college or university also should include the role of the faculty. More specifically, we agree with arguments made by others that there is an intersecting authority within higher education institutions which, in an ideal world, would involve the relatively coequal contributions of presidents, governing boards, and faculty members.[1] Because we have an entire chapter devoted specifically to the impact of faculty members, however, we will defer our discussion of their role in governance for the time being.

## Governing Boards and Their Members

Who exactly do we mean when we use the term "governing board members"? Typically, these are the individuals known collectively as the "board of trustees." However, in other colleges and universities throughout the nation they also are called "boards of governors," "boards of visitors," "boards of curators," and "boards of overseers." Regardless of the nomenclature, however, they are the body of individuals who bear the final authority on all matters related to the business of the university.[2]

The direct impact of governing board members on higher education's ability to meet the needs of communities seems to have been downplayed in the academic literature. One reason for this modulation may stem from the belief that governing board members, and especially those involved in public institutions of higher learning, are more focused on fiscal accountability than they are on larger societal enhancements.[3] Fiduciary responsibility certainly is a significant component of the governing board member's job description, as is strategic planning, setting institutional policies and procedures, and, ultimately, retaining hire/fire authority over the president or chancellor.

Another significant component, however, is the need for governing board members to function as a direct representative of the larger community served by higher education institutions. Here, these individuals are portrayed as "guardians of the public trust" who are supposed to ensure that universities are in fact meeting certain societal needs and demands—so much so that governing board members have been discussed by at least one source as being positioned to play a critical role in the civic engagement efforts of universities by serving as a bridge between campus and community.[4] Particularly important in this line of thinking is the need for board members to safeguard the need to embed such community-building activities directly and emphatically into the mission and vision statements of the university, those fundamental guideposts by which institutional direction and progress are evaluated.

The presidents and chancellors we interviewed portrayed the impact of governing board members on meeting the needs of communities as a bit of a mixed bag. On the one hand, there was widespread acknowledgment that boards can be powerful advocates for the university and its work in communities. Specific examples were offered that painted a picture of board members as important liaisons to community stakeholders for these senior administrators, for example. Also emphasized was a reliance on members of governing boards to offer presidents and chancellors some perspective on life outside of academia, including what it was like to live and work in communities that were directly touched by the university. The following statement made by one senior administrator captured these positive sentiments quite well:

> Our trustees are very interested in communities and their needs. There is a committee of the trustees that is very active in dealing with government affairs at both the federal and state level. They are a great sounding board for the university as we attempt to meet the needs of communities. They don't dictate what we actually do for communities, unless it happens that one of them makes a philanthropic gift in order for the university to implement a program that they value. They speak by being generous, in a certain way. They are incenting this kind of work, but not dictating what we do and do not do. (president/chancellor pers. comm.)

In contrast, other senior administrators lamented that their board members tended to offer a lot less help in terms of strategic guidance and advice about community engagement. Instead, these presidents and chancellors perceived their board members as involving themselves in deliberations about management decisions and issues that were thought of as being unhelpfully "in the weeds," and ultimately providing distraction away from the needs of communities. Here is another representative quote from one senior administrator which captured this decidedly less positive take:

> My perspective on this is that governing boards are getting more and more into a managerial role versus a policy role. And it is the managerial role that these governing board members are least well suited to take on. When you have lay individuals from the private business sector directing higher education instead of the people who are experts in this area, you have problems. You would never expect higher education experts to run a private business. Why is the reciprocal case appropriate? I see an increased number of consequential mistakes being made. Not with ill intent. But there are people making lots of managerial decisions that they have no business making. (president/chancellor pers. comm.)

On a related note, some of the presidents and chancellors took exception to the types of individuals who were being chosen to serve on the governing boards. These senior administrators believed that the political appointment process led to the selection of elitist and self-reinforcing members who had lost touch with the needs of communities. In the words of one senior administrator,

> As a president, I have been surprised by the arrogance of many governing board members, borne in large part by their being selected from a very small pool of well-connected professionals. While I believe they understand the personal and thus private benefits accrued from a college education, I do not believe they understand the public benefits of public education. Said a bit differently, I don't think they understand the role that public education plays in the ongoing health of a democratic society. (president/chancellor pers. comm.)

Another group of presidents and chancellors complained of outright obstruction by board members when it came to undertaking activities designed to meet the needs of communities in one fashion or another. In these situations, governing board members were described as creating barriers to such work because those community-focused activities were thought of as a distraction from other, "more important" university business. The typical examples of higher-priority agenda items for these board members were linked directly to some of the themes discussed in the previous chapter and further addressed below, including the emphasis on research prowess and factors that contributed to higher national rankings. Hence, for these presidents and chancellors, the message they sometimes heard was, "Stop doing these unimportant things and put more effort into the critical stuff."

To be fair here, we need to highlight the idiosyncratic way in which the personality characteristics and interactional styles of senior administrators and their governing board members either mesh or clash over time. The presidents and chancellors we interviewed were consistent in their declarations that the points of view and relational qualities of board members played a huge role in determining the course of actions taken by the university. While our interview questions were specifically focused on the issue of meeting the needs of communities, the senior administrators often spoke much more broadly on the topic of governing board members. Many stories were told about colleagues who had very difficult times working with their boards, and in those places the board members were portrayed as making the president's job increasingly unworkable until the point of dismissal. Because personality clashes and diametrically opposed points of view between board members and senior administrators were thought to be the root cause of such relationship dysfunction, the development and maintenance of positive relationships with board members were emphasized by the presidents and chancellors we interviewed.

Therefore, presidents and chancellors who wished to focus the attention of their land-grant universities on meeting specific community needs knew that they had to do this with the direct and unequivocal support of their boards. For many of the senior administrators who were interested in creating or enhancing outreach and engagement activities, this meant having to take the time to build coalitions among governing board members in ways that would move the university into a more engaged position with the community. Here is what one senior administrator told us about this process:

> As we bring board members new ideas, and give good rationale for why it's important to do what we propose to do for communities, they have been very supportive of those ideas. But you've got to do your homework. Board members also are responsive to information about how our university compares to what is going on or what is typical at other land-grant universities. This is especially true when you can say that what we are proposing will make things remarkably better for our students. (president/chancellor pers. comm.)

As we continue to note, all such efforts take place within a matrix of competing issues that test the very definition of how land-grant universities act in the interest of the public good. We address some of these concerns in the sections that follow.

## Perceptions about Board Member Understanding of the Land-Grant Mission

In previous chapters, we noted how the presidents and chancellors we interviewed were nearly unanimous in their agreement that the public at large had little understanding of the land-grant university mission and how land-grant universities contributed directly to the well-being of communities. These same senior administrators also spoke directly to the fact that, even among themselves as a peer group, they did not always share a common understanding of the twenty-first-century land-grant mission. It should come as no surprise, then, that many of these university leaders also had serious reservations about the degree to which the members of their governing boards were knowledgeable about land-grant issues and concerns. Here is how one senior administrator put it:

> My experience as the senior administrator of two different land-grant universities is that governing board members just don't get it. They don't understand what the term land-grant implies. This is made even more murky when the governing board is responsible for multiple institutions, of which the land-grant is only one of many universities under their jurisdiction. In general, they know little about us, and they do little to help us meet the mission of the land-grant university. (president/chancellor pers. comm.)

Thus, the scope of responsibilities inherent to the governing board itself seemed to greatly impact the ability of governing board members to understand the land-grant mission in the eyes of the presidents and chancellors we interviewed. That is, some governing boards retained authority over a single university, while others were placed in charge of the entire state's higher educational system. In general, the senior administrators we interviewed believed that those governing board members who singularly focused on one institution were easier to pull into alignment about what a land-grant university is supposed to do, including its ability to meet the needs of communities, as compared to those board members who had statewide responsibilities. When governing board members had a broader set of charges, in contrast, senior administrators believed that land-grant universities were put into the more defensive position of having to make the argument that they were the primary institutions the community tapped to solve their problems and address their concerns. Here is how another senior administrator explained this phenomenon:

> We have a unified governing board. Our challenge here is that we all kind of get treated the same. You would think if our land-grant mission was to serve the whole state, then it would be reasonable to charge a different tuition, or we might be supported by our governing board to get a differential amount of state or federal funding. Unfortunately, that doesn't really happen for us. A part of the problem is the governing board members don't really understand the land-grant mission, and another part relates to their desire to treat everyone equally. It's kind of like the sentiments underlying a movie like *Sophie's Choice*. You want to treat all of your children equally, you don't want to play favorites. So, the fact that one of us is a land-grant institution and has some different mission obligations doesn't mean that much to our governing board members. (president/chancellor pers. comm.)

The scope of responsibilities (single vs. multiple institutions) also seemed to be related to the depth of board member involvement in various management issues and decisions discussed above. Here, it is important to note that there was never one "right" scope of responsibilities for board members proffered by the senior administrators we interviewed. Instead, these presidents and chancellors discussed a series of trade-offs that they had to remain sensitive to as they worked with their governing boards. One senior administrator we interviewed had experience with both types of governing boards and had this to say about the key differences:

> I think the impact of governing board members depends on the type of system you are in. If you exist within a statewide system of governance, there is a lot less potential for meddling, micromanagement, and other monkey business. And the really great aspect of a statewide system is that there are people who are looking out for the needs of the entire state when it comes to higher education. On the other hand, there are certain good things about an institutional board, noting that everything of course depends on the quality of the people who make up such a board. One particularly good thing about a local board is that there are less worries about succession issues. The local board can really help a university stay the course throughout various leadership changes. They are the keepers of the mission, which hopefully saves

universities from ever veering too far off course. (president/chancellor pers. comm.)

Of course, the idiosyncratic nature of the state in which the land-grant university is located also plays an important role here. As noted in our first chapter, it is important to acknowledge that there are 50 states across the country and, as a result, there are 50 different ways of managing higher education. Presidents and chancellors repeatedly emphasized the fact that public higher education in America is not a national organization, but rather a very state-specific one. Thus, while individuals interested in higher education issues may be prone to evaluating statistics and processes across states and then comparing which states seem to have legislatures and governing boards that are more and less supportive of universities, the reality is that every state is different in terms of how higher education is governed. In many respects, it will always be a comparison of apples and oranges, and bananas, kumquats, and many other types of fruit.

Other presidents and chancellors were decidedly more upbeat in their assessment of the support they received from governing board members to implement various aspects of the land-grant mission, but only as the result of not employing specific land-grant terminology. In the words of one senior administrator,

> Governing boards typically do not have a lot of historic background, so we don't talk to them about land-grant [mission]. We talk to them about being relevant. We talk to them about wanting to be the university that seeks to engage communities and help them solve problems. The interesting thing that I noticed over the years is that the governing board—which oversees all of the universities across the state—views us as the worker university in the state. I had one board member say to me, "you just solve problems and you don't whine about it." (president/chancellor pers. comm.)

We do appreciate the can-do spirit here, as well as being in favor of nearly anything that results in more support for the mission of land-grant universities. At the same time, we worry about the dilution of the land-grant message, and we wonder out loud about how often this sort of repackaging (i.e., being "relevant" instead of being "land-grant") has been part of the problem instead of part of the solution. We will have more to say about this later in the book.

## Perceptions about Board Member Involvement
## in Fiscal Concerns

Perhaps unsurprisingly, one of the most salient challenges in working with governing board members raised in the interviews we conducted with the senior administrators of land-grant universities revolved around fiscal matters. Reactions to the general decline in state support experienced by land-grant universities over the past several decades were covered extensively in the previous chapter and were couched in terms that often left presidents and chancellors questioning whether land-grant universities could afford to maintain excellence in all three areas of their mission (teaching, research, and service). Readers will recall that some of these senior administrators were worried particularly about their ability to maintain current levels of outreach and engagement activities in the communities they were designed to serve.

Some of the presidents and chancellors we interviewed believed that their governing board members were some of the strongest advocates their universities had when it came to lobbying legislators and governors for greater state support. Others believed that their board members were either indifferent to or complicit in the state funding declines their universities were experiencing. In the latter case, these senior administrators spoke about governing board members in terminology such as "with friends like this, who needs enemies." Here, the political appointment process was blamed for installing governing board members who believed that their primary responsibility was to serve as a sort of "jealous watchdog" over public funds. In these instances, senior administrators reported having very negative interactions with board members who would not support university requests for additional state subsidies.

At the same time, some of the senior administrators we interviewed were displeased that board members were not even more forceful in their attempts to hold the university's feet to the fire, fiscally and otherwise. This is what one of them said:

> Trustees of all higher educational institutions have been way too compliant. They have been too reluctant to press for necessary changes or push for better performance. I know way too many people who, in their professional lives, are tough-minded and results-oriented and impatient with excuses for poor performance. And yet they get all weak in the knees when it comes to their alma mater's excesses or sloppy performances. (president/chancellor pers. comm.)

Similar sentiments were expressed by some of the other senior leaders, especially including those who had a background of governmental experience. This makes a great deal of sense, given that these individuals previously had been in positions that required them to see things from the "other side" of the equation.

Another common difference of opinion found in the interviews of these senior administrators concerned the relative level of support received from governing board members when it came time to discuss raising tuition levels. Some presidents and chancellors reported that their board members were wholly supportive of tuition increases that were designed to offset reductions in state subsidies. Others recounted opposition that seemed to run the gamut from tepid reluctance to steadfast and vehement opposition. Here is how one senior administrator described the more negative version of this situation:

> The most important new threats to our viability include our board members. But maybe you shouldn't put that in your report. Over the years public universities—land-grants included—became very dependent on public funding. Two decades ago, most of us were getting 50% to 60% of our operating costs from the legislature. And now we're down to 30% or less, and that support is going south fast. So, the question becomes how we replace that revenue. And our board is strongly opposed to any tuition increase right now, and has been for several years. I think that's our biggest challenge. (president/chancellor pers. comm.)

The senior administrators we interviewed also displayed significant variation in their expressions of concern about gaining support from board members in terms of a longer-term funding strategy that would redress fluctuations in state support. Again, some expressed their steadfast belief that governing board members were full and willing participants in such planning activities for the future. For at least some of the other presidents and chancellors we interviewed, however, it seemed to be the case that this was easier said than done. In the latter regard, one senior administrator used the phrase "flitting from one yearly financial crisis to the next" to describe the lack of a more strategic conversation among governing board members regarding the stabilization of revenue streams into the foreseeable future.

## Perceptions about Board Member Concentration
## on Research Efforts and Rankings

Land-grant presidents and chancellors openly and uniformly described their governing board members as being most knowledgeable about the research component of the tripartite university mission. There were many comments made surrounding the notion that, for most public universities, their prestige resided ultimately within their research portfolio. And because that prestige is so highly valued, what seemed to matter most to many board members was how many grants the university received from the National Institutes of Health, from the Department of Energy, and so on. One senior administrator put it this way:

> I've been at four land-grant institutions, and have spent a lot of time both observing and being in front of boards. Quite frankly, the land-grant mission doesn't come up in conversation very much. I think it's taken for granted, a part of the history or tradition that isn't fully explored. Unfortunately, it doesn't necessarily translate into questions about the daily operation of the university. Of course, what does translate is the counting up of research dollars, because research plays such a critical role in land-grants. I just don't think that the traditional land-grant mission is on the minds or on the agendas of most governing board members. In almost 30 years of being in administration, I have yet to hear a board member talk about the land-grant mission to any great length. (president/chancellor pers. comm.)

Of course, research prowess can be assessed in ways beyond grant dollars. For instance, great weight also is placed on how many award-winning faculty you have who are Nobel Prize winners and nominees, how many faculty members are elected as fellows to the American Association for the Advancement of Science (AAAS), and so on. Regardless of the example, however, these awards and honors typically are connected to research efforts, not to teaching activities or outreach and engagement efforts.

The presidents and chancellors indicated that a great deal of the reasoning behind this lopsided viewpoint on the part of governing board members rested on the relative ease with which research prowess could be tallied. In the words of one senior administrator,

> People love to count things. Anything that can be counted is counted, and assumes a level of importance well beyond its actual significance. This is one of

the main reasons why board of trustee members are so heavily focused on research. It's easy to count, plain and simple. Service to communities is really tough to quantify. So is quality teaching. It's the nature of the beast, but it's probably getting worse, not better. (president/chancellor pers. comm.)

As we will see in the next chapter regarding faculty and the promotion and tenure process, this is a challenge that extends well beyond what governing members are considering. Simply put, university administrators and faculty members have been struggling mightily to quantify excellence in teaching and excellence in outreach and engagement, and thus they have been challenged to find ways to reward such excellence.

There is an old maxim that goes "what gets counted gets done." We might add here that what gets counted gets ranked as well. In our third chapter, we discussed the dynamic tension that seemed to exist between wanting to climb ever higher in national rankings and the desire to focus on issues surrounding access and affordability. While these issues are not mutually exclusive per se, they do reflect differences in emphasis and strategy. The presidents and chancellors we interviewed typically reported that they felt at least some pressure from board members to take actions that would conceivably lead to upward movement in the rankings, both in terms of academic reputation in general and, more specifically, in terms of research expenditures. The price paid here, of course, is less emphasis on access and affordability, among other important factors discussed in the previous chapter.

## Geography and Perceptions of Board Member Support for Community Engagement

In our second chapter, we discussed the stereotypical way that land-grant universities are sometimes thought of in terms of their rural and agricultural connections. In our third chapter, we reported on presidents and chancellors as they discussed the dynamic tension that exists between meeting the needs of more rural communities and addressing the issues and concerns of more urbanized communities. It should not be surprising, then, that geography would be thought of as a salient issue among governing board members as well.

In states where agriculture remained an important part of the economy, the presidents and chancellors thought that governing boards were more likely to be sensitive to the needs of land-grant institutions and the needs of communities, or at the very least those communities that their agricultural schools served. In large part, this was thought to be the result of having more agriculturally inclined people on the board, individuals who were much more likely to be supportive of Cooperative Extension Service activities and other forms of outreach and engagement stemming from rural and agricultural roots. In this context, it was either implied or directly stated that governing board members in these more agriculturally oriented states tended to take on roles where they became de facto guardians of the relationship between the agribusiness community and the university.

Conversely, senior administrators contended, when the land-grant university was situated in a state where agriculture was not nearly as important to the economy, the support for community engagement among governing board members tended to lessen. One senior administrator stated it this way:

> My guess, and I haven't done the research so this is just a guess, is that land-grant university boards in earlier periods of time may have had more farmers and farm industry people as board members who were more community oriented. This would have been during a time in which our colleges of agriculture were seen as playing a more important role in our university, and when farming was seen as a more critical part of the economy of the United States. The decline of agriculture's status in our state coincides with a much smaller proportion of board members who are farmers or are knowledgeable about the farm industry. (president/chancellor pers. comm.)

Continuing this line of reasoning, it was asserted that states without a strong agricultural presence tended to have board members who were more philanthropic in their orientation, often placed on boards because of their specific fundraising capabilities or more general political connections. As a result, presidents and chancellors portrayed these board members as being less inclined to focus on community needs (rural or urban), unless those issues were specifically addressed within the scope of the university's current capital campaign goals.

## The View from the Governing Board

For over 300 years, America's distinct model of board governance has provided leadership and oversight for colleges and universities. Institution and board leaders continue to respond to the challenges and opportunities facing their campuses—focusing on the issues of greatest consequence to their communities and to higher education as a whole. We thought it would be helpful to position the comments of the land-grant presidents and chancellors in a context that included the viewpoints of those individuals and organizations that work on behalf of governing board members. We begin by examining the work of the Association of Governing Boards of Universities and Colleges (AGB), which provides leadership and counsel to member boards, chief executives, organizational staff, policymakers, and other industry leaders.[5] In this capacity, AGB serves trustees, regents, presidents, chancellors, CEOs, senior-level administrators, and board professional staff members. AGB's leadership focuses on board governance and policies/practices that are of importance to public and private two-year and four-year colleges and universities.

Over the years, AGB has addressed many critical issues that have been covered to some extent in the pages of this book so far, including free speech on campus and the governing board's role in financial oversight.[6] Among the most notable is a newer series of offerings from AGB called the Guardians Initiative. Particularly significant is the subtitle of this initiative, which reads, "Reclaiming the Public Trust." Here, there is an explicit recognition that governing board members can and should play a critical and appropriate role in helping community stakeholders better understand institutions of higher learning, including their core missions, how they operate, what they cost, and how they impact society.

The first resource to come out of AGB's Guardians Initiative is an informational brief entitled *The Business of Higher Education.*[7] This document begins by asserting that colleges and universities typically employ what was termed "an unconventional business model," one that made these institutions distinct from any other industry in the American economy. The unusual nature of the higher education business model, the document goes on to say, is reflected in the fact that the cost of its main product—classroom instruction—is tied up rather opaquely in many other activities undertaken by colleges and universities. Further exaggerating the uniqueness of this model is the historic reliance on government subsidies, which largely have become unpredictable sources of revenue, especially in the past two decades.

*The Business of Higher Education* provides a platform for board members to take an active role in creating a compelling narrative regarding the return on investment which a college degree provides. To make such a contribution, this AGB resource asserted that governing board members must have sustained one-on-one conversations with friends, colleagues, community stakeholders, and even fellow board members to provide those individuals with pertinent and accurate information about the enigmatic business of higher education. Four key propositions were offered to help guide these sorts of conversations:

1. The cost of attending college is not as high as many people believe
2. The value of a college degree has never been higher
3. Institutions of higher learning are highly complex and unusual businesses
4. Colleges and universities are engaged in more transparent cost-cutting efforts

We had the chance to discuss the Guardians Initiative and related topics with Rick Legon, AGB president and former governing board member of Virginia State University (an 1890 land-grant university). This conversation centered largely on the "upside-down" nature of higher education's relationships with many of its stakeholders. That is, despite a relatively robust economy and a strong demand for a college-educated workforce, more and more individuals in society are expressing unfavorable views of higher education. Factors contributing to this growing discontent, according to Mr. Legon, include rising costs and corresponding increases in student debt, as well as our society's growing inability to differentiate between the private good and public good outcomes of a college education (recall these discussions from chaps. 1 and 2). As a result, governing board members are challenged to respond to this increasingly complex environment in a manner that is both supportive of the institution of higher learning and sensitive to the concerns of parents, legislators, accrediting bodies, and other stakeholders.

The Guardians Initiative, according to Mr. Legon, was created to mobilize the individual and collective voices of our nation's college and university board members to share the value proposition of our diverse higher education system. The Guardians Initiative encourages board members to articulate the value proposition offered by institutions of higher learning at present while concurrently encouraging these board members to assert their fiduciary duty to ask difficult questions about those business practices that can and should be changed to meet the needs of twenty-first-century America. Legon went on to say,

> Trustees realize that higher education is perhaps the richest sector of our economy when it comes to opportunity, and therefore a part of their responsibility is to help stakeholders realize just how special and unique this resource is for the country. This is the framework of the Guardians Initiative. Rather you

acknowledge the disconnect, take ownership for what needs to change while clarifying misunderstandings and misconceptions about affordability, outcomes, and return on investment. Ultimate fiduciary authority falls on trustees—and they understand how institutions can improve communities. They can and should articulate this value. (pers. comm.)

Next up for the Guardians Initiative is to unpack some of higher education's most valuable components. This will include an upcoming paper that explicates the return on investment realized by communities when its citizens seek and acquire college degrees, including the contributions that higher education makes to the development and maintenance of the best of our democratic ideals. Again, the emphasis here is on the provision of resources to governing board members which allow them to become strong and vocal advocates for the role that colleges and universities play in shaping our destiny as a country and as a society in which we can live and prosper.

## The Impact of Elected Officials

As we noted at the beginning of this chapter, issues related to the impact of governors and state legislators consistently were raised in our interviews with the land-grant presidents and chancellors. In response, we decided to address the impact that state-level politicians and policymakers had on land-grant universities in this chapter, even though we did not pose direct questions to senior administrators about these individuals. Most specifically, we wanted to provide readers with a context for understanding the issues facing governors and state legislators as they grappled with higher education issues.

Recall here that the initial theme we discussed in our third chapter centered attention squarely on the concerns presidents and chancellors had about the funding declines their universities were facing as the result of cuts in state support (alongside pressures to become more cost efficient in their expenditures). While it is axiomatic to note that these funding declines were the result of decisions made by state lawmakers and governors, what may be less obvious is the sense of betrayal that at least some of these university leaders felt as the result of these fiscal cutbacks. Here is what one senior administrator shared with us:

Why is it that state governors and legislators have become so distrusting of their public universities? This despite the fact that all of these land-grant and public universities have had such a long history of direct involvement in the communities across the state. How is it that this history has been forgotten?

I continue to be puzzled by the extent to which 150 years of this service seems to be getting us no benefits politically. That's problematic, because it doesn't give us many incentives to keep investing there. (president/chancellor pers. comm.)

In turn, some of these same university leaders expressed amazement that politicians had managed to convince the public that the rising costs of a college degree were the fault of universities rather than the state legislators and governors who were reducing the state's subsidies for higher education. Rather than solely blaming these legislators, however, other presidents and chancellors believed they bore direct responsibility for the predicament they found themselves in regarding the funding reductions their universities faced. In part, these senior administrators believed they had not formulated their supportive arguments very well, or at the very least had not influenced perceptions more positively in terms of how state funds were expended by their institutions of higher learning (and therefore "deserved" to have their support reduced). Regardless of where culpability was placed, however, many of these senior administrators were convinced they had thoroughly lost this debate in the court of public opinion over the past several decades.

What are state politicians thinking about when it comes to higher education? Do they feel they have "won" the debate? Where do they believe funding for higher education is going to come from in the future? One way to answer these questions is to investigate what is being promoted on websites connected to those organizations providing services to state lawmakers. Our search revealed at least two organizations dedicated to state legislators—the National Conference of State Legislators (NCSL) and the American Legislative Exchange Council (ALEC)—which help to organize and otherwise offer resources for these lawmakers.[8] Even a casual visit to the websites of these organizations leaves visitors struck with the wide variety of issues that these elected officials are facing at present, extending far beyond higher education: transportation, energy, environmental issues, tax reform, international trade, health, criminal justice, and pension reform, to name but a few of the larger and more expensive concerns. At the same time, there are very visible task forces, trainings, publications, and other resources dedicated specifically to higher education issues.

There also is one major organization focused on the needs of governors—the National Governors Association (NGA).[9] The NGA website, similar to the NCSL and ALEC websites described above, covers a wide variety of concerns mentioned in the preceding paragraph which shine a light on all of the issues competing for attention with higher education. In addition, the NGA website includes ample coverage of topics related to colleges and universities through its education division. Recent work within NGA's Center for Best Practices, for example, includes the release of a strategic plan covering educational issues from birth through college and career which focuses on equal access, organizational alignment, and data-driven approaches to challenges.[10]

Our review of these organizations and their websites led us to conclude that higher education is very much on the minds of state legislators and governors, yet it is just one of many concerns facing these lawmakers and administrators. There also is solid evidence that, at least in terms of the governors, there is a great deal of potential loyalty to land-grant universities as a function of alumni pride which campus leaders may not be fully accessing. While not a part of our initial exploration plans, we were drawn to the fact that the NGA website touted the educational backgrounds of the governors. Interestingly, we found that 20 out of the 50 state governors (40%) at the time of this chapter's writing held at least one degree from a land-grant university. We would hazard a guess that a significant number of state legislators also earned at least one degree from a land-grant university and therefore also would be proud graduates. These are hopeful signs, to be sure, but again are predicated on the notion that these elected officials understand the land-grant mission of their alma maters.

What was still missing, however, was a deeper glimpse of the ways in which these politicians thought about higher education. Fortunately, as this chapter was being compiled, your authors were invited to participate in an event sponsored by ALEC and hosted by George Mason University which included state legislators, governors, and thought leaders in higher education.[11] Sessions at this conference covered topics ranging from university spending and state budgets to the promotion of free speech and inquiry on campuses. There also was a session entitled "Rethinking State Universities" which provided Gavazzi with the opportunity to showcase some of the work contained in this book, including most importantly the themes developed from the interviews with land-grant presidents and chancellors described in our third chapter.

The gist of Gavazzi's presentation to the ALEC audience went something like this: For their part, land-grant (and other public) institutions must invest more time and effort in those activities that have a direct and positive impact on the communities they were designed to serve. This means that higher education leaders must place the highest value on exactly those sorts of community-enhancing endeavors, which could take on various forms, including how students are taught to become more civically engaged and how faculty are rewarded for those research and engagement activities that are directly traceable to community benefits. In return, legislators and policymakers must do their part to consistently value those community-focused activities in terms of both serving as vocal champions of the public higher education system and providing more predictable funding streams for those colleges and universities that have devoted significant time to the creation of such "public goods."

The reactions of the state legislators who participated in this presentation at the ALEC conference provided us with some additional (if somewhat informal) insights into the questions we raised in terms of what politicians are thinking about when it comes to higher education. For starters, as a group they professed to want their state public universities to succeed, especially at the task of serving as excellent educators in the classroom. They were less keen on empirical activity overall, yet they seemed genuinely to like the idea of research efforts that had an immediate and recognizable impact on community needs, as well as those activities that promoted the civic engagement of students.

This event was not all rainbows and unicorns, however. There were plenty of complaints about faculty members who didn't teach enough, for example, and lots of skepticism about the ways in which universities spent money overall (especially when it came to the topic of hiring more administrators). There also was a palpable sense of frustration expressed by many of these state lawmakers. Part of this exasperation came in the form of statements made by the legislators indicating that there simply wasn't enough money to go around for all the agencies and organizations that relied on state appropriations. Another portion of this vexation had to do with the perception that university leaders were not always good partners, at least in the sense that they were not uniformly willing to devote the time and energy necessary to build personal relationships with these politicians.

One final point we wish to share about our experiences at the ALEC event is this: When state legislators heard about the historic land-grant mission—providing an education that was accessible to the sons and daughters of toil, excellence in applied and practical pursuits, and service to communities—most of them got downright excited. They recalled having previously heard something wonderful and positive about this land-grant mission, even as they wondered aloud why it was the case that they themselves—the elected officials of the state—couldn't always tell you which of their state's public universities were land-grant institutions. And therein lies the fundamental challenge to university leaders: making sure that the political representatives of the people can easily identify the people's universities and how they generate significant and immediate positive impact on meeting the needs of their communities.

## The Impact of Accrediting Bodies

Once the impact of elected officials began to be more fully explored, we realized that we also initially had neglected to consider the ways in which higher education accreditation bodies also played a role in providing guidance and feedback related to implementation of the land-grant mission. We had not asked the presidents and chancellors any questions regarding the impact of accrediting bodies, just as we had not posted any questions about elected officials. What is different here, however, is that these senior officials did not mention accrediting bodies at all. This is most likely due to the relatively long period of time that transpires between accreditation visits, which is when the impact of these organizations is most acutely felt. Nevertheless, we included the influence of the regional institutional accreditors who review degree-granting postsecondary institutions in the United States to round out the picture of external forces that can influence the ways in which universities implement the land-grant mission.

There are approximately a dozen regional and national accrediting organizations for higher education institutions across the United States.[12] By law, these accreditors work in partnership with the US Department of Education to determine eligibility for federal government assistance. The most important component of this federal assistance is centered on access to student financial aid. Hence, in the most drastic form, if an institution loses its accreditation, its students cannot use federal financial aid to pay for attendance at that college or university.

To illuminate the potential impact of these accrediting bodies on land-grant institutions at slightly less dramatic levels, we chose to focus on the Higher Learning Commission (HLC), which serves colleges and universities in 19 states contained within what is termed the North Central region of the United States.[13] The HLC catchment area includes both Ohio and West Virginia, the two states in which Gavazzi and Gee live and work. Further, Gavazzi is part of the HLC Peer Corps, meaning that he is one of approximately

1,600 faculty members and administrators who volunteer their time as reviewers in the process of maintaining quality control within these institutions of higher learning.

The HLC review process typically stretches over a 10-year period. During the first three years, various documents are prepared by university personnel and entered as "evidence" into that institution's "assurance argument." The fourth year is marked by a comprehensive evaluation, which includes a site visit by HLC Peer Corps members. The comprehensive evaluation is based on five overarching criteria: (1) the quality of the university's mission statement, which must be clearly stated and publicly available; (2) the level of institutional integrity as a function of the ethical and responsible conduct of its employees; (3) the quality, resources, and support directed toward teaching and learning; (4) the evaluation of and efforts to improve those teaching and learning activities; and (5) overall institutional effectiveness as a function of strategic planning and resource allocation. Subsequent activities include institutional responses to the comprehensive evaluation in years five through nine, as well as additional document preparation for the assurance argument that will undergo the next comprehensive evaluation, which occurs in the 10th year.

We wish to highlight a few components of this accreditation process so that readers can gain a sense of how HLC and other accrediting bodies can and do have an impact on the ability of land-grant universities (and other institutions of higher learning) to meet the needs of communities. One example is contained within the first HLC criterion involving the university's mission statement, where there is a section that focuses on the institution's demonstration of its "commitment to the public good." This includes one specific indicator that "the institution engages with its identified external constituencies and communities of interest and responds to their need as its mission and capacity allow."[14] In practice, colleges and universities as often as not include a lengthy inventory of their outreach and engagement activities. Frequently listed in these evidentiary statements are service-learning courses and extracurricular student activities specifically designed to meet various community needs. In addition, if they have acquired it, institutions of higher learning also will highlight the Carnegie Community Engagement Classification designation we detailed in our second chapter, as part of their verification that they have met or exceeded this criterion.

More specific to one of the topics raised in the present chapter, another HLC criterion focuses specific attention on how well a given university's governance and administrative structure enable that institution to fulfill its mission. Many of the indicators in this section of the review are focused wholly or partially on the activities of the governing board. This includes items that evaluate the degree to which governing board members are knowledgeable about and provide oversight of the institution, including its financial and academic policies and practices. This HLC criterion also assesses the degree to which the institution successfully employs procedures that engage all internal university stakeholders—the governing board, administrative leadership, faculty, staff, and students—in the process of governing the institution.

In short, the monitoring of a given university's compliance with these sorts of accreditation demands typically has the net effect of maintaining high standards within these institutions of higher learning, including the actions of its governing board members. We spoke at length on this topic with Barbara Gellman-Danley, the current HLC president, whose background included previous stints as a university president (for both the University of Rio Grande and Antioch University McGregor), a vice chancellor for the Ohio Board of Regents (now Ohio Department of Higher Education), and a vice chancellor for the Oklahoma State Regents for Higher Education. Dr. Gellman-Danley indicated that board members have essential roles to play in the operation of a university and hence are pivotal in the accreditation process:

> What we often see as accreditors are the difficulties that result when board members go awry. As a result, these problems are often in evidence across many of our criteria. When individuals receive little to no training in terms of how to be a good board member, we can tell. It's pretty easy to figure out which institutions have boards that are in sync with the university's administration and which ones are involved in pitched battles. Other times, there is infighting within the board itself. Again, this is both easy to spot and often has a decidedly negative impact on our evaluation of how well the university is conducting its business, which at the end of the day is about educating students. (pers. comm.)

While accrediting bodies focus on the internal activities of governing boards, administrators, faculty, staff, and students, they also monitor and respond to actions that fall outside of the immediate control of universities. Dr. Gellman-Danley recounted several recent episodes where the HLC became either directly or indirectly involved in cases in which there was clear-cut external interference in university governance, typically by a governor and/or a state legislature. Examples included actions resulting in the removal of presidents, threats to disband an entire governing board, and attempts to rewrite university mission statements. In each case, HLC was there to protect the integrity of the university by reminding these external entities about the stipulations of the accreditation process, including where certain actions taken would violate specific standards and thus place the university's accreditation in jeopardy.

Although much of this kind of work is handled more discreetly, sometimes these issues take place in a very public setting. Consider, for instance, the recent two-year budget stalemate that has been occurring in the state of Illinois.[15] The continued lack of funding for public higher education, largely the result of a breakdown in budget negotiations between a Republican governor and a Democratic-controlled statehouse, was deemed by HLC to be a direct threat to the well-being of students who were enrolled in the state's public colleges and universities. In a letter sent directly to the governor and the leadership of the Illinois General Assembly (and which ended up on the front page of the *Chicago Tribune*), HLC articulated its concerns about the diminishing quality of public higher education in Illinois, as well as the attendant consequences of failing to live up to the HLC standards, which could include withdrawal of accreditation and restricted access to federal financial aid.[16] As fortune would have it, the budget impasse was resolved a short time after that letter was delivered.

## Summary

We began this chapter with an overview of the roles and responsibilities assigned to governing board members. We then reported on the replies that land-grant presidents and chancellors gave to our question about the impact governing board members have on the land-grant university's ability to meet the needs of the communities they were designed to serve. These responses highlighted concerns about a general lack of understanding about the nature of the land-grant mission, the governing board members' concentration on research prowess and rankings, and the connection between geography and support for community engagement. In addition, we introduced topics related to elected officials and accrediting bodies, as both groups were thought to have considerable additional impact on how land-grant universities are able to meet community needs.

# CHAPTER 5

# The Critical Role of the Faculty

Here we present the comments made by the land-grant presidents and chancellors we interviewed regarding the impact faculty members had on how well land-grant universities were meeting the needs of the communities they were designed to serve. This work builds on the themes developed in chapter 3 regarding the strengths, weaknesses, opportunities, and threats faced by land-grant universities as they attempt to fulfill their mission. We again use direct quotations as examples of the main issues generated by the land-grant presidents and chancellors, as well as providing supplemental information as needed from referential material available on applicable topics.

We begin with a description of the differing types of faculty members (i.e., tenure-track and non-tenure-track), as well as how these distinct roles contribute to the tripartite land-grant university mission regarding teaching, research, and service. Next, we cover the main responses of the presidents and chancellors to the question of the impact of faculty members, who typically were viewed by senior administrators as most involved in meeting the needs of communities through their applied research focus and other related engagement activities. In reaction to some comments made by the senior administrators we interviewed, we raise the concern of how these efforts often seem to be siloed in certain quarters of the campus. The issue of promotion and tenure is given our full attention, as we firmly believe that the reward structure of universities has a tremendous impact on the activities of faculty members over the long haul. Other than curriculum development and implementation, there is no greater role in governance played by faculty than the evaluation of each other's performance regarding the tripartite mission of the land-grant university. Finally, we also examine the evaluation of the tripartite mission of teaching, research, and service over time. This penultimate section of the chapter includes a focus on the efforts of the Engaged Scholarship Consortium (ESC), a multi-institutional effort designed to promote the development of robust campus–community partnerships that are grounded in rigorous scholarship and meaningful capacity-building activities.

## Tenure-Track and Non-Tenure-Track Faculty Members

The gold standard for university employment is a tenure-track position. The typical course of this sort of employment goes as follows: A graduate of a doctoral program is hired by an academic department as an assistant professor either directly upon completion of the PhD degree or after serving a relatively short time in what is termed a "postdoc" (i.e., postdoctoral) position, which usually involves working as a research associate under the tutelage of an established (and typically tenured) faculty member. After approximately six years of probationary status, the teaching, research, and service record of the assistant professor is reviewed internally by the tenured faculty of that individual's department and college, as well as externally by a select group of prominent faculty members from similar departments at other universities. If the assistant professor's record is judged to meet certain standards of excellence, that individual is given tenure, almost always with the promotion to associate professor.

In general, the granting of tenure is a guarantee of lifelong employment at that university, barring fiscal emergency within the university or criminal conduct or other grossly inappropriate behaviors on the part of the professor. Why do universities grant tenure? According to the American Association of University Professors (AAUP), tenure has two main purposes: (1) the protection of academic freedom, allowing professors to teach and conduct research on whatever subject matter they wish to pursue as scholars; and (2) the offering of enough economic security to make the position financially appealing to individuals with high ability.[1] We would add that, while the tenure process results in permanent employment, the lengthy probationary period that precedes the granting of tenure is used to maintain the highest standards of academic value within the university. Said slightly differently, it's not easy to get tenure, and for good reason.

Noted throughout this book is the tripartite mission of the land-grant university: teaching, research, and service. Evaluation of tenure-track faculty at land-grant universities closely adheres to this mission.[2] Applying standards of excellence that are developed over time by academic departments, colleges, and institutions, probationary faculty (i.e., assistant professors) are judged on the merits of their ability to effectively teach, to conduct important scholarly work and generate creative activity, and to fulfill service obligations to their tenure initiating unit within the university, to their academic field, and—at least for land-grant universities (we hope)—to the communities those institutions were designed to serve.

Issues surrounding accountability and productivity have been seen by some as altering the balance between teaching, research, and service over time. In recent times, for example, there has been a rather robust insistence from the public in general and state legislators (see chap. 4) more specifically that faculty members spend more of their time teaching in the classroom, with a corresponding devaluation of their research efforts.[3] Tenure itself also has been under almost constant scrutiny, from the fiscal emergencies of the 1970s and 1980s which triggered the firing of tenured faculty members to more recent efforts in Wisconsin and elsewhere to strip protections typically associated with tenured status.[4]

It should be noted that not all university faculty members are on the tenure track, however. In fact, it has been estimated that three out of every four faculty members across the country fall into the non-tenure-track category.[5] There are various titles that are used to describe these non-tenure-track faculty members, including but not limited to the following: lecturer, adjunct faculty, auxiliary faculty, contingent faculty, clinical faculty, professional faculty, professor of practice, and research faculty. Some of these labels are used to reflect a specific set of job responsibilities. Research faculty, for example, are employed only to conduct research and thus do not have teaching or service responsibilities. As a result, the efforts of these non-tenure-track faculty members are not evaluated as broadly or as comprehensively as are those of tenure-track faculty, and their employment over time is not automatically assumed.

This is not to say that non-tenure-track faculty members are any less important to the land-grant mission, however. In fact, quite the contrary. Non-tenure-track faculty members are responsible for teaching the majority of courses being taken by students and thus make significant contributions to the teaching mission of land-grant institutions.[6] Similarly, many of the research programs at land-grant universities are as productive as they are because they employ full-time, non-tenure-track research faculty members who can concentrate solely on their empirical work. Finally, we note the heavy lift in service and outreach activities historically done by Extension faculty members, who are equally likely to be non-tenure-track as they are to be on a tenure track.[7]

## Faculty Member Impact on the Community

The presidents and chancellors we interviewed left no doubt that faculty members were the workhorses of the land-grant university. They were described as especially dedicated to upholding the highest standards of scholarship, whether in their classrooms, in their research laboratories, or in applying their empirical findings in the real world. While asked about faculty efforts, some of the comments made by these senior administrators were very student-centric, that is, they centered on the role that faculty played in terms of setting high expectations for their students and, concurrently, actively involving themselves in the preparation required to send those students successfully back into the community as productive members of society.

Relatedly, there were consistent reports about the variety of mechanisms faculty put into place to make sure students are actively engaged in projects that positively and significantly impact the well-being of communities. Here is how one senior administrator summed this up:

> We have faculty members who are completely committed to the land-grant mission. They are here precisely because we are supposed to be combining our teaching, research, and service in ways that ultimately bring benefit to communities. Our approach is to place community engagement in the context of disciplinary learning. So, community service is not something that students would see as being separate from their learning, but rather their engagement would be presented as part of a best practices model inside of the discipline. That's an opportunity to connect community engagement more closely to the teaching and scholarship efforts of the faculty members. In fact, if you can't connect engagement to teaching and scholarship, it's not going to go anywhere. By connecting engagement to curricula and pedagogy, we are trying to make those connections so that faculty will see this as a way of teaching their students in more impactful ways. That's the viewpoint we

are trying to establish for the second 150 years of the land-grant university. (president/chancellor pers. comm.)

Forging linkages between community engagement efforts and both the instructional and empirical activities of faculty members is very much in alignment with similar calls to action made previously by the Kellogg Commission on the Future of State and Land-Grant Universities, the Carnegie Foundation for the Advancement of Teaching Classification for Community Engagement, and the Association of Public and Land-Grant Universities (APLU) as described in our second chapter. As we shall see toward the end of this chapter, the evolution in thinking about the tripartite mission of the land-grant university increasingly emphasizes the interconnections between the three components (i.e., engaged teaching and engaged research).

Other comments made by senior administrators were more scholarship-centric and left us with the impression that there was a consensus belief that faculty involvement in the community as a function of their research interests was where the rubber hit the road and where the important action was really occurring inside of land-grant universities, at least insofar as community needs were being addressed. Further, these presidents and chancellors recounted specific examples of community engagement in which faculty members really "bought into it" to the point where it was obvious they were enjoying themselves. Said slightly differently, these faculty clearly had made engagement activities an essential part of their fundamental professional and personal identity.

On the other hand, administrators also acknowledged that there were faculty who were resistant to the idea of community engagement. Here, senior administrators differentiated between those faculty members who were intentionally at a land-grant institution—that is, they sought a position at a land-grant university because they were invested in the traditions and the mission—and those who were coincidentally at a land-grant institution, but with no real investment in the land-grant mission. Said one,

> We have attracted some great faculty members who came to our university purposefully. They are who are very productive and active in meeting the needs of communities. In fact, often as not they serve as sobering reminders of what that land-grant mission is. But then we also have faculty members who came to us more conveniently because we had an open position, and not because they were truly invested in the land-grant mission. These are the faculty members who end up creating a dynamic tension and confusion about

what the mission really is for the land-grant university. (president/chancellor pers. comm.)

This "dynamic tension" was mentioned by a fair number of senior administrators as an ongoing issue among their faculty. As a direct result, we see here a reflection of the dialectic of basic versus applied research—or in the parlance of our themes, knowledge for knowledge's sake versus a more applied focus—in action. While some faculty members value the contributions made by both sides of this empirical dialectic, others have a far more one-sided take. As suggested by the quote above, at a land-grant university the great danger comes from those faculty members who would insist that applied research efforts are subordinate to basic research efforts. In its most exaggerated form, that sort of stance is a strong repudiation of the land-grant mission itself.

At the same time, we wish to emphasize that there are difficulties associated with an extreme stance taken the other way as well. That is, it is very difficult for us to imagine a land-grant university that does not also place value on basic research efforts. This exact sentiment was expressed poignantly by Daniel M. Fogel, the former president of the University of Vermont who in 2012 helped to lead a sesquicentennial commemoration of the Morrill Act, which included a three-day symposium and an edited book entitled *Precipice or Crossroads? Where America's Great Public Universities Stand and Where They Are Going Midway through Their Second Century* (both the symposium and edited book are discussed in more detail in chap. 7).[8]

We had the opportunity to discuss with Dr. Fogel those sesquicentennial activities and the aspiration to jump-start a national conversation about the land-grant mission, especially regarding the land-grant mission of meeting the needs of communities. While agreeing that applied research activities were important elements within the mission of land-grant universities and other public institutions of higher learning, Fogel also expressed explicit concerns about losing the ability to focus on what he termed "disinterested learning and research." Here is what he said:

> In line with Jim Duderstadt's trenchant essay in *Precipice or Crossroads*, I worry that governments used to support the purposes of higher education, but that now it seems more and more the case that governments are making demands on higher education to serve the needs of government, ironically even while they are giving us less and less support. It is not at all clear that being enlisted to serve economic and workforce development serves the purposes of research universities and their teaching and learning, and especially disinter-

ested learning. That's why, in my essay on the place of arts and humanities in public research universities, I put so much stress on disinterested and basic non-applied scientific research. This is analogous to the seeming uselessness of analyzing a text by Shakespeare, something that would appear to be impractical to most people. But so is string theory, and so is a lot of basic research that eventually makes lives better, healthier, and longer. A lot of stuff is not anticipated. So, I worry that, although service to the community is all well and good, there is something that needs to be guarded against as well. If you are a chemist working on applied research for Merck or Pfizer, you work on what they tell you to work on. And it either works within a given time period or it doesn't. And if it doesn't, you are re-tasked or you're out. If you are a chemist in a research university, however, you can follow your nose. You can go anywhere. To me, that's what a research university has to be able to do at the highest level. And it's not clear that the emphasis on applied research and service to the community and state is able sufficiently to cherish, support, and fund the pursuit of knowledge for its own sake. (pers. comm.)

Essentially, Fogel warned that there was something very important at stake and in need of protection—the university researcher's ability to follow his or her own instincts and intellectual curiosities. That is, land-grant universities must emphasize and value basic research activities alongside those applied empirical efforts that serve the more immediate needs of the state and its economy. This comports with an idea attributed to George Smoot of the Lawrence Berkeley National Laboratory, who stated that "people cannot foresee the future well enough to predict what's going to develop from basic research. If we only did applied research, we would still be making better spears."[9]

Taken together, the impact of land-grant faculty members on meeting the needs of communities was portrayed by senior administrators as significant, both in the shorter term, through their more applied research activities, and over the long run, through their more basic research efforts. And regardless of where they fell on the basic versus applied research continuum, land-grant faculty members were portrayed as doing critically important work that either immediately or eventually touched citizens' lives in every county of their home states, as well as across the nation and throughout the world. Repeatedly, presidents and chancellors spoke glowingly of this impact through faculty efforts that focused on such critical issues as renewable energy, clean water, food security, and transportation, to name but a few of the more significant areas.

Of course, taking on such big challenges concurrently meant grappling with unique obstacles that often hampered this sort of work. Presidents and chancellors proudly noted the additional labors that land-grant faculty members often took on to overcome such roadblocks. Their sensitivity to the high degree of difficulty these sorts of efforts entailed is clearly seen in the words of one senior administrator:

> Land-grant faculty run toward the most complex difficulties the world is facing today. Yet in so doing, they must learn to work with big stakeholders who control lots of resources surrounding those issues, and often as not those stakeholders tend to be resistant to change. For example, these big issues typically are associated with a significant amount of government interface and regulation. Hence, the challenge for us is to be able to work in this heavily regulated environment, with an audience of lots of people who care a great deal about these issues, in a way that moves our work forward. The land-grant mission asks us to stay ahead of all this without drowning under our own weight. So, faculty members are invested constituents. They must be flexible enough to adapt themselves and what they are doing to that future. And it's tough for these invested constituents in these highly regulated times to be able to be that nimble, at least at times. (president/ chancellor pers. comm.)

In addition to a willingness to grapple with such external complications, senior administrators pointed out certain internal impediments as well. Perhaps most often cited was the inherent danger of faculty members only working to meet those community needs that fall within their immediate interest areas. Here, presidents and chancellors talked about the need to encourage faculty members to spend more time asking specific questions about what community members needed from their land-grant universities. We turn to the words of one senior administrator to explain:

> Academics, as it turns out, usually approach things in a uniquely egocentric manner. That is, faculty members have a certain area of expertise, they know how to apply this expertise in a certain way and, as a result, they believe community members should be happy to receive the benefits of their knowledge in exactly that way. But they didn't bother to check out whether anyone in the community really needed that expertise applied in *that specific way*. What we need to do to become more effective as land-grant institutions is find out what the people really want and need. Let's not just do

what I want to do. Let's do what the community wants and needs us to do. (president/chancellor pers. comm.)

As scholars in this area have asserted repeatedly, this sort of reciprocity or interaction around mutually beneficial and cocreated goals and objectives speaks to the very definition of community engagement.[10] While this noble goal might seem obvious to some, these senior administrators acknowledged that at least some land-grant faculty members may require targeted assistance in opening lines of communication with stakeholders to facilitate more efficient and more readily recognizable ways of applying their expertise to those community needs and issues that will have the greatest impact.

## Silos of Community Involvement

In addition to the personal decisions faculty members make about the degree to which their teaching, research, and service activities are undertaken with community needs in mind, the presidents and chancellors we interviewed also expressed concern about the uneven contributions that different disciplines across campus make toward the land-grant university's engagement mission. One senior administrator put it this way:

> Many faculty members are heavily invested in the idea that they are supposed to be engaged in meeting the needs of communities. Now, that's not true of all faculty members. You tend to see this most often from faculty members in agriculture, who are fairly cognizant of the need to be engaged. Education faculty sense the need to engage with communities as well. But the typical English professor, in contrast, doesn't seem to be aware of the fact there is a world outside of his or her office. You tend to see faculty members in service-oriented professions getting more involved, especially licensed professions. There is much less engagement in the liberal arts fields, of course with some interesting exceptions. (president/chancellor pers. comm.)

In addition to agriculture and education, other more frequently mentioned academic disciplines with significant direct involvement in community outreach and engagement efforts included architecture, engineering, medicine, human development and family science, and social work. Further, business schools typically were mentioned as having established important partnerships with local businesses, as well as containing faculty members who serve as consultants to the business community or otherwise are called upon by larger corporations for technical assistance.

That said, we cannot overstate the amount of emphasis that was placed on the role agriculture was thought to play in community engagement efforts. For most presidents and chancellors, the involvement of agriculture faculty members was a given in terms of both historical tradition and their current areas of content expertise. These senior administrators typically noted the great amount of pride that surrounded these efforts in terms of what was being done for farms and farm systems. Similarly, these same faculty also were portrayed as being involved in many (mostly rural) economic development projects, activities that often were described as having created concurrent opportunities for students to become more immediately involved in their communities as well.

The focus on the dominant role that agricultural faculty often play in community engagement is further intensified by their historical interconnectedness with Cooperative Extension Services. Senior administrators noted that those areas that traditionally have been close to Extension—plant and soil sciences, for instance, and the vestiges of home economics and consumer science departments—have had a more service-based orientation and thus have recruited and retained faculty members that continue to seek out opportunities for outreach and engagement activities. Importantly, the presidents and chancellors we interviewed were aware of the importance of the community-oriented work undertaken by Cooperative Extension Services faculty, yet they were also mindful of the fact that these faculty members often are poorly recognized for their work on behalf of communities. Here is what one senior administrator said about this subject:

> Extension faculty members play a critical role within our county Extension offices through their funded research and their teaching efforts. The faculty at large tend not to understand or recognize the importance of Extension faculty, however. I think that's because of a number of reasons. Most importantly, Extension faculty typically are not tenured, and they are not eligible for tenure. Faculty senates by and large exclude you from membership in the senate if you are not tenure eligible. So, you don't really "count" in the same way if you are an Extension faculty member. (president/chancellor pers. comm.)

The large footprint of the agricultural colleges, in combination with the parallel presence of Cooperative Extension faculty in many community-oriented activities, sometimes has had the unintended consequence of ghettoizing or otherwise creating silos on land-grant university campuses when it comes to engagement activities. According to the presidents and chancellors we interviewed, faculty members from other disciplines at times will act genuinely perplexed when asked about their becoming more involved in meeting community needs. This is so precisely because the perception is that such work can and should fall under the strict purview of the agricultural and Extension faculties.

One of the best inoculations against this way of thinking is an orientation toward interdisciplinary work, some senior administrators argued. Great things tended to happen when faculty members crossed academic boundaries, worked with people in other departments, and collaborated with faculty colleagues in other universities to create solutions to community-based issues. The value of bringing faculty members from various disciplines together to focus on societal problems has long been recognized by university administrators,[11] as reflected in the emphatic endorsement of this idea by one senior administrator we interviewed:

> I am very proud of our faculty members and their ability to address community needs. Like everywhere else, we have specialists, but at the same time we have a lot of people who work across disciplinary lines. There are a lot of joint appointments that bring out a lot of creative messiness that contributes to the work conducted as part of the land-grant mission. And we have a board that has been supportive of that work and that messiness. Our capacity to approach community problems in an interdisciplinary fashion has helped us enormously. (president/chancellor pers. comm.)

One more common way of facilitating this sort of work is through the development of centers and other units that are administered by multiple academic units (departments and colleges) and/or through use of joint faculty appointments. Some of the senior administrators citing the use of these sorts of interdisciplinary enhancements noted that, while there are higher transactional costs and a certain amount of messiness that doesn't always yield an optimum productivity profile, the ability of faculty to freely participate in groups and joint activities promotes a greater agility and responsiveness to community needs.

## Promotion and Tenure

In the previous chapter, we asserted that the most functional governance structures inside institutions of higher learning included the voices of faculty members. The ideal situation would involve the relatively coequal contributions of senior administrators, governing board members, and faculty in terms of deliberation on a wide spectrum of issues that were essential to the primary mission of the university. At the same time, faculty members always have wielded the greatest amount of power in various mission-critical areas, including what is taught (curriculum) and student evaluation (grades). Further, there is an even more essential area that serves as the most important expression of faculty self-governance: the promotion and tenure process.

As we indicated earlier in this chapter, internal and external reviews of the teaching, research, and service record of assistant professors are used to ensure that certain standards of excellence are met prior to the granting of a lifetime guarantee of employment. While there are various levels of the university through which a candidate's dossier must pass, in practice there is a tremendous amount of weight placed on the conclusions of that faculty member's home department. That departmental unit is composed of those faculty members who are most similar to the candidate in terms of their general area of study (i.e., anthropologists are organized in a department with other anthropologists, mechanical engineers are all grouped together in their own departmental unit, etc.). So, if faculty members within a department place higher value on community engagement vis-à-vis engaged scholarship and/or engaged teaching, then the untenured assistant professors in that unit will be rewarded accordingly for their participation in those sorts of activities (i.e., they will be tenured and promoted to associate professor). Alternatively, if those same departmental colleagues instead do not place much value on such engagement activities, more than likely the candidacy of the assistant professor participating in those sorts of efforts is doomed.

The presidents and chancellors we interviewed spoke directly to the role that the departmental unit played in positively appraising community engagement activities as part of the promotion and tenure process. This underscores the fact that the power to positively evaluate engagement activities rests primarily in the hands of the faculty members themselves. Here is the way one senior administrator put it:

> How much value is placed on engagement is highly variable by department. I think there is a greater appreciation for scholarship that concerns our impact on communities. There is support for a teacher-scholar model that is based on engagement with students and engagement with communities. I would have to say that, when it comes to votes on tenure and promotion, community engagement does not count as much as other things on one's dossier. That said,

I think we have a little more balanced approach across the campus than other land-grant universities would have. You should be giving presentations at national and international conferences, and you should be publishing research in high-quality journals. But you also should be positively recognized by your peers for being more involved in the community when you are in a land-grant university. (president/chancellor pers. comm.)

This statement underscores a commonly held notion that community engagement does count for something among one's peers. However, what seems to be at issue here is how much it matters. And this is where the land-grant mission, at least in terms of meeting the needs of the communities, is seen to be at its most vulnerable state. When faculty members feel connected to the land-grant mission, they are going to think about how their scholarship engages with the communities that they are serving. But at the end of the day, they are going to do what they need to do to be successful in achieving tenure, being promoted, and receiving annual raises.

Several university presidents and chancellors expressed the belief that there is a lot about the promotion and tenure process that is out of date, especially regarding faculty activities that are directly related to community engagement. In the words of one senior administrator we interviewed,

Faculty will be most active where they see themselves as being rewarded. Out of all the things we have figured out in higher education and land-grant universities regarding faculty rewards, we probably have failed most miserably on engagement. I think we have figured out how to reward great teaching, and certainly we have figured out how to reward great research and scholarship. But when it comes to engagement, I don't think we do a very good job. And we can give a lot of lip service to it as a land-grant university, and we often do just that. But when it comes right down to it, to evaluating faculty and giving them rewards, I think engagement is undervalued. In fact, it is often just ignored. (president/chancellor pers. comm.)

One particularly frequent lament centered around the desire of presidents and chancellors to meet the needs of business and industry partners within the community. Here, these senior administrators found themselves wanting to emphasize the innovation and entrepreneurship of their faculty, all the while knowing that faculty member involvement in startup companies and the acquisition of patents was not going to be measured or counted in the same way as papers in a peer-reviewed journal.

The notion that the promotion and tenure process is outdated is an indictment of a reward structure that strongly emphasizes excellence in research at the expense of great teaching and distinguished engagement. Presidents and chancellors who found themselves at these sorts of land-grant universities were frustrated with what they believed to be a "vacuous lip service" being given to community engagement work. Particularly galling to some of these senior administrators was the belief that faculty members could in fact make something very different happen, yet instead what they discovered was that faculty who got tenure through one set of criteria were not terribly excited about changing those standards to allow others to forge a different path.

Other presidents and chancellors whom we interviewed, however, were much more positive about the reward structure that existed at their land-grant universities. Many of these senior administrators were witnesses to more recent and dramatic shifts in promotion and tenure policies within their institutions, as reflected in the following statement:

> I think our faculty are proud of their land-grant assignment. We talk about it a lot at our university. I think they share a general pride that this is who we are. We just revised our promotion and tenure policy, and I would like to think that it has strengthened the engagement component in at least a couple of ways. It reaffirmed that engagement is one path toward promotion and tenure, and that it is our expectation. In addition, I would like to think that we modernized it a bit. For example, our policy now says explicitly that entrepreneurial activity and tech transfer activity will be recognized and rewarded in future tenure cases. My point of view is that the purest form of engagement today is to move knowledge out into the community, the state, the region, and the world in ways that create new opportunities—economic and otherwise—for people. We are very explicit about that now. (president/chancellor pers. comm.)

The senior administrators in this camp firmly believed that having a balanced portfolio of the tripartite mission was entirely possible at a land-grant institution. They spoke forcefully about faculty members not having to feel they had to give up on one thing to do something else within the land-grant tradition.

While we wish to acknowledge the tremendous weight placed on departmental preferences regarding the promotion and tenure process, it is important to realize that different types of institutions of higher learning are thought to vary significantly in terms of their responsiveness to the community engagement activities of their faculty.[12] Research-intensive public and private universities have been portrayed as being less likely to make the organizational changes necessary to make a wholesale institutional commitment to engagement, for example, because they continue to experience successes surrounding their traditional empirical focus. In contrast, colleges and universities that primarily serve local students who will remain close to home upon graduation, that emphasize teaching and learning more than research, and that exist inside of host communities with significant economic challenges are more likely to choose to adopt an engagement focus at an institutional level. As a result, those institutions place greater value on the civic engagement efforts undertaken by their faculty.

While the land-grant mission and traditions would lead one to believe that those institutions would naturally embrace an engagement framework, they have been portrayed as lagging in this capacity.[13] We had the opportunity to discuss engagement at land-grant institutions with Barbara Holland, Distinguished Professor of Community Engagement at the University of Nebraska Omaha and the creator of the Holland Matrix, a system of identifying institutional levels of commitment to civic engagement.[14] By way of explaining what was different about land-grant universities on the topic of community engagement, Dr. Holland asserted that perceptions regarding the relationship between research and engagement are what distinguishes land-grant universities from all other institutions of higher education. In part because of their land-grant history, which long emphasized community connections through Extension and outreach services, she argued that it is harder for land-grant faculty members to understand that research and engagement are not separate activities. As a result, Dr. Holland believes that land-grant universities have struggled with understanding this relationship more than any other institutional type. In short, because faculty members at land-grant institutions believe that their university has always done community engagement through its Extension programs, they have difficulty in seeing it as a form of disciplinary scholarship.

Our earlier discussion about the siloed nature of community involvement is echoed in Dr. Holland's remarks here:

> The historic role of Extension can create a mind-set among faculty that "those people" do that kind of work, so I don't have to. It is largely subconscious, and yet it is pervasive. It creates this idea that community engagement is a separate and distinctive activity and not necessarily connected to core traditional research. And then you add on to that the historic culture of all research

universities, which creates an environment that says research is individualized to the specific interests of each faculty member. While that may be all well and good for a traditional view of academic culture, these universities struggle to tell the story of how they are making contributions to the public good because those lines of research are so often individualistic. The best story for a land-grant to tell, after all, is how the university is having a significant impact on issues that are of the utmost importance to the citizens and context of the state through its teaching, learning, and research efforts. Engagement is a method of teaching, learning, and research. A focused agenda of interdisciplinary scholarly engagement is the best path toward increased levels of both intellectual discovery and public support. (pers. comm.)

In the end, then, we believe that there must be shared responsibility for the valuation of community engagement as part of the promotion and tenure process. Faculty members within departmental units must recognize its worth, for starters, and the college and university committees must affirm its merit along the way.

There did seem to be some fundamental disagreement among the presidents and chancellors we interviewed regarding the degree to which engagement activities are measurable and therefore able to be evaluated. Some of these senior administrators expressed the opinion that the scholarship of engagement was no more difficult to appraise than any other form of research and creative activity. Others, however, believed that it was much harder to demonstrate excellence because questions had not yet been answered in terms of what engaged scholarship was and how you would evaluate the excellence of that sort of work. Here is what one senior administrator said:

> We are driven on the scholarship side by the need for peer evaluation. Your peers must authenticate that your work is important and that it has impact. With engaged scholarship, this is still hard to do, and there is plenty of work ahead in trying to establish the legitimacy of these efforts. We haven't quite gotten there yet. We need to have systems established that help us to evaluate the importance of this sort of work. Once this is done, then the work will flow quite naturally. (president/chancellor pers. comm.)

It is our opinion that, while the framework for determining excellence in engagement activities continues to be developed, sufficient efforts have been undertaken to allow faculty members and administrators alike to pass judgment on these sorts of endeavors. What more likely is lagging is academicians' understanding of just how much progress has been made on this front in the realm of engagement.

## Evolution of the Tripartite Mission and the Engaged Scholarship Consortium

Boyer's work on the reconsideration of scholarship in academia, first introduced in our second chapter, discussed the need for universities to become more dynamic partners with community stakeholders through their teaching, research, and service efforts.[15] Four components of scholarship were asserted in this reconceptualization of university faculty activities: teaching, discovery, application, and integration. The scholarship of teaching was meant to include not only the imparting of knowledge by faculty members but also the transformation and extension of that content in meaningful ways. The scholarship of discovery concerned basic research that contributed new knowledge to academic fields, whereas the scholarship of application focused on applied research that created solutions to real-world problems. Finally, the scholarship of integration called for the amalgamation of teaching, discovery, and application efforts by faculty members in ways that cut across academic fields and provided higher-order understanding not achievable within a single discipline.

Boyer's reconsideration of scholarship was thought to demand certain worldview changes within institutions of higher learning.[16] As a result, over time the tripartite mission of teaching, research, and service was relabeled. Teaching was recast as "learning," signifying a more active and bidirectional relationship between professor and student. Owing to the significant emphasis on basic research effort within many universities, research was relabeled as "discovery," although more liberal interpretations, of course, included applied research in this category of activities. And finally, as we noted in our second chapter, as a result of the influence of the Kellogg Commission, the service component was rebranded as "engagement" to reflect the reciprocal nature of the relationship between the university and its partners.

More recently, there have been further attempts to refine the epistemological basis of the tripartite mission to reflect the impact that universities have on economic development. An effort led by APLU and the University Economic Development Association (UEDA) was organized around the need to transition university personnel away from thinking about contributing to the twentieth-century industrial economic model and toward their full participation in the global knowledge economy of the twenty-first century.[17] In so

doing, teaching/learning was recast as "talent" to reflect the lifelong development of human capital, research/discovery became "innovation," and service/
engagement was relabeled "place" to illuminate the role universities can play
in being stewards of more vibrant communities. Taken together, only
higher-intensity efforts in each of the talent-innovation-place components
were asserted to yield what is termed "high-impact economic engagement."

Although it is nuanced, what readers may notice there is a shift in thinking about engagement itself, spoken about as the *combination* of efforts in the
talent-innovation-place activity centers. We believe that, as the tripartite mission has evolved, so too has our understanding of how universities are connected to community stakeholders. In earlier times, service to communities
was portrayed as being distinct from teaching and research. More recently,
however, involvement in the community has been framed in terms that have
demanded more direct and functional connections to activities in both the
classroom and the laboratory.

Principles have been laid out for public and land-grant universities to increase their community engagement activities in ways that enhance all aspects of the tripartite mission.[18] First, there is the need to *generate scholarship*
that focuses empirical attention either on the act of engagement itself or on
the product of the engagement. Second, there is the need to *integrate efforts*
in ways that combine various aspects of teaching, research, and service within
each engagement effort (vs. seeing engagement as located separately in only
one aspect of the tripartite mission). Third, the activities must be *mutually
beneficial* to both campus and community stakeholders, as we have emphasized repeatedly throughout this book. And fourth, engagement must support
the *democratic ideals* of our nation.

Seen from this vantage point, engagement encompasses all aspects of a faculty member's existence inside of the university rather than being relegated
to an "other" category—so much so, in fact, that more recent calls have been
made to move engagement into the center of all conversations about the ways
public and land-grant universities are contributing to the public good.[19] To
accomplish this, however, universities will have to realign certain internal aspects, not the least of which includes funding models and reward structures. It has been asserted that these institutions of higher learning also will
have to adopt more systemic ways to connect with community partners and
to help solve the most pressing problems society faces at present.[20]

The Engaged Scholarship Consortium (ESC) is the most well-known
organization dedicated to the strengthening of campus–community relation-

ships through an engagement framework that permeates all aspects of the tripartite mission.[21] The roots of ESC can be traced back to 1999 and the hosting of the first National Outreach Scholarship Conference by three land-grant entities: The Ohio State University, Pennsylvania State University, and the University of Wisconsin's Extension Services. Since that time, the organization has grown to over 40 members, approximately half of which are land-grant universities. ESC brings university personnel together through an annual conference and various professional development workshops and academies, recognizes outstanding engagement efforts through an awards program, and provides outlets for engaged scholarship through the maintenance of two peer-reviewed journals: the *Journal of Community Engagement and Scholarship* and the *Journal of Higher Education Outreach and Engagement*.

We had the opportunity to speak about ESC and its activities with former ESC president Hiram Fitzgerald, who also is a distinguished professor in psychology at Michigan State University and that university's associate provost for outreach and engagement. Much of what Dr. Fitzgerald shared with us underscored his belief that engaged scholarship can and should be evaluated in much the same way that any other rigorous research efforts would be judged. In fact, he went on to state that there was much to be said for the superiority of engaged scholarship activities that were the result of collaborations with community partners, especially in terms of comparing the legitimacy of testing hypotheses in the real world versus the sterility of a research laboratory exercise.

Because we knew that Dr. Fitzgerald had worked with dozens of land-grant universities on their engagement efforts, we asked him about the disagreements we had discovered among the presidents and chancellors we had interviewed regarding the ability to evaluate engaged scholarship. His response was first to point to one of the dialectics that emerged from our qualitative data—basic versus applied research—and the notion that there are people in the academy who hold strong views about the superiority of the former over the latter. He went on to state,

> Some people can't get it in their heads that when you go into a community that has a serious problem, you have to learn a whole lot about that community from the folks who live there in order to design and conduct a study addressing that problem. It's this notion that the indigenous knowledge of community, both the tacit and explicit knowledge, contribute[s] to our understanding of the problem at hand. And without the voice of the community members, how

could we possibly ask the right questions? That is what engaged scholarship is all about, and that is no less rigorous than any other approach to scholarship. In fact, it's probably more authentic, because the sustainability of outcomes is higher than if you went in there and did a traditional efficacy study, one where you walked away with your results and the community members are still sitting there with the problem. (pers. comm.)

Dr. Fitzgerald went on to say that he recognized that there were colleagues and senior administrators across the country who did not share those same beliefs about the value of engaged research. However, in large part owing to the efforts of ESC over the years, he believed that the number of those individuals has been shrinking over time, and he remained genuinely optimistic about further increased respect for engaged scholarship efforts in the years ahead.

## Summary

We began this chapter with a description of both tenure-track and non-tenure-track faculty members and described the part that each type of faculty member contributes to the tripartite land-grant university mission regarding teaching, research, and service. We then reported on the responses of the presidents and chancellors to the question of faculty member impact on the land-grant university's ability to meet the needs of the communities they were designed to serve. Our central focus here was on faculty applied research activities and related outreach and engagement efforts. We also raised concerns that the senior administrators had about the siloed nature of engagement on land-grant campuses. Further, the issue of promotion and tenure was also discussed, with significant emphasis on the local control that faculty members have regarding how engagement is rewarded by land-grant universities. Finally, we also reported on the evolution of the tripartite mission of teaching, research, and service, with special attention given to the efforts of the ESC.

# CHAPTER 6

# Our Students

## *Vanguard in the Community*

The present chapter focuses on the set of remarks made by the land-grant presidents and chancellors we interviewed regarding the impact students have on how well land-grant universities were meeting the needs of the communities they were designed to serve. Where possible, we attempt to situate these comments within the themes developed in our third chapter regarding the strengths, weaknesses, opportunities, and threats faced by land-grant universities as they attempted to fulfill their mission. To remain consistent with the other chapters that reported on our qualitative data, we continue to use direct quotations as examples of the main issues generated by the land-grant presidents and chancellors, as well as providing supplemental information as needed from referential material available on applicable topics.

We begin with basic descriptions of the undergraduate and graduate levels of study within land-grant institutions. We present a portrait of undergraduate study which reflects attempts by universities to reconcile the dynamic tension between the desire to provide a well-rounded liberal arts education and the demand for more targeted career readiness and workforce development efforts. The graduate study experience, while impacted by some of the same strains, additionally is depicted as being heavily influenced by the research aspirations of the typical land-grant university.

The focus of this chapter then moves to the responses given by the presidents and chancellors we interviewed to the specific question we posed concerning student impact on the land-grant university's ability to address community needs and concerns. Many of these university leaders emphasized the important effect that students had on communities while currently enrolled in their degree programs, most typically through service-learning. Interestingly, some of the senior administrators focused more exclusively on the graduation of students and their return to the community as productive members of the workforce. In other words, they framed student impact as being most significant once they have become alumni. Because the presidents and chancellors also raised concerns about student activism and the promotion of democratic ideals through civic engagement activities, we deal specifically with these student-oriented issues in this chapter as well.

## The Undergraduate and Graduate Student Experiences at Land-Grant Universities

Let us begin by highlighting the fact that the presidents and chancellors we interviewed took great pains to note that undergraduate and graduate students were the very lifeblood of the land-grant university. One senior administrator put it this way:

> Our students are our hope. They bring energy, they bring ideas, and they bring drive. They are better prepared than they have ever been before when they reach us, so they really do push us all the time. To meet their needs, we are required to move ahead. And if we are to meet their needs as a leading institution, we need to run as fast as we can to stay ahead of them. Students are a great stimulating force that makes us who we are, and who we will become. (president/chancellor pers. comm.)

These university leaders also recognized that students applied to land-grant institutions precisely because they were looking for experiences that would allow them to understand the world that encompasses them and to apply the knowledge they gain directly to their surroundings. As a result, they believe that the education offered at a land-grant university provides an effective path toward both personal enlightenment and preparation for the kinds of careers that students wish to pursue in their lives.

Are land-grant universities able to offer all of that? At first glance, some observers would raise doubts. Among other things, the birth of the land-grant universities has been blamed for the schism that has developed between the classic liberal arts education on the one hand and a more vocationally oriented academic program on the other.[1] What exactly is that schism? Most simply, we might see this as a clash of viewpoints about the need to offer a more general educational curriculum versus more specific and vocationally oriented coursework. The liberal arts tradition is the more general viewpoint and seeks to offer a well-rounded education on various subjects in the arts, humanities, natural sciences, and social sciences. In contrast, as we have recounted in previous chapters, land-grant institutions originally were charged with the specific task of focusing on more practical areas such as agriculture and the mechanical arts (engineering), areas of study that certainly retain a more professional orientation.

We know from various historical accounts, however, that such a schism is not as large as might be expected, at least in terms of the real-world experiences of educating undergraduate students at land-grant universities.[2] These institutions of higher learning developed and offered many programs of study that have combined the best of both worlds, that is, a well-rounded general education with more vocationally specific coursework—so much so, in fact, that land-grant institutions have been portrayed as highly integrative in their approach to undergraduate education, uniting not only the essentialist (liberal arts) and pragmatic (professional) needs of students but also their existential need for self-discovery and personal meaning.[3]

What about graduate education at a land-grant university? We first need to distinguish between work on the master's degree level and the pursuit of a doctoral degree. Most master's-level programs aim to grant an advanced degree in a specific vocational area, often meeting professional licensing requirements along the way. Well-known examples here include the MBA (master of business administration), the MSW (master of social work), the EdM (master of education), and the MFA (master of fine arts). These are thought of as "terminal degrees" in the sense that the completion of the master's program provides the student with everything they need for employment in that professional realm.

Doctoral degrees, in contrast, are designed to grant an advanced degree that is connected to the acquirement of research and other scientifically oriented skills. While some of the earliest American doctoral programs were created within private institutions, the Morrill Land-Grant Acts and the Hatch Act together were thought to play particularly significant roles in the founding of PhD programs within land-grant universities.[4] Essentially, appropriations from the federal government have guided and directed the development of science-based graduate education at the doctoral level across our nation.

While the master's and doctoral degree programs represent somewhat differing approaches to graduate education—professional preparation versus research and science skill development—together they remain a contrasting approach to the more generalist framework of the classic liberal arts education.[5] Also embedded here is some dynamic tension between the operation of the undergraduate and graduate programs themselves. Master's and doctoral programs are much more expensive to operate, for example, and as a result they are often subsidized by revenue generated by undergraduate tuition.

While graduate education is much more closely aligned with research efforts, in more recent times there has been tremendous growth in undergraduate student participation in empirical activities, and this sort of experience has enhanced the land-grant university's ability to meet community needs.[6] Several presidents and chancellors mentioned this specifically in their remarks, represented here by the following quote:

> The connection I see there, and I think all land-grant universities do this to some degree, relates to the student's ability to work elbow to elbow with faculty members in the production of research. To ensure they are not just sitting in a classroom, we enlist undergraduate students—not just our graduate students, who are expected to do research—to work directly with our most senior faculty members on big research projects. And a lot of those projects are translational. They're not just bench science. I think these interactions make enormous contributions to the land-grant mission of meeting the needs of communities. (president/chancellor pers. comm.)

Interestingly, a few of the senior administrators who focused on undergraduate research experiences went on to share some remarkable stories about students whose lives had been radically altered as a direct result of the work they had undertaken as a community-based research project assistant. The unprompted disclosure of these anecdotes served to confirm our belief in the transformative nature of these sorts of extracurricular activities for undergraduate and graduate students alike.

One last topic we wish to share in the introductory section of this chapter concerns the remarks made by land-grant university presidents and chancellors regarding the counterbalancing of the selective admissions process with student perceptions of access (or lack thereof) first discussed in our third chapter. Most simply put, these senior administrators were exposed to a great deal of frustration expressed by prospective students (and the parents of those individuals) who did not gain admittance into the land-grant university of their choice. In the words of one university leader,

> A whole lot of students, and those students' families, have come to believe that all students can get into a land-grant university. I can't tell you how many talks I give to alumni groups that are frustrated with the fact that we have become more selective in our admissions process. That's a reflection of the number of people who are applying and the fact that we are increasingly judged by the success of our students through graduation rates and other similar performance indicators. Quite simply, this is how we are funded in our state. So, the way that students think about us is that we should be serving the masses through a more open admissions process. And this is of course not true for us, and is not a reflection of what most land-grant universities across the country are doing right now. (president/chancellor pers. comm.)

This is a contentious issue, to be sure, especially if the land-grant institution also is the flagship university of the state, meaning they are the largest research institution.[7] The original land-grant mission of educating the offspring of working-class parents does not stand up well to the continued use of such high admission standards, especially when the data indicate that these flagship universities increasingly are serving students from families in higher income brackets.[8]

In the meantime, we believe that some of the disappointment and annoyance experienced by such undergraduate student prospects and their parents can be alleviated by the offering of a high-quality academic experience on a branch or regional campus as an "alternative front door" to the university. This situation is made even better when there are clearly articulated steps in place that allow students who start on those remote locations to transfer to the main campus in relatively short order. Those land-grant universities without such alternative campus options or transfer policies and procedures are in more dire straits in terms of this access issue, of course.

## Engagement through Service-Learning

The presidents and chancellors we interviewed consistently named service-learning courses as the vehicle by which students had the greatest impact on the land-grant university's ability to meet the needs of communities. The following quote is emblematic of how many of these senior administrators described the use of service-learning:

The most significant way that students are connecting to the land-grant mission is through service-learning. Now, they don't necessarily see that as part of being a student at a land-grant university. However, the more that we can have our students working in the communities that we serve, and connect their educational success to direct involvement in the community, the more we are fulfilling the land-grant mission and preparing our students to leave the university as fully committed citizens. And God knows we need more of those kinds of students. (president/chancellor pers. comm.)

Many of the senior administrators were quick to point out the continued growth their land-grant universities were experiencing through this form of community engagement, most often by citing significant increases in the number of service-learning credit hours that had been generated over the past several years. Others pointed to statistics related to the overall number of service-learning courses being taught, the number of faculty members and departments teaching such courses, and the number of community partners who participated as collaborators in the design and delivery of such coursework.

What exactly is service-learning? The seminal work of Robert Bringle and Julie Hatcher, "A Service-Learning Curriculum for Faculty," is most often cited in journal articles and book chapters that provide a basic working definition of service-learning. These scholars formulated a definition of service-learning that emphasized its academically oriented roots as a "course-based, credit bearing educational experience in which students (a) participate in an organized service activity that meets identified community needs, and (b) reflect on the service activity in such a way as to gain further understanding of course content, a broader appreciation of the discipline, and an enhanced sense of personal values and civic responsibility."[9] While related to other university-based efforts to increase student appreciation for social justice, civic engagement, and involvement in other forms of community service,[10] all forms of service-learning are distinguished from these other activities by their embeddedness in a curriculum of study. The literature currently is replete with scholarly publications that outline best practices for faculty members interested in the implementation and evaluation of service-learning offerings, and service-learning courses are thought to be central to the Carnegie Foundation for the Advancement of Teaching Classification for Community Engagement, first introduced in our second chapter.[11]

The presidents and chancellors we interviewed were struck by just how enormous the impact of high-quality service-learning offerings could be on students, faculty members, and community partners. These senior administrators were particularly impressed with the persistent contact students had with community stakeholders throughout the semester or academic year covered by such service-learning courses. This high level of involvement over time was thought to generate substantial evidence that the students were firmly committed to these sorts of curricular-based community engagement efforts.

## Civic Engagement Activities beyond the Classroom

Regardless of the exact mechanism used to create greater student involvement in the community, there was broad consensus among university leaders that their students were extremely socially aware and therefore needed little prompting to become involved in community engagement efforts. Students were described invariably as "wanting to change the world" as part of their higher education experience, at least to some degree because they already had some exposure to land-grant personnel carrying out such work. Here is what one senior administrator told us about this point:

> Students come to use prepared to do a lot of work on subject matter related to the environment, sustainability issues, and social justice concerns. Because we are a land-grant institution, we can provide these sorts of opportunities. It's also important to point out that students who are coming for agriculturally based degrees likely have grown up around Extension agents and other land-grant personnel who were modeling the behaviors we associate with community involvement. At other public universities that I have been to that were not land-grant institutions, I felt that there was much less desire to become involved in the community. It's as if land-grant institutions tend to attract those students who wish to have a significant impact on communities as the result of their educational experience. (president/chancellor pers. comm.)

Other comments made by these senior administrators included observations that the generation of students now attending college was very much aligned with the land-grant mission in that they were very interested in seeing the application of their learning directly in the community. This was portrayed as a core characteristic of this most recent cohort of students, who were thought to demonstrate a great deal of enthusiasm for these sorts of activities. Because many of these students already had done a substantial amount of volunteer work in their high schools, it was reasoned, community involvement seemed to be the norm for them.

Even more impressive in the eyes of the presidents and chancellors we interviewed was how much of the community-based work was being led by college students themselves. Here is how one senior administrator described this:

> Our students continuously surprise me. I am amazed at how active our students are in doing community service kinds of things. Our students get together regularly and go out in the town to do service projects. They will paint buildings in low-income areas, or physically clean up an area that has fallen into disrepair. And they do the same thing on our campus, I might add. Two to three thousand students will participate once a month in projects that spruce up the campus. I'm really pleased to see and hear about their attitudes toward community outreach and community service. And this is all done under student leadership. It's not like our administration went out and told these students to do these things. They just decided they wanted to do community service, so they started these projects by themselves. (president/chancellor pers. comm.)

Another related issue was how often student-led community engagement efforts involved athletes. Several senior administrators spoke proudly of the fact that their athletic teams had some form of contest every year to see who could do the most community service. University leaders uniformly described these sorts of competitions as being great for both the athletes and the community members who benefited from that contact, whether it was a world-class swimmer out in the community giving children their first pool experience or an NFL-bound football player mentoring a youngster in improving their reading skills.

The overall emphasis these presidents and chancellors placed on the significant impact that students have on the land-grant university's ability to meet the needs of communities comports with the findings of studies examining the differential influence of various campus representatives on positive campus–community interactions. For example, one study led by Gavazzi reported that community member perceptions of students were the most salient factor in those residents' assessments of town–gown relationship quality, outstripping the impact of faculty members, administrative staff, and governing board members.[12] These sorts of results are thought to support the notion that impressions of students and their behaviors—for better and for worse—tend to drive overall perceptions regarding how well campuses and communities are working together.

## Other Issues Impacting Student Engagement with Communities

The demographics of the state in which the land-grant university was situated and the characteristics of the university itself were also thought to play a role in determining the relative impact of student involvement in the community. Said one senior administrator,

> We are a very small state and a relatively small university inside of that state. Therefore, community service from our athletes, honors students, fraternity and sorority members, and students from any of our clubs and organizations becomes a very important part of what we do for communities as an institution. Whether it's working in a food pantry or working on recovery efforts from natural disasters, our efforts are exceptionally meaningful. We are very visible, and that helps lift up the importance of our efforts inside of the communities we serve. (president/chancellor pers. comm.)

In turn, there also was a clear connection made between community engagement and other cocurricular activities sponsored by the residential life units on the campuses of the land-grant universities. Those senior administrators who talked about getting beyond coursework and the need to study hard and do well on examinations and papers were the ones who asserted that student interactions with the community often generated significant learning experiences not replicable in the classroom. And at least one university leader framed student–community interaction as part of the "long-term salvation of residential campuses," in that these kinds of activities—especially if coherently connected to living-learning environments and relevant coursework—simply cannot be duplicated in either web-based or traditional educational approaches.

We note here that the presidents and chancellors we interviewed were mindful of the fact that definitions of community engagement varied from person to person and from institution to institution. Relatedly, there was open wonderment about the degree to which other land-grant leaders would be able to agree on a common definition of community engagement. Some of these senior administrators were concerned particularly when characterizations of engagement became self-limiting. Here is how one university leader described her apprehensions:

Unfortunately, I think the word "engagement" has come to mean something that is extremely narrow. When engagement is defined solely in terms of interaction with the community, it becomes largely irrelevant in the twenty-first century. Engagement must be viewed as a commitment to the full undergraduate experience, one that provides structured activities within a set of expectations that students will be fully and personally engaged in their learning. To the extent they learn new knowledge in the classroom and the laboratory, it must become knowledge that is substantiated in a sense of self that is embedded within the community [where] they live and work. And this must be impressed upon these students to an extent that it drives their lives postgraduation. (president/chancellor pers. comm.)

We found that the arguments made for more fully integrated engagement efforts by these senior administrators sounded very similar to the most recent iteration of the tripartite land-grant university mission discussed in our fifth chapter—where the classic teaching, research, and service model was converted for more modern (and economically grounded) sensitivities into activities that focused on talent, innovation, and place—as it calls for more direct and purposeful connections to activities in the classroom, the research lab, and the community. In this sort of environment, as students become more active learners in all aspects of their education, their impact on communities only increases.

## The Impact of Alumni

When asked about the impact of students on the land-grant university's ability to meet the needs of the communities they were designed to serve, several presidents and chancellors made remarks indicating that students are important first and foremost because, after graduating, they go back into their communities as more enlightened adults and more productive members of the workforce. While not necessarily downplaying the role that currently enrolled students may play in meeting community needs, it was clear that this group of senior administrators believed that alumni had much greater impact overall. The general tenor of these comments positioned individuals with conferred degrees as a "primary product" of land-grant universities when it came to serving communities. Here is how one senior administrator put it:

Graduates are the key to understanding the impact that students have on meeting the needs of communities. We graduate thousands of students every year, and they occupy every field. They become the intellectual human capital of the state. I think that's where you see the real impact of students. When they graduate and go on to become leaders in the community, that's when they really begin to make a difference. (president/chancellor pers. comm.)

Previous interviews of university and municipal leaders have underscored the important role that alumni play in building higher-quality campus–community relationships. The 2016 book *The Optimal Town–Gown Marriage*, written by Gavazzi, contained interviews of former university presidents and city managers on the topic of what leadership actions most contributed to harmonious campus–community interactions.[13] The importance of developing and maintaining relationships with alumni was so critical to these leaders that it became one of the "ten commandments" of town–gown relationships, stated as "Thou shall know the power of your alumni, especially those living in communities immediately surrounding the campus." Here, it was stressed that students who graduated and decided to remain as longer-term residents of the community can and should have a special place in leaders' thinking about town–gown relationships, as they are thought to represent "the perfect blend" of campus and community interests.

The importance of establishing alumni relationships in the process of fostering healthy campus–community relationships—with special emphasis on connections to the business community, we might add—was echoed in remarks made by university presidents and chancellors in interviews conducted by Francis Lawrence, the former president of Rutgers University. His 2006 book *Leadership in Higher Education* reported on material culled from responses given by 12 university leaders to a series of questions, including one that requested commentary on the role of the university within the communities that surrounded their campuses.[14]

Two examples culled from these previous interviews of land-grant leaders shall suffice to support our main point here. Witness first the remarks made by Brit Kirwan, former president of The Ohio State University and chancellor of the University of Maryland system, who admitted to not really understanding the importance of campus–community linkages or being aware of the role that alumni played in this space when he first became a university president. Through a sustained focus on numerous external relations fronts, however, including specific efforts to reinvigorate the alumni operations office, he reported having experienced much greater success in all aspects of his leadership as a result. Similar remarks were made by David Ward, former chancellor of the University of Wisconsin–Madison. In sharing his thoughts on the complex relationships that existed between his university, alumni, and the business community, he noted, "I tended to work through the UW alumni association and the UW foundation to reach the business community to focus on people who already had some connection and loyalty to Madison."

The presidents and chancellors who participated in our more recent interviews similarly reported having learned to pay attention to the impact that alumni had on the relationship between campuses and communities, especially those graduates who became business leaders. These individuals, who were thought to represent an amalgamation of alumni, employer, and donor roles, wore "multiple hats" as advocates for both the university and the communities in which they resided. As such, senior administrators believed that they ignored these specific alumni at their own peril.

Returning full circle to the point we made at the beginning of this section, we wish to note here that land-grant universities would be best served by a long-term investment strategy that focuses attention on the community impact of both present students and alumni. We were reminded about this point in the middle of a discussion with one senior administrator who was discussing tech transfer issues, intellectual property, and student entrepreneurs. This is how that conversation went:

> We've created a lot of minors within colleges and have created a certificate program that any student can take regardless of their major that allows them to learn the fundamentals of business. We have many different types of competitions and awards that allow our students to transition into these economic incubators within their communities. Basically, what we are saying in this space is look, you can decide that you must go to San Francisco to create your company—there's capital there and there are a lot of people doing these kinds of things—but you are going to live in a crummy place and you are going to eat ramen noodles. Or you can have a university that helps you to be successful, and eat hamburgers and live in a decent place, and build your student company in your community. In my mind, this is a student role in the land-grant mission because we are enabling the student to be successful within their home communities. Now, the university doesn't get their intellectual property, but I have the feeling that if the student believes we really helped them with their company, and they become successful, some future president will be really happy with this situation when they are fundraising. (president/chancellor pers. comm.)

Such a long-term investment strategy would seem to bode well for land-grant universities, which have everything to gain and comparatively little to lose by linking their tripartite mission specifically to the activities of their present and former students. Previous scholarship has documented the various ways universities have reshaped their development activities to gain greater support for community engagement efforts,[15] and much of this fundraising highlights the role that students play in addressing community issues and concerns. Pointedly, student involvement in engagement has been clearly highlighted by institutions that have applied for the Carnegie Foundation for the Advancement of Teaching Classification for Community Engagement in ways that have attracted internal university resources and have set the stage for the solicitation of external funding to support such engagement activities.[16]

We had the opportunity to talk about these issues with David Weerts, associate professor of organizational leadership, policy, and development at the University of Minnesota, whose scholarship focuses on the intersection of higher education leadership, institutional advancement, and university–governmental relations. We were interested particularly in his thoughts about certain advantages land-grant institutions might enjoy through an emphasis on the mission-specific components of the work their faculty, staff, and especially students do in communities. Here is what he shared with us:

There is a camp that says we do this because it's the right thing, it's in our charter. What I have been trying to do is ask questions that help people position a strategy of engagement that aligns with the goals that everyone agrees on: better student graduation rates, more economic development within communities, and so on. In other words, we are engaged with communities because it's the right thing to do, but it's also because it is connected strategically to a future that's healthier for our own campuses. It's trying to help people get the right mind-set about all of this. And given what we know about people's legacy giving, we can anticipate that these sorts of activities will prove to be immensely attractive from a donor perspective as well. Certainly, making an appeal to a potential benefactor about their ability to support the university making a difference in communities is far superior to a pitch that asks an alum to give to the department they took classes in 40 or 50 years ago simply because it contained one of their favorite professors at the time. (pers. comm.)

Dr. Weerts went on to point out that studies also have indicated that the impact of higher levels of community engagement extends beyond donor relationships with alumni and other benefactors. Perhaps most importantly, universities with higher engagement tend to be more well funded by their state legislatures.[17]

One other consideration verbalized by several presidents and chancellors focused attention on the necessity of thinking that the land-grant mission continues to touch the lives of graduates long after they leave the university. In other words, it's not only the case that land-grant students have an enormous impact on communities as alumni living productive lives as educated and involved citizens. Here, these senior administrators argued, land-grant institutions need to remain connected to these graduates in ways that continue to provide those individuals with continuous learning throughout their lives, including those ways that increase their value as citizens. In the words of one senior leader,

> The value proposition is not simply to move to our campus and spend four years with us and then leave and never have contact with us again. Instead, we hope to make those first four years the foundation of a lifelong relationship that ensures you will continue to be a more productive citizen. I think a lot of schools are beginning to think along those lines. If we are going to remain viable two or three decades from now, we will have to offer something beyond the residential four-year experience. (president/chancellor pers. comm.)

## Nurturing Democracy through Higher Education

Several presidents and chancellors we interviewed also suggested that land-grant universities could be doing more to meet the needs of communities by placing additional emphasis on educating students for life as active citizens in a democratic society. Most pointedly, their recommendations surrounded actions that would prepare students to make community contributions through their participation in a broader civic life. One senior administrator put it this way:

> At one time, preparing college students to be more civically engaged was thought to be fundamental to sustaining our American democracy. I believe we need to be reasserting that as part of our land-grant mission. I think we do a great job of educating engineers, and doctors, and biologists, and agronomists, but what are we doing to make sure that our students are prepared to be civic leaders? On a related note, I believe we need to think about how we are

preparing people to go into government and perform those necessary roles as well. (president/chancellor pers. comm.)

At risk of stating the obvious, many of the service-learning courses, civic engagement opportunities, and other acts of volunteerism described in earlier sections of this chapter were designed specifically to increase student involvement as committed and enthusiastic citizens in the communities they reside in throughout their undergraduate and graduate years.

We believe that while such activities bear fruit after graduation when students return to their home (or other) communities, they also do much to diminish the impact of student misbehavior on those neighborhoods immediately adjacent to campuses and near-campus student housing complexes. After all, individuals who are active in the life of the community they reside in as students discover a sense of ownership about the place, one that creates a sense both of pride and of protectiveness about its value. When such proprietary sensitivity is absent, in contrast, we argue that you will more readily find increased rates of everything from public urination to property destruction and worse.

Of course, student activism has its darker side as well, and presidents and chancellors made remarks about the worries they had regarding recent events on college campuses across the country. Student protests aimed at disrupting the planned appearances of controversial speakers were the focal point of this concern, an issue that has sparked widespread apprehensions about what students are learning in college courses on the democratic process.[18] Special attention was given to actions taken that resulted in the suppression of free speech, as indicated in the comments of this senior administrator:

> Students have an enormous impact, and overall it is very positive. Students are becoming more active because they are paying more attention to the needs of communities. The only danger here is when student activism becomes a form of political catechism, one that is dogmatic and that they believe everyone should adhere to one way of thinking on campus. Universities are supposed to be messy places in the world of ideas, where things need to be said and then debated. If we move to censuring ideas and the wide expression of thoughts, then the university will no longer be the marketplace of ideas. (president/chancellor pers. comm.)

While we touched on this issue in our first chapter, we wish to say a bit more about this topic here. Based on the comments made by the presidents and chancellors we interviewed, we believe that there is a bit of a balancing act that universities must accomplish. Every precaution must be taken to ensure the personal safety of students and other campus and community stakeholders, of course, and there should be zero tolerance for hate crimes. At the same time, the ability of all parties to be heard on our campuses, regardless of the palatable nature of the beliefs associated with their voices, is essential. Therefore, we must never conflate the necessary prevention of bodily harm with the misguided hindrance of psychological and emotional challenges to the sensitivities of our students (let alone our faculty members and other campus denizens). As the quote immediately above asserts, universities must remain the leader in the marketplace of ideas, no matter how idiotic some beliefs and opinions might seem at the time.

Happily, and despite the amount of headline-grabbing attention gleaned by some recent events on college campuses which did raise legitimate questions about free speech rights, most activities involving students as participants in the democratic process remain positive and vibrant. Leading the way on this important set of student-focused activities is Campus Compact, a national organization representing over 1,000 colleges and universities that, in their words, "build democracy through civic education and community development."[19] Having just celebrated its 30th anniversary, Campus Compact maintains both a national headquarters and either state-level or regional affiliate offices dedicated to the provision of resources and organizational efforts surrounding campus-based civic engagement activities.

We had the opportunity to speak to Andrew Seligsohn, who has been the president of Campus Compact since 2014. Our conversation began with an exploration of five contentions that, according to Seligsohn, provide the foundation for higher education's public mission. The first four contentions are as follows: the assertion that no one has the right to rule over others without their consent, the requirement to ensure every individual the equal opportunity to shape the future of their community, the obligation each individual in a society has to ask critical questions, and the individual citizen's parallel need to display openness to all potential answers to those critical questions. The fifth and final contention focuses attention on the special role colleges and universities play in shaping those other democratically oriented positional statements. Here, it was asserted that an engaged institution needed to reflect the values intrinsic to those contentions in order to protect those values.

We were particularly excited to speak to Dr. Seligsohn because he had more than just a passing familiarity with land-grant institutions. In part, this was the result of the contact he had had with land-grant universities since assuming the role of president, as well as the experiences he had acquired through both his doctoral training at the University of Minnesota and his prior position as the associate chancellor for civic engagement at Rutgers University. Hence, we asked Dr. Seligsohn to weigh in on any special issues or concerns related to the land-grant mission and the work of Campus Compact.

Dr. Seligsohn began with the acknowledgment that most land-grant universities are large and complex institutions, making it more difficult to speak with a unified voice about practically any matter. In comparison, it was asserted that many smaller colleges and those institutions with a religious orientation find it much easier to focus on civic engagement as a core component of their mission. In addition, Dr. Seligsohn was keenly aware of the many ways land-grant presidents and chancellors were focused on making connections between their universities' efforts and the economic well-being of the state in which they were located. At the same time, he believed that university leaders, at land-grant institutions and otherwise, generally were not as articulate in terms of their institutions' impact on healthy civic culture, despite the fact that there is tremendous evidence that the two are strongly associated with one another. In his own words,

> I generally think this is a weakness in the leadership of our institutions. I think we must do a better job of preparing those who are in leadership roles and those who are heading toward those positions to understand the democratic and civic role of colleges and universities. If institutions of higher learning are focused on the role they play in creating a healthy civic culture, the other roles they seek to play, including economic well-being, will be made all the easier to accomplish. On the other hand, if leaders are solely focused on innovation and prosperity, they will likely fail in their efforts precisely because they are not working to strengthen our political culture in ways that are necessary to support economic success. And if we think we can educate students without educating them about democracy, we end up not educating them very well at all. (pers. comm.)

In this light, Campus Compact exists to maintain a spotlight on this essential role, providing ongoing opportunities for university representatives to gather together to discuss best practices and policies that support student civic learning both in the classroom and in the community.

## Summary

We began this chapter with some basic descriptions of the undergraduate and graduate levels of study within land-grant institutions. This included discussion of the dynamic tension between the provision of a well-rounded liberal arts education and the demand for a more vocationally oriented curriculum at the undergraduate level, as well as the heavy influence of research aspirations on graduate study at a typical land-grant university. Our focus then shifted to the responses given by the presidents and chancellors we interviewed regarding the impact that students had on the land-grant university's ability to address community needs and concerns. Student involvement in service-learning courses was predominantly featured in the comments of these senior administrators, while others focused more exclusively on the graduation of students and their return to the community as productive members of the workforce. Finally, student activism and the promotion of democratic ideals through civic engagement activities also were covered in this chapter.

# CHAPTER 7

# Charting the Future of American
# Public Education

In our final chapter, we provide an interpretation of the interview material we gathered from land-grant university presidents and chancellors through use of two frameworks that were more thoroughly discussed in our first chapter. First, we examine the qualitative data, augmented by our further conversations with higher education thought leaders, through the lens of our marital metaphor to discuss how land-grant universities can use the material contained in this book to build more harmonious relationships with stakeholders who represent the multiple communities served by land-grant institutions. Second, we revisit the servant university construct introduced in the first chapter as an additional bold step toward developing a more compelling narrative about the role land-grant institutions can play in terms of meeting the needs of various community constituencies as the "people's universities."

Because we believe so strongly that our students need to be as knowledgeable about the land-grant mission as they are about every other subject matter our universities offer, we also provide the framework for an undergraduate course that can be offered in the general education curricula as an intentional way of building land-grant advocates and leaders for the twenty-first century. Finally, as we synthesize the material covered in this book, we offer ideas we believe can contribute to a reboot of Mr. Lincoln's universities for the remainder of this century and beyond.

## Creating Harmonious Relationships
## with Multiple Constituencies

Taking the entire contents of this book into account, we now want to address the relevance of our work, in effect answering the "so what?" question. What, we hope you are asking, does all of this tell us in terms of the need to take bold action aimed at restoring the American citizenry's confidence in its public institutions of higher learning through the establishment and maintenance of more harmonious relationships with community stakeholders? And further, how do we account for the fact that these stakeholders represent multiple audiences, and ones that shift their orientation over time? As you will recall from our first chapter, this means generating higher levels of effort that contribute to correspondingly higher levels of comfort in partnership with communities, all the while reflecting both capital and countryside sensibilities. This is a tall order for sure. Let us briefly reflect on some of the main issues and concerns illuminated in the chapters of this book in order to further explore how that material can be seen in such a comprehensive light.

In our second chapter, the efforts of the Kellogg Commission, the Carnegie Foundation for the Advancement of Teaching, and APLU were presented as having helped scholars and practitioners to better define and otherwise codify the meaning and scope of community engagement. By association, one would have hoped that these activities also would have served to sharpen our understanding of the land-grant mission itself, at least insofar as it concerned that part of the mission focused on meeting the needs of community stakeholders. Unfortunately, however, the jury seems to still be out on that notion, at least in terms of agreement among senior administrators about the level of importance ascribed to community engagement. Witness the mixed reactions university leaders had to the resource constraints they faced as discussed in the third chapter, for example. Some university presidents believed that it was time to double down on engagement efforts with communities, while others quite oppositely expressed doubts they could continue to provide funding for these same activities indefinitely. This is not exactly an unqualified endorsement of the importance of community engagement in the hierarchy of land-grant institution activities, at least at present.

Despite a lack of concurrence among land-grant presidents and chancellors on this point, it is our contention that the development of more harmonious relationships with community partners across a wide spectrum of interest areas must include an emphasis on community engagement activities.

We believe that land-grant institutions by design—if not in the original 1862 Morrill Act, then certainly through the 1914 Smith-Lever Act—were built and funded specifically to meet the needs of communities in each state of the Union. And we wish to argue vociferously that most of the present-day fiscal challenges facing land-grant and other public institutions of higher learning are the result of their inability to *demonstrate* the return on investment their citizens are receiving for those tax dollars directed toward state-supported colleges and universities.

The inability to exhibit or otherwise document community impact is one of the main reasons so many university leaders struggle to articulate a clear and consistent message about the public good their campuses generate. This point cannot be made too fervently. If we cannot make a strong case for continued public funding based on what institutions of higher learning provide to the communities of citizens who are handing over their hard-earned tax dollars, we shall be passed over for other pressing issues that demand state government funding.

What then can we learn from the seven themes that emerged from our interviews with land-grant presidents and chancellors which were introduced in our third chapter? We believe that the results of the research study we completed indicate that now is the perfect time for the leaders of land-grant universities to take swift and decisive action that aims to restore the general public's confidence in its public institutions of higher learning. Our major premise is that this renewed trust among America's citizenry will be produced through the establishment and maintenance of more harmonious relationships with community stakeholders who represent multiple audiences that, at least at times, have diametrically opposed viewpoints. We believe that our analysis of the qualitative data generated from the presidents' and chancellors' responses to our interview questions provided us with some initial clues about what those harmonious relationships will have to look like and exactly whom we must be addressing at present.

The capital versus countryside audiences we discussed in our first chapter loom large here. Certainly, this speaks first and foremost to the theme that emerged on the needs of rural communities versus the needs of a more urbanized America. Land-grant universities historically have been rooted in rural America, yet we feel compelled to ask whether these institutions of higher learning have lost their edge in terms of being able to rally support from the portion of the countryside audience which traditionally has seen benefit to their farms, families, and livelihoods through the efforts of

Cooperative Extension Services and the agricultural colleges. Plugging back into the relationship dimensions of the marriage metaphor discussed in our first chapter, are land-grant universities involved in efforts that no longer create the same level of comfort they once did in the eyes of these stakeholders? Or are the effects of budget cuts on meaningful activities undertaken by entities such as Cooperative Extension Services already showing up as decreased satisfaction (or disaffection) levels in the populations they were meant to serve?

On the other side of the coin, what are land-grant universities doing in metropolitan areas to find favor with more capital-inclined audiences? We wonder out loud about the extent to which more recent efforts to impact the lives of urban-located populations are being developed into partnerships that build greater comfort levels and then translate into meaningful support from the recipients. We also wish to raise the specter of possibility that, in a resource-constrained environment, an element of "robbing Peter to pay Paul" may be seen by some as unavoidable in terms of serving these geographically distinct entities. And if this is the cold hard reality of a given university's situation, then in those cases are representatives of land-grant universities speaking openly and honestly about the choices being made here? Are more rurally located stakeholders being prepared for a decrease in the amount of support they have come to expect? And have land-grant institutions calculated what the political costs will be if this were to happen?

Most of the remaining themes we put forward in our third chapter seem to signal decision-making directions for university leaders to consider which are relatively uniform across the constituencies of land-grant universities, at least in terms of those efforts that these institutions of higher learning should be undertaking to increase comfort levels inside of relationships with the public at large. Regarding the theme of global reach versus closer-to-home impact, we think that all internationalization efforts are going to carry the significant risk of decreasing comfort levels with both capital and countryside audiences. Many a citizen would ask, if a given activity does not provide some immediate benefit to those citizens whose tax dollars are providing support to the university, why are those resources being squandered (yes, that is the word that will be used) in that way? Bring this back to the concept of marriage for a moment if the point is not decidedly clear in your head. A spouse might well ask, what in the world are you doing investing so much time and energy in relationships outside of our marriage when I don't feel like you are paying much attention to me?

The two research-oriented themes also seemed to break decidedly in one direction. Regarding the theme of research prowess versus teaching and service excellence, the public at large strongly believes that a university's first purpose is to provide high-quality instruction. Research seems more like a luxury activity to most people outside of academia, or at least a secondary activity that should be undertaken only after teaching excellence is secured. As for the theme of basic versus applied research, it's axiomatic to state that stakeholders are going to value immediate returns on investment (applied) over disinterested (basic) research every time. When placed together, we hear the public saying, "Do research if you must, but please make it immediately relevant to our lives if we are asked to pay for it."

The two "money"-related themes similarly point in one uniform direction, at least as far as increasing comfort among the public at large through efforts that "count" is concerned. On the theme of funding declines versus the need to create efficiencies, it is rather obvious to state that stakeholders are not going to be sensitive to the fiscal plight of land-grant universities unless and until they are portrayed as efficient and streamlined enterprises. Regarding the focus on rankings versus an emphasis on access and affordability, one would have to search far and wide to find a tax-paying citizen who would complain that not enough was being done to help their land-grant university receive a higher ranking in *U.S. News and World Report*. Instead, we witness what seem to be almost daily tirades in our local papers about the high cost of tuition, books, fees, room and board, and so on.

If the customer is always right, what implores us to believe that we should ignore what they are saying to us? Or worse, what has brought us to the place where we think we should be arguing with our customers? The latter strategy virtually guarantees a further loss of market share in any business sector. We feel obliged once again, however, to note that the customers of land-grant universities are not of one singular mind about what these institutions of higher learning should be offering, nor are individual customers always displaying internal consistency in their demands. As but one example of the latter issue, we juxtapose the calls for low tuition and fees to the demand for "country club" campuses which has led to an arms race among universities competing for students who seek greater amenities as part of their college experience.[1]

Let us turn our attention now to what was learned from the information we gathered on governing board members, elected officials, and accrediting bodies in our fourth chapter. From the results, it is our belief that one of the biggest sticking points getting in the way of stronger public support for our nation's public universities—including land-grant institutions—is the issue of rising tuition levels and other escalating costs associated with the pursuit of a college degree. These growing costs seem to trigger very strong negative reactions from the public in general and those state and federal lawmakers and policymakers more specifically who make critical decisions about the provision of fiscal support. Predictably, this leads some individuals to conclude that the pursuit of a college degree just isn't worth the price, and it leads others to determine that the public should decrease (or eliminate) its support of higher education. What will it take to get beyond this impasse? What should be done to move land-grant institutions back toward more harmonious relationships with the communities they were designed to serve? And for the purposes of this chapter, how can governing board members, elected officials, and accrediting bodies make a difference here?

We are mindful of scholarship that has been done on factors associated with rising tuition levels at public institutions of higher learning, including work that has been done to explain tuition inflation as a set of competing narratives.[2] The first of these stories, well known by now to our readers, focuses on tuition increases as the direct result of declines in state appropriations (i.e., state lawmakers are to blame). The second narrative blames rising Medicaid costs that crowd out all other publicly supported activities, including higher education. The third account holds that greater academic program quality is driving tuition spikes, which is to say that you get what you pay for in terms of the worth of your college degree. The fourth story lays blame on the universities themselves, with special attention paid to the assumed irresponsible spending patterns of presidents, chancellors, and other senior administrators. Finally, the fifth narrative insists that there really isn't an affordability issue at all, as tuition increases coexist alongside continued enrollment increases. Here, it is assumed that people rationally pay only what something is worth, and thus market forces would prevent universities from pricing their product beyond its current value.

Which narrative is correct? The evidence suggests that each of these five stories has some merit, meaning that tuition increases are the result of many complex factors. So, how do we envision finding a new way forward for land-grant universities and their constituents, one where there is shared responsibility for the achievement of mutually beneficial goals—including most centrally the achievement of a well-educated workforce and society—instead of engagement in activities that largely seek to assign shame and blame to one aggrieved party or the other?

We had the opportunity to speak to Donald Heller, a national expert on higher education policies, who has written extensively on the coexistence of rising tuition levels and increasing enrollment figures.[3] Having been a faculty member at both Michigan State and Penn State (he currently is the provost at the University of San Francisco), Heller had a keen appreciation for the difficult situations in which leaders of land-grant institutions find themselves at present.

Although Heller was steadfast in his belief that state appropriations on a per-student basis likely were never going to return to previous levels in many states, he did believe that presidents and chancellors could significantly alter the current negative tone of public discourse if they could find new ways to communicate about the return on investment which land-grant institutions yielded. He also believed that these universities were doing themselves no favors by taking actions that smacked of elitism. More specifically, he stated,

> In many institutions of higher learning, and particularly in land-grant universities and other flagships, there is enormous pressure to become more selective, to move up in the rankings, and to become more nationally and internationally recognized. In many instances, these sorts of activities are in direct conflict with the land-grant mission, especially in terms of providing broad access to higher education across the state. For instance, the move toward more selective admissions makes it harder for students from low- and moderate-income families to be accepted into land-grant universities, due in large part to the significant correlation between socioeconomic status and standardized test scores. Couple this with steady increases in tuition levels, and you can see how access for these students becomes diminished over time. That's not supposed to be the case in land-grant institutions. (pers. comm.)

Hence, access and affordability indeed are always in the eyes of the beholder. If you cannot gain entrance to a university, then cost is a moot point. Similarly, a college degree at an even modestly expensive cost certainly is a great deal more affordable for the offspring of higher-income families than it is for those on the lower end of the socioeconomic spectrum.

The selective admissions policies adopted by many public universities also would seem to slant the field against students from more rural areas. School districts in less urbanized locations, for instance, typically have fewer educational resources for students, which suppresses achievement on those standardized test scores (ACT, SAT) that are heavily weighed in admissions decisions. There also are a host of other factors that not only suppress the aspirations of more rurally located students to go to college but also decrease the likelihood of their returning to their communities if they do complete a degree.[4]

This brings us back to the main point we made in our first chapter in terms of how comfort levels inside of campus–community relationships will fluctuate as a direct result of how university activities are interpreted as being in alignment with or against the core values of its *multiple* audiences. If land-grant universities are viewed as the playground of more wealthy and urbanized populations, then those citizens who are less well-off and who live in more rural locations are going to be less inclined to support those institutions of higher learning. By association, state legislators, governors, and other policymakers are going to adopt a similar viewpoint, one that does not bode well for the future support of land-grant institutions.

Therefore, it is our belief that governing board members of land-grant universities must provide the necessary oversight and motivation to have their institutions uphold the traditional mission of serving the broadest range of students. Among other things, this means an insistence on recruitment and retention activities that support diversity in its widest definition. Culture and race will continue to be crucial aspects in these efforts, of course, but so too should be the socioeconomic and geographic factors we have been discussing throughout the chapters of this book.

Interestingly, the 2016 presidential election results already may be reverberating within public higher education's admissions departments. According to a recent *New York Times* article, university admissions officers now are "discovering" the rural student.[5] This piece begins with the admissions director of Texas A&M, a land-grant institution, stating that "in terms of diversity, geography is just as important as racial and ethnic." The article goes on to argue for a better connection between rural citizens, who by and large cast their votes out of deep-seated anger over the lack of economic opportunities, and institutions of higher learning, which hold the educational keys to future prosperity. We can extrapolate here and suggest that those who lead our land-grant universities—presidents, chancellors, and the governing board members who provide oversight—must find ways to highlight and expand these connections in ways that are highly visible to and valued by politicians and voters alike.

## Applying a Servant University Orientation

We now wish to address the servant university orientation introduced in our first chapter to further refine the more compelling narrative we wish to create regarding the role that land-grant universities can play in terms of meeting the needs of various community constituencies. In large part, we believe that this sort of emphasis is necessary because our institutions of higher learning in general, and land-grant universities more specifically, seem to be missing an explicit recognition of the difficulties associated with having to communicate the worth of our activities to multiple audiences representing, at least at times, conflicting values and loyalties. And this may be one of the reasons contributing to the lack of consensus among the senior administrators about the importance of community engagement. In other words, exactly who is being referenced in statements made about the need for involvement with community stakeholders may be far from clear to these presidents and chancellors. And when the community is well defined at other times, there may be a lack of consensus about the value of partnering with or otherwise working for that group of individuals.

Therefore, we believe that the time is exactly right for a robust national conversation on the land-grant institution and its community-focused mission for the twenty-first century, with special emphasis on its servant university orientation. Said slightly differently, how do we reclaim the mantle of the people's universities? Opportunely, this sort of dialogue on land-grant and other public universities was initiated by APLU around the celebration of the Morrill Act's 150th anniversary. This sesquicentennial commemoration in 2012 included a three-day symposium hosted by the University of Vermont, as well as an edited book entitled *Precipice or Crossroads? Where America's Great Public Universities Stand and Where They Are Going Midway through Their Second Century.*[6]

The symposium consisted of a series of lectures, presentations, and panel discussions by a veritable who's who of public and land-grant institutions and related organizations. A variety of subjects were covered throughout this gathering, including but not limited to changing institutional and instructional models, conducting and financing research and other forms of scholarship, tuition and strategic resource investment, access and affordability, and the role of the humanities and the arts. While community engagement was not a specific topic designated for coverage, it certainly was brought up repeatedly by presenters and audience members alike. This proved to be particularly true in discussions surrounding the right balance that needed to be struck within the tripartite mission of teaching, research, and service.

The contributors to *Precipice or Crossroads* represented some of the more prominent thought leaders in higher education at the time, and, as might be expected, there was substantial overlap between the authors and the symposium presenters. Therefore, topics from the symposium were covered in the edited chapters, albeit in substantially greater detail. Additionally, community engagement activities seemed to have been given significant and direct consideration by certain authors in the edited book. Most notably, this included Nancy Zimpher and Jessica Neidl's discussion of community-building efforts undertaken by universities that recognize their role as "anchor institutions" and John Hudzik and Lou Anna Simon's emphasis on the mutual engagement demanded of campus and community partners who wish to collaborate on local and global initiatives.[7]

Unfortunately, at present the national dialogue on the land-grant mission for twenty-first-century America seems to have snagged. One senior administrator interviewed for our study specifically referenced the sesquicentennial activities and the subsequent cessation of conversation as follows:

> Around the time of the Morrill Act's 150th birthday, there was a national conversation about a new land-grant act, so to speak. There is a history of the land-grants having made a significant contribution to the development of our nation, and they have built up significant infrastructures as a function of that work. The task at hand now is to turn our attention to how these resources will be applied to the twenty-first-century needs of this country. This conversation seems to have stalled, unfortunately, as soon as the sesquicentennial celebrations died down. I think we became distracted by some of the more immediate challenges we were facing, instead of continuing to focus on the long-term bigger picture. (president/chancellor pers. comm.)

We strongly believe that this conversation needs to be picked back up again, especially regarding the importance of community engagement and given the fact that we are compelled to sell the value of our activities to multiple audiences. As representatives of the people's universities, presidents, chancellors, other senior administrators, faculty, staff, students, and alumni collectively need to work in collaboration with community stakeholders to figure out how land-grant institutions will retool their activities for the twenty-first century to better serve communities across our great nation.

We had the opportunity to make this exact call to action for university leaders at the 2017 APLU Annual Conference, the theme of which was "The Age of Disruption: Navigating, Innovating, and Excelling." Jointly hosted by two APLU councils—the Council on Outreach and Engagement and the Council on Innovation, Competitiveness, and Economic Prosperity—we participated in a special panel session designed to address the land-grant mission of the twenty-first century.[8] The session was moderated by Randy Woodson, chancellor of North Carolina State University, and we were joined by Rebecca Blank, chancellor of the University of Wisconsin–Madison.

Dr. Woodson set the stage for the ensuing discussion by making a set of opening remarks that focused attention on linkages between the APLU conference theme of disruption and the evolution of the land-grant institution and mission. Here, the point was driven home that land-grant universities have been at the center of a great deal of disruptive growth throughout their history as pillars of American society. Next, we presented the seven themes contained in the third chapter of this book and provided additional context to clarify the central point of our thesis: land-grant institutions have been and were always meant to be the people's universities. Dr. Blank closed out the panel discussion with an updated reaffirmation of the Wisconsin Idea, one of the first models to be developed out of the land-grant tradition demanding strong and deep connections between universities and communities in order to tackle the most pressing public issues and concerns of the day.

The APLU conference audience displayed strong receptivity to the call for a fresh and vibrant national conversation about the value of public higher education's crown jewels and their place in building a brighter future for our country. Readers will recall from the first chapter our argument that there is nothing quite as uniquely American as its land-grant universities. Forged amid tremendous domestic conflict, these institutions of higher learning trained those citizens who went on to heal our disrupted and divided nation and set it on a path to greatness. Once again, we believe that it is time for higher education leaders to answer the call, to gather together as the people's universities and chart a course for the land-grant mission of the twenty-first century.

Let us reflect a bit more on the themes that arose from the interviews of the land-grant presidents and chancellors, including and especially the seventh and final theme. In many ways, we see that the theme of the benefits of higher education versus the devaluation of a college diploma is an exponential outcome of the other six themes in combination. That is to say, the general public would seem to be most comfortable with—and therefore most likely to value the efforts of—those land-grant universities that were maximizing their efficiency efforts in ways that made them affordable or otherwise accessible to students across socioeconomic levels, were best known for their excellence in teaching, were conducting research studies with results that immediately applied to the well-being of local citizens, and had a balanced approach to meeting the needs of both rural and urban populations.

If a narrative built on these themes were to be used consistently by senior administrators in ways that became ingrained in the consciousness of the public at large, we believe that the benefits of higher education and a college diploma from a land-grant university would never be in doubt. Fortuitously, we believe that these themes help form the basis for a solid working definition of the people's university. That is, the land-grant institution as a servant university is within the financial reach of all qualified students seeking admission, it prioritizes its teaching and research efforts to maximize community benefit, and its activities are balanced across the geographic regions within the state where it operates.

We wish to tackle headlong the potential criticism that this is merely putting old wine into new skins, that is, taking the historic land-grant mission of meeting the needs of communities and simply repackaging those activities as something emblematic of the servant university. We are certainly mindful of the past, and to some extent we do believe that land-grant institutions have lost their way, at least insofar as their senior leaders are not employing community-based work as a guiding principle for decision-making about what is and what is not considered to be mission-critical work. We do believe that this artifact of our history needs to be rediscovered, and exalted, by land-grant universities across our country.

Yet we are reasserting something not only about our past but also about our future. The land-grant institution of the twenty-first century must be the go-to university for state citizens across a wide range of academic, business, and technological needs. And for that to happen, there needs to be a directional alignment among many competing priorities which could never have been experienced, much less imagined, in the nineteenth century. To achieve mastery over this collection of agendas, then, requires intentional leadership on many fronts. Presidents and chancellors are at the forefront of this effort, of course. However, this sort of undertaking also requires the buy-in of a core group of additional individuals—governing board members, faculty, and students—who together determine the mission and actions of the land-grant university. And it is precisely those three groups of university stakeholders that we paid attention to in the fourth, fifth, and sixth chapters of this book.

More specifically, we believe that the information we have gathered on the impact that governing board members, elected officials, and accrediting bodies have on the ability of land-grant universities to meet the needs of the communities they were designed to serve sets the stage for a prescriptive set of actions to be undertaken amid the rededication of land-grant institutions as the people's universities. First and foremost, we must keep in mind the persistent fiscal challenges all public universities will continue to face in the years ahead. There is strong evidence that higher education sits within a range of other very important and competing demands for state dollars, coupled with the likelihood of continued economic constraints and instability of elected officials in the statehouse (especially where term limits have been established). As such, the relationship between higher education and state politicians will remain strained for the foreseeable future, especially if the present status quo is maintained.[9]

In the previous section of this chapter, we proposed the issues of access and affordability as fundamental concepts that must be addressed in such an economic climate. That said, what else can leaders of land-grant universities do to change the calculus of what is going on in statehouses across the country? We posed that question to Richard Vedder, who is a distinguished professor emeritus of economics at Ohio University and the director of its Center for College Affordability and Productivity.[10] Having devoted the bulk of his career to advancing issues related to the costs of a college degree, Dr. Vedder frequently has been called upon by state legislators to testify on various bills and other governmental actions that surround higher education funding.[11] As a result, he has expert knowledge of the way these lawmakers think about state support for college and universities.

One of the main problems with higher education at this specific point in time is the insular nature of most colleges and universities, Dr. Vedder explained. This has led to a litany of complaints from the public that universities are not as connected to community needs and concerns as perhaps they once were. He went on to say that many of the state legislators he has known throughout the years have been very aware of this growing disgruntlement, and as a result they have felt less and less inclined to continue providing high levels of support for higher education. This is a radically different political environment in comparison to the past, as indicated in the following remarks:

> As far back as 40 years ago, governors and state legislators wanted to spend more money on higher education. They were adding new campuses, and older campuses were expanding. It was very popular politically to be pro-higher ed. Today, that sentiment is gone, or at least has been severely diminished, as the public increasingly questions the return on investment that a college degree yields. Additionally, a variety of factors outside of any university's control, including the expansion of Medicaid and the dramatic economic slowdown in this country, make it especially painful for legislators to fund higher education today. To do so, they believe, means that they either cut somewhere else or alternatively they will have to raise taxes, and that is anathema to members of both parties these days. (pers. comm.)

Dr. Vedder went on to state his belief that land-grant universities, at least in principle, would seem to be well positioned to win back the favor of the people, especially if any of these institutions of higher learning decided to act like the "people's university" again. While the electorate clearly has been disenchanted with the elitism of "ivy league gated communities," he continued, they may be quite open to the real-world values and accomplishments of the engineers, doctors, and farmers that the land-grant institution more typically produces through its educational efforts. Skepticism about the exclusivity emanating from many present-day universities and the necessity of getting back to the more egalitarian roots set down through the Morrill Land-Grant Act has been expressed elsewhere.[12]

We see obvious connections between these sentiments and the servant university framework we have been espousing throughout the pages of this book. Again, we believe that governing board members can and should play a critical role in realizing these ambitions. Greenleaf's work on servant leadership often pointed directly toward governing boards when writing about the need for universities to work for the betterment of societies.[13] Further, Wheeler's application of the servant leadership principles to higher education also highlighted the essential role that governing board members play here. Among other things, he stated, "At an institutional level, trustees and higher education administrators should be asking questions that address what the needed service is to make a better society: Do we have the appropriate vision and mission to make a difference to our clientele? Do we need to review our vision and mission to more accurately be a servant organization?"[14] Wheeler concluded this section of his writing by pointing out the ways in which universities are distracted from their servant mission—including most notably by buying into the "institutional rating game"—instead of focusing on the creation of leaders who are dedicated to a service orientation. We believe that these words are well worth pondering at length.

## An Undergraduate Course to Develop Land-Grant Advocates and Leaders

We remain steadfast in the belief that our students must be as knowledgeable about the land-grant mission as they are about every other subject matter in which our universities offer coursework. Our history is a source of pride, tradition, and hope which is unsurpassed by the foundations of any other college or university, public or private. It is our heritage, and thus it is both our privilege and our responsibility to transmit a basic understanding of the land-grant university's strengths and challenges to those present and future generations of bright, young scholars who will pass through our hallowed academic gates. Therefore, we include in this chapter the outline of an undergraduate course that can be offered in the general education curricula as an intentional way of building land-grant advocates and leaders for the twenty-first century.

Readers will not be surprised to discover that our syllabus for a course entitled "Land-Grant Universities: Mission and Leadership" (see app. A) closely follows the outline of chapters contained in this book. The match is purposeful, in that we sought to make this book accessible to students in a manner that reflects the logic of a university-based course. For the course itself, we hope that readers on both sides of the podium—that is, students and faculty members—recognize our effort to provide a progressively stronger understanding of the core constructs that together constitute the past, present, and future story of the land-grant mission and university.

There are four main student learning objectives for this course:

1. Students will understand the connection between the historical underpinnings of land-grant universities and the present efforts land-grant leaders and other university representatives are undertaking to meet the needs of diverse communities.

2. Students will become familiar with the ways in which governing boards, faculty members, and college students impact and are impacted by the land-grant mission.
3. Students will gain an appreciation for the various ways in which the quality of campus–community relationships influences public support for our nation's public institutions for higher learning.
4. Students will be able to identify leadership characteristics and actions taken by senior administrators, with special attention paid to the current political context in which these university leaders operate, and apply those facets to their own emergent leadership capacities.

Our main aspiration for the course, comparable to our hopes for the book, is to give students the opportunity to learn about land-grant institutions and their place in American history as the building blocks of the nation's public higher education system. If we are to reclaim our title as the people's universities, the thinking goes, we must understand the historical activities that first set us on that path. At the most basic level, this would include the need to understand how the Morrill Acts of 1862 and 1890 created the incentives to educate the sons and daughters of toil, how the Hatch Act of 1887 incentivized research efforts, and how the Smith-Lever Act of 1914 provided the structure for Cooperative Extension Services and other efforts to translate or otherwise apply empirical findings.

The evolving nature of the land-grant mission in twenty-first-century America, as well as how higher education leaders are reconfiguring our nation's preeminent public institutions to meet the needs of the communities they were designed to serve, brings into focus the impact that various campus representatives have on the continued development of the people's universities. Among other things, this demands a familiarity with how governing board members, elected officials, and accrediting bodies all influence the parameters within which land-grant universities and other public institutions of higher learning operate. This also requires a working knowledge of the ways in which faculty members are rewarded for various activities they pursue, as well as how the involvement of students in civic engagement efforts is perceived as part of a longer-term investment in our democratic traditions and the recentering of the university in the public commons of discourse on the issues of the day.[15]

A better understanding of the land-grant institution's evolution over time, coupled with a greater familiarity with how various campus representatives interact, prepares students for exposure to more advanced topics, including the development and maintenance of more harmonious relationships between campuses and communities. This allows for the introduction of various town–gown issues that have been demonstrated to impact everything from donor relationships to funding levels from state legislatures. Further, such deliberation spotlights the important inherent advantages that land-grant institutions enjoy when it comes to campus–community relationship quality.

Finally, the contents of this course set the stage for students to locate their leadership potential through the narratives of present-day presidents and chancellors and the universities they represent. With special attention paid to servant leadership principles, students are invited to explore the various ways their desire to make a difference in the world they live in can be achieved through the curricular and extracurricular activities they choose to become involved in at their land-grant university. In addition, these students are encouraged to develop a plan for how they will take the next steps in realizing their life's calling postgraduation.

Keeping in mind the statistic that land-grant universities hand out over one million diplomas every year, we wish to encourage greater preparation of these students to become informed citizens who can advocate for the land-grant mission of the twenty-first century. In addition, recall the fact that 40% of our current governors have received at least one degree from a land-grant institution. If those elected officials had taken a course on the land-grant university, and if the many state legislators who also hold degrees from land-grant institutions similarly had such a course on their transcripts, how different might the relationship be right now between statehouses across our country and Mr. Lincoln's universities? There are just too many compelling reasons to put coursework like this into place, and soon.

There is at least one higher educational model already in existence that provides a "home base" for the course we propose to deliver to students at land-grant universities. Here, we wish to draw attention to a framework known as Active Concerned Citizenship and Ethical Leadership (ACCEL). Developed by Robert Sternberg, who has been both a faculty member and an administrator at two land-grant universities, the ACCEL model speaks directly to the need for universities to become more deeply involved in the development of its students.[16] Couched in the Jeffersonian ideal of higher education for the masses (the very heart of the land-grant tradition), Sternberg focuses attention on a variety of methods designed to promote greater community involvement through servant leadership activities. We were struck particularly by the overlap between the ACCEL plan of action for institutional change and many of the themes and issues we have covered throughout this book.

## Overthrowing Tyranny in All Its Forms

What will it take to move land-grant institutions closer toward the reaffirmation of their role as the people's universities? In this section we wish to mention several additional related topics that bear directly on this question. These issues are identified as stumbling blocks that can obstruct and delay the land-grant institution's ability to adapt successfully to the challenges and needs of twenty-first-century America. This includes what we term the tyranny of the departmental structure of the university and the tyranny of the university gerontocracy, both of which contribute to the tyranny of university complacency. If land-grant universities can overcome these self-inflicted forms of oppression, we believe that the future indeed will look all the brighter for Mr. Lincoln's universities.

Let us first examine the tyranny of the university's departmental structure. We have indicated in previous chapters that promotion and tenure decisions at the departmental level are weighed quite heavily by decision-makers at other university levels. And there is a certain sense to be made of this. After all, who better to pass judgment on an individual's demonstration of excellence in teaching, research, and service than that faculty member's most immediate academic peers? Decision-making authority regarding curriculum—in essence, what will and will not be taught—also resides primarily at the department level. Again, this seems reasonable, as those faculty members who are experts in their field should have keen insight into the subject matter students would most need to learn. After all, this is how the modern research university was founded, based on the "virtues of specialization" wrought by the German higher education model.[17]

The difficulties pertaining to the departmental structure of universities are most evident when demands for change arise, especially when adjustments are needed across the entire university. For instance, it is our belief that, to be the people's universities once again, land-grant institutions must establish a reward structure that incentivizes faculty activities that meet a wide variety of community needs. Currently, high research productivity is the coin of the realm at the departmental level, a situation that is firmly ensconced across many land-grant universities. Yet while communities ostensibly served by land-grant institutions have needs reaching well beyond what empirical work can provide in areas linked to available faculty member expertise, we see a great deal of foot-dragging by faculty within these academic units.

This sort of departmental rigidity in turn is nurtured by a parallel concern: the tyranny of the university's gerontocracy. The lack of mandatory retirement ages, coupled with the extraordinary hiring boom that occurred in the 1960s and 1970s, has led to an aging faculty workforce.[18] And in the midst of this, we are witnesses to the fact that our younger faculty members largely are the ones who have been insisting that we rethink the nature of the land-grant university, especially in terms of how it should be more actively serving the needs of communities. Older faculty members, in contrast, typically are more supportive of the status quo and often are quite resistant to the introduction of alterations in "what counts." Because these senior professors tend to have greater clout within departments, they control the agenda of everything from what is discussed at faculty meetings to what kinds of issues are presented for further discussion at the college and university levels. Unfortunately, we need faculty members who are agents of change, not change-adverse obstructionists, at this critical point in our evolution as land-grant universities.

Whether unnoticed or discounted by other campus stakeholders, these related forms of inflexibility have over time contributed to a climate of complacency within the land-grant institution. Importantly, the word "complacency" was an often-used term by the presidents and chancellors we interviewed when responding specifically to the question we asked them about future threats. Here is a typical example:

> There are so many threats to higher education today that I don't know where to begin. I think our biggest threat is complacency. What we do well, we do very well, but we have lost sight of other opportunities to meet the needs of our communities because we are so focused on continuing to do well in those areas in which we have always excelled. In turn, there is complacency among our political leaders that have celebrated us for so long, who now believe we are no longer a priority. They have become complacent about what we do. (president/chancellor pers. comm.)

Other related remarks indicated that land-grant universities are largely victims of their own success. For example, it was stated that, because land-grant institutions often are the flagship research university, complacency gradually settled in as the result of playing such a dominant role in comparison to other universities in the state.

The presidents and chancellors we interviewed noted that another factor contributing to this sense of self-satisfaction is the set of tremendous accomplishments land-grant universities have displayed in agriculture and engineering. These achievements have prompted university leaders to rest on their laurels, according to these university leaders, and have made them more reluctant to expand their sights and encourage other academic areas to focus on meeting community needs. In the words of one senior administrator,

> We have forgotten that we have some opportunities to serve society in an increasingly meaningful way by bringing other disciplines to the engagement arena beyond agriculture and engineering, which we have always done. If we truly want to embrace the mission of serving communities as land-grant institutions, then we need to bring those other disciplines to bear on those communities. (pers. comm.)

This gives us some further insight into one of the root causes of community engagement as a siloed enterprise within the land-grant institutions. Here, this lack of an expanded way of approaching societal needs may be as much a function of our arrogance and conceit as anything else—a conceit, we might add, that ends up contributing to "mediocracy," a term Robert Sternberg employed to discuss how mediocrity becomes rewarded by universities when there is a systemic failure to connect one's academic work to any sort of external standards of performance excellence.[19]

In short, and in agreement with many of the presidents and chancellors we interviewed, we do believe that complacency in all its forms is the number one threat to the future of land-grant universities. Universities generally are supposed to be places of creativity, and so we gather together those individuals who are always thinking about discovering how to grow a better potato and how to build a sturdier bridge. At the same time, the land-grant institution also should want to gather people together who wish to discover a cure for cancer, who wish to write the next great American novel, and who wish to figure out what to do about educating children from impoverished families.

Ironically, although all faculty members employed by land-grant universities are naturally inquisitive about topics in their field, they typically have little curiosity about how to make their university better. In fact, as we have noted above, at least some of them want the land-grant institution to remain much the same as they have found it. We find it very strange that these people display wonder about their craft but not about their place of work. In closing, we would ask these individuals to reflect on the possibilities associated with freedom from departmental restrictions and a moribund reward structure, among other issues we raise here and throughout this book. Then and only then will the aspiration to become the people's universities be realized.

## The Audacity of Hope and Making America Great Again

The finishing touches on this book were being applied in early 2018, a little over a year into the presidency of Donald J. Trump. Our first chapter contained quite a bit of discussion about the 2016 US presidential election, and it is to that topic that we now return as we close out our writing. It seems impossible to exaggerate the increased polarization we have witnessed on both sides of the political aisle over the course of these past 12 or so months. The Left and the Right, Democrats and Republicans, citizens of red and blue states, or, in our favorite parlance, denizens of the capital and the countryside are alternately yelling at each other more and more vociferously and then ignoring or otherwise turning their backs on each other when they finish speaking.

Now more than ever before in the history of our country, we believe that it is important for land-grant universities to step into this breach. As our nation abdicates the middle ground in politics, the center must be taken and held at all costs. This is a struggle we must immerse ourselves in because, first, it is part of our overall mission to serve the most pressing needs of our communities and, second, our institutions of higher learning will not be allowed to sit on the sidelines anyway. Try as we might, we will find ourselves in the same position as the character Michael Corleone in *The Godfather, Part III*, when he exclaimed, "Just when I thought I was out, they pull me back in."

We are familiar with some of the major complaints lodged by both factions about the "impossibility" of working with the other side. From the left, we hear the voices of those who ask what can possibly be done when there are a group of people in power who hold beliefs running counter to those values that universities hold dear. From the right, we recognize the expressions of dismay about dealing with people who want to stifle the speech of anyone who disagrees with them. And from politicians catering to both sides of these laments, we watch with dismay as they throw "red meat" to their constituents, shoring up their bases at the expense of any sort of bipartisan dialogue.

These forms of extremist thinking must be countered by the activities of our land-grant institutions. As the heirs of Mr. Lincoln's universities, we can and should be the adults in the room, pulling people back together time and again to discuss the issues of the day. Neither side holds the upper hand on an ethical or moral level, despite the rhetoric. Those who would proclaim "fake news" are guilty of contributing to the suppression of scientific fact. And those who would declare "safe spaces" and demand "trigger warnings" are making a mockery of free speech on campuses. All of this contributes to the "truth decay" recently discussed in a Rand Corporation report, described as accelerating disagreement about facts and their interpretation, a blurred distinction between what is fact and what is opinion, a profound lack of understanding about the difference between personal experiences and verifiable facts, and an increased skepticism about the availability of trusted sources to acquire factual information.[20]

How do we counter this truth decay and the related devolution of civil discourse in communities across our nation? Can we help make America great again? The audacity of our hope lies within our modest suggestion to incorporate the themes we reported in our third chapter as a starting point. Conversations about funding declines should coexist with discussions about the need to create efficiencies, with special emphasis on channeling those savings to the students who are most in need of assistance. Yes, our land-grant universities should be recognized for their research prowess, but how about developing (and sustaining) a real emphasis on teaching and service excellence as well? And speaking of research, can't we all agree that the application of scholarship has been and should remain the *primary* task of the land-grant mission? This is the same land-grant mission that has always emphasized access and affordability, by the way, and not national rankings of one sort or another.

Some readers might ask, but haven't we tried all of this before? Certainly not all in one narrative, we would reply, and clearly not with the additional need to focus on the remaining themes we have developed out of the interviews conducted with land-grant presidents and chancellors. Who has talked about finances, the tripartite mission, and access and affordability while simultaneously comparing and contrasting the needs of rural and urban communities? And where do we see all of those issues being concurrently addressed within a dialogue that recognizes the importance of university activities both at home here in the United States and abroad?

If we succeed in combining these themes together in one seamless narrative about the land-grant mission, we believe we will have created the proper environmental context for coaxing the vast majority of our nation's citizens back into the middle ground, and thus back to the family table where we can talk about our differences and find our commonalities. And if we do well on this task, we will have demonstrated one of the true benefits of higher education and the acquirement of a college diploma.

## Summary

We began this final chapter with our interpretation of the land-grant president and chancellor interview material through the lens of the two conceptual frameworks we introduced in our first chapter: the marital metaphor surrounding the development of more harmonious campus–community relationships, and the servant university construct we used to describe the reaffirmation of the land-grant institution as the people's university. Both constructs were used in service to the development of a more compelling narrative about the role land-grant universities can play in terms of meeting the needs of the communities they were designed to serve. We then provided an outline for an undergraduate course meant to be offered in the general education curricula as an intentional way of developing land-grant advocates and leaders for the twenty-first century. Finally, we provided some concluding ideas that we believed were important considerations in elevating the importance of Mr. Lincoln's universities in this century and beyond.

## *Syllabus* Land-Grant Universities
### *Mission and Leadership*

**Course Description:** This course provides students with the opportunity to learn about land-grant institutions and their place in the American higher education system. Special attention is paid to issues surrounding the evolving nature of the land-grant mission in twenty-first-century America, as well as how higher education leaders are reconfiguring our nation's preeminent public institutions to meet the needs of the communities they were designed to serve. Students are invited to locate their leadership potential through the narratives of present-day university presidents and chancellors.

**Course Objectives:**
1. Students will understand the connection between the historical under-pinnings of land-grant universities and present efforts that land-grant university leaders are undertaking to meet the needs of diverse communities.
2. Students will become familiar with the ways in which governing boards, faculty members, and college students impact and are impacted by the land-grant mission.
3. Students will gain an appreciation for the various ways in which the quality of campus–community relationships impacts public support for our nation's public institutions for higher learning.
4. Students will be able to identify leadership characteristics and actions taken by senior administrators, with special attention paid to the current political context in which these university leaders operate, and apply those facets to their own emergent leadership capacities.

**Textbook:** Stephen M. Gavazzi and E. Gordon Gee, *Land-Grant Universities for the Future: Higher Education for the Public Good* (Baltimore: Johns Hopkins University Press, 2018). (Assigned readings are denoted as LGUF chapters below.)

**Additional readings:** In addition to reading the book chapters as assigned, students also are responsible for the supplemental material as assigned in the weekly reading schedule below. Students are responsible for one (1) of the three (3) readings for each topic area in addition to the book chapter assignment.

**Commentary on the readings:** Starting in week 2 and continuing through week 13, students are expected to submit a reaction both to the book chapter assignment and to one (1) of the three (3) additional readings for each topic area. More specifically, students will post a 250-word commentary for the assigned book chapter and a 250-word commentary on the selected article (500 words total). This commentary will be posted no later than 48 hours prior to class. Total student commentaries: 12.

**Peer commentary:** Starting in week 2 and continuing through week 13, students will provide 100 words of commentary on one (1) of the web postings written by other students prior to class. This commentary will be submitted no later than two hours prior to class. Students will be asked to be ready to read that posting out loud, as well as lead a discussion on the topic they have discussed in their posting. Total student peer commentaries: 12.

**Post-class commentary:** Following each class in weeks 2 through 13, students will submit a commentary of 100 words in length describing the most interesting and/or important point that came out of the class for each student. This will be posted no later than 48 hours immediately following the class period. Total post-class commentaries for students: 12.

**Attendance/Quizzes:** Attendance is expected for every class session. Students are expected to be on time and to stay for the entire length of the class session. Students are also expected to complete the reading assignments before each class session and participate in class discussions, and will take a quiz on those readings at the beginning of each class. You will receive up to five (5) points for each week that you fully attend a class session (1 point) and answer all quiz questions correctly (4 points).

**Papers:** There are two (2) papers that, in combination, are worth 100 points. The breakdown is as follows: Paper #1 is worth 25 points. Paper #2 is worth 75 points. The papers will focus on one of the following topics:

- Free speech issues on college campuses
- Student diversity
- Service-learning courses
- Student involvement in university research
- Volunteerism efforts of college students
- Tuition and other issues related to the costs of college
- Student debt after college
- Title IX
- College admissions issues and concerns

- Student leadership
- Other student-focused issues with prior permission from instructor

For Paper #1, due on week 7, students will locate three (3) online stories from mainstream media sources (newspapers, magazines, other news outlets, etc.) about the chosen topic area which were written and published in the past two years. Students will provide the citations as specified below, as well as writing a summary (3–5 pages in length) of the articles and their connection to the assigned readings.

Students will provide the media citations in the following format:

Schmidt, Peter. "Charlottesville Violence Sparks New Worries about Safety during Campus Protests." *Chronicle of Higher Education*, August 15, 2017, www.chronicle .com/article/Charlottesville-Violence/240927.

For Paper #2, due on the last week of regular classes, students will extend their first paper by locating three (3) scholarly articles or book chapters about the chosen topic area that were not part of the assigned readings for this class. Students will provide the citations in the format specified below, as well as writing a summary (6–10 pages in length) of the articles and their connection to the assigned readings. Students will provide scholarly article/book chapter citations as follows:

Scholarly article example:

Gavazzi, S. M., M. Fox, and J. Martin. "Understanding Campus and Community Relationships through Marriage and Family Metaphors: A Town–Gown Typology." *Innovative Higher Education* 39 (2014): 361–74.

Book chapter example:

Lawlor, J., and E. Boyle. "The Merger Phenomenon in Higher Education." In *Contemporary Corporate Strategies*, ed. J. Saee, 131–38. New York: Routledge, 2007.

**EVALUATION:**

| | |
|---|---|
| 12 sets of commentaries on the articles | |
| 5 points per commentary | 60 points possible |
| 12 sets of peer commentaries | |
| 5 points per meta-commentary | 60 points possible |
| 12 sets of commentaries on the class | |
| 5 points per commentary | 60 points possible |
| 14 classes | |
| 5 points per class attended/quiz grade | 70 points possible |
| Paper 1 and Paper 2 | 100 points possible |
| | 350 points total |

A    315–350    points
B    280–314    points
C    245–279    points
D    210–244    points
E    <209      points

P/F  245 points or better is a pass

## Weekly Reading Schedule

### Weeks 1–2

LGUF Introduction: Whither the Land-Grant?
LGUF Chapter 1: The Land-Grant Study, Campus–Community Relationships, and the Servant University

Additional readings:
Scala, Dante J., and Kenneth M. Johnson. "Political Polarization along the Rural-Urban Continuum? The Geography of the Presidential Vote, 2000–2016." *Annals of the American Academy of Political and Social Science* 672, no. 1 (2017): 162–84.

Gavazzi, Stephen M. "Engaged Institutions, Responsiveness, and Town–Gown Relationships: Why Deep Culture Change Must Emphasize the Gathering of Community Feedback." *Planning for Higher Education* 43 (2015): 1–9.

Greenleaf, Robert K. *The Servant as Leader.* Westfield, IN: Greenleaf Center for Servant Leadership, 1970.

### Weeks 3–4

LGUF Chapter 2: The Land-Grant Institution and Mission in Service to Communities

Additional readings:
Kellogg Commission on the Future of State and Land-Grant Universities. *Returning to Our Roots: The Engaged Institution.* Washington, DC: Association of Public and Land-Grant Universities, 1999. www.aplu.org/library/returning-to-our -roots-the-engaged-institution/file.

Driscoll, Amy. "Carnegie's Community-Engagement Classification: Intentions and Insights." *Change,* January/February 2008, 38–41.

Price, Steven C., Ron D. Duggins, and Stephen W. S. McKeever. "Economic Development." In *The Modern Land-Grant University,* ed. Robert J. Sternberg. West Lafayette, IN: Purdue University Press, 2014.

**Weeks 5–6**

LGUF Chapter 3: Land-Grant Strengths, Weaknesses, Opportunities, and Threats

Additional readings:
Gee, E. Gordon. "The Modern Public University: Its Land-Grant Heritage, Its Land-Grant Horizon." In *Precipice or Crossroads: Where America's Great Public Universities Stand and Where They Are Going Midway through Their Second Century*, ed. Daniel M. Fogel and Elizabeth Malson-Huddle. Albany, NY: SUNY Press, 2012.

Sandmann, Lorilee R., and William M. Plater. "Leading the Engaged Institution." *New Directions for Higher Education*, no. 147 (2009): 13–24.

Crow, Michael M., and William B. Debars. "University-Based R&D and Economic Development: The Morrill Act and the Emergence of the American Research University." In *Precipice or Crossroads: Where America's Great Public Universities Stand and Where They Are Going Midway through Their Second Century*, ed. Daniel M. Fogel and Elizabeth Malson-Huddle. Albany, NY: SUNY Press, 2012.

**Weeks 7–8**

LGUF Chapter 4: The Impact of Governing Board Members, Elected Officials, and Accrediting Bodies

Additional readings:
Longanecker, David. "State Governance and the Public Good." In *Higher Education for the Public Good: Emerging Voices from a National Movement*, ed. Adrianna J. Kezar, Tony C. Chambers, and John C. Burkhardt. San Francisco: Jossey-Bass, 2005.

Eckel, Peter D., and Adrianna Kezar. "The Intersecting Authority of Boards, Presidents, and Faculty." In *American Higher Education in the Twenty-First Century*, 4th ed., ed. Michael N. Bastedo, Philip G. Altbach, and Patricia J. Gumport. Baltimore: Johns Hopkins University Press, 2016.

Wheeler, Daniel. "Principle Eight: Leave a Legacy to Society." Chapter 8 of *Servant Leadership for Higher Education*. San Francisco: Jossey-Bass, 2012.

**Weeks 9–10**

LGUF Chapter 5: The Critical Role of the Faculty

Additional readings:
Atiles, Jorge H., Chris Jenkins, Patricia Ryas-Duarte, Randal K. Taylor, and Hailin Zhang. "Service, Cooperative Extension, and Community Engagement." In *The Modern Land-Grant University*, ed. Robert J. Sternberg. West Lafayette, IN: Purdue University Press, 2014.

Fitzgerald, Hiram E., Karen Bruns, Steven T. Sonka, Andrew Furco, and Louis Swanson. "The Centrality of Engagement in Higher Education." *Journal of Higher Education Outreach and Engagement* 16, no. 3 (2008): 7–28.

Philip G. Altbach. "Harsh Realities: The Professoriate in the Twenty-First Century." In *American Higher Education in the Twenty-First Century*, 4th ed., ed. Michael N. Bastedo, Philip G. Altbach, and Patricia J. Gumport. Baltimore: Johns Hopkins University Press, 2016.

**Weeks 11–12**

LGUF Chapter 6: Our Students: Vanguard in the Community

Additional readings:
Penn, Jeremy D., John D. Hathcoat, and Sungah Kim. "Undergraduate Academic Experience." In *The Modern Land-Grant University*, ed. Robert J. Sternberg. West Lafayette, IN: Purdue University Press, 2014.

Van Delinder, Jean, and Sheryl Ann Tucker. "Graduate Academic Experience." In *The Modern Land-Grant University*, ed. Robert J. Sternberg. West Lafayette, IN: Purdue University Press, 2014.

Quaye, Stephen John. "Let Us Speak: Including Students' Voices in the Public Good of Higher Education." In *Higher Education for the Public Good: Emerging Voices from a National Movement*, ed. Adrianna J. Kezar, Tony C. Chambers, and John C. Burkhardt. San Francisco: Jossey-Bass, 2005.

**Weeks 13–14**

LGUF Chapter 7: Charting the Future of American Public Education

Additional readings:
Duderstadt, James J. "Creating the Future: The Promise of Public Research Universities for America." In *Precipice or Crossroads: Where America's Great Public Universities Stand and Where They Are Going Midway through Their Second Century*, ed. Daniel M. Fogel and Elizabeth Malson-Huddle. Albany, NY: SUNY Press, 2012.

Saltmarsh, John, Dwight E. Giles, Elaine Ward, and Suzanne M. Buglione. "Rewarding Community-Engaged Scholarship." *New Directions for Higher Education*, no. 147 (2009): 25–35.

Wheeler, Daniel. "Principle Three: Foster Problem Solving and Taking Responsibility at All Levels." Chapter 6 of *Servant Leadership for Higher Education*. San Francisco: Jossey-Bass, 2012.

# National Institute of Food and Agriculture Land-Grant Colleges and Universities, 1862, 1890, and 1994

**ALABAMA**
Alabama A&M University, *Normal*
Auburn University, *Auburn*
Tuskegee University, *Tuskegee*

**ALASKA**
Ilisagvik College, *Barrow*
University of Alaska, *Fairbanks*

**AMERICAN SAMOA**
American Samoa Community College, *Pago Pago*

**ARIZONA**
Diné College, *Tsaile*
Tohono O'odham Community College, *Sells*
University of Arizona, *Tucson*

**ARKANSAS**
University of Arkansas, *Fayetteville*
University of Arkansas at Pine Bluff, *Pine Bluff*

**CALIFORNIA**
D-Q University, *(Davis vicinity)*
University of California System—
Oakland as Headquarters, *Oakland*

**COLORADO**
Colorado State University, *Fort Collins*

**CONNECTICUT**
University of Connecticut, *Storrs*

**DELAWARE**
Delaware State University, *Dover*
University of Delaware, *Newark*

**DISTRICT OF COLUMBIA**
University of the District of Columbia, *Washington*

**FLORIDA**
Florida A&M University, *Tallahassee*
University of Florida, *Gainesville*

**GEORGIA**
Fort Valley State University, *Fort Valley*
University of Georgia, *Athens*

**GUAM**
University of Guam, *Mangilao*

**HAWAII**
University of Hawaii, *Honolulu*

**IDAHO**
University of Idaho, *Moscow*

**ILLINOIS**
University of Illinois, *Urbana*

**INDIANA**
Purdue University, *West Lafayette*

**IOWA**
Iowa State University, *Ames*

**KANSAS**
Haskell Indian Nations University, *Lawrence*
Kansas State University, *Manhattan*

**KENTUCKY**
Kentucky State University, *Frankfort*
University of Kentucky, *Lexington*

**LOUISIANA**

Louisiana State University, *Baton Rouge*

Southern University and A&M College,
*Baton Rouge*

**MAINE**

University of Maine, *Orono*

**MARYLAND**

University of Maryland, *College Park*

University of Maryland Eastern Shore,
*Princess Anne*

**MASSACHUSETTS**

University of Massachusetts, *Amherst*

**MICHIGAN**

Bay Mills Community College, *Brimely*

Keweenaw Bay Ojibwa Community
College, *Baraga*

Michigan State University, *East Lansing*

Saginaw Chippewa Tribal College, *Mount
Pleasant*

**MICRONESIA**

College of Micronesia, *Kolonia,
Pohnpei*

**MINNESOTA**

Fond du Lac Tribal and Community
College, *Cloquet*

Leech Lake Tribal College, *Cass Lake*

University of Minnesota, *St. Paul*

White Earth Tribal and Community
College, *Mahnomen*

**MISSISSIPPI**

Alcorn State University, *Lorman*

Mississippi State University, *Starkville*

**MISSOURI**

Lincoln University, *Jefferson City*

University of Missouri, *Columbia*

**MONTANA**

Aaniiih Nakoda College, *Harlem*

Blackfeet Community College, *Browning*

Chief Dull Knife College, *Lame Deer*

Fort Peck Community College, *Poplar*

Little Big Horn College, *Crow Agency*

Montana State University, *Bozeman*

Salish Kootenai College, *Pablo*

Stone Child College, *Box Elder*

**NEBRASKA**

Little Priest Tribal College, *Winnebago*

Nebraska Indian Community College,
*Winnebago*

University of Nebraska, *Lincoln*

**NEVADA**

University of Nevada, *Reno*

**NEW HAMPSHIRE**

University of New Hampshire,
*Durham*

**NEW JERSEY**

Rutgers University, *New Brunswick*

**NEW MEXICO**

Institute of American Indian and Alaska
Native Culture and Arts Development,
*Santa Fe*

Navajo Technical College, *Crownpoint*

New Mexico State University, *Las Cruces*

Southwestern Indian Polytechnic
Institute, *Albuquerque*

**NEW YORK**

Cornell University, *Ithaca*

**NORTH CAROLINA**

North Carolina A&T State University,
*Greensboro*

North Carolina State University,
*Raleigh*

**NORTH DAKOTA**

Cankdeska Cikana Community College,
*Fort Totten*

Fort Berthold Community College,
*New Town*

North Dakota State University, *Fargo*

Sitting Bull College, *Fort Yates*

Turtle Mountain Community College,
*Belcourt*

United Tribes Technical College,
*Bismarck*

**NORTHERN MARIANAS**

Northern Marianas College,
*Saipan, CM*

**OHIO**

Central State University, *Wilberforce*

Ohio State University, *Columbus*

**OKLAHOMA**
College of the Muscogee Nation, *Okmulgee*
Langston University, *Langston*
Oklahoma State University, *Stillwater*
**OREGON**
Oregon State University, *Corvallis*
**PENNSYLVANIA**
Pennsylvania State University, *University Park*
**PUERTO RICO**
University of Puerto Rico, *Mayaguez*
**RHODE ISLAND**
University of Rhode Island, *Kingston*
**SOUTH CAROLINA**
Clemson University, *Clemson*
South Carolina State University, *Orangeburg*
**SOUTH DAKOTA**
Oglala Lakota College, *Kyle*
Si Tanka/Huron University, *Eagle Butte*
Sinte Gleska University, *Rosebud*
Sisseton Wahpeton College, *Sisseton*
South Dakota State University, *Brookings*
**TENNESSEE**
Tennessee State University, *Nashville*
University of Tennessee, *Knoxville*

**TEXAS**
Prairie View A&M University, *Prairie View*
Texas A&M University, *College Station*
**UTAH**
Utah State University, *Logan*
**VERMONT**
University of Vermont, *Burlington*
**VIRGIN ISLANDS**
University of the Virgin Islands, *St. Croix*
**VIRGINIA**
Virginia State University, *Petersburg*
Virginia Tech, *Blacksburg*
**WASHINGTON**
Northwest Indian College, *Bellingham*
Washington State University, *Pullman*
**WEST VIRGINIA**
West Virginia State University, *Institute*
West Virginia University, *Morgantown*
**WISCONSIN**
College of Menominee Nation, *Keshena*
Lac Courte Oreilles Ojibwa, Community College, *Hayward*
University of Wisconsin, *Madison*
**WYOMING**
University of Wyoming, *Laramie*

## Introduction · Whither the Land-Grant?

1. Robert J. Sternberg, ed., *The Modern Land-Grant University* (West Lafayette, IN: Purdue University Press, 2014).

2. Robert J. Sternberg, *What Universities Can Be: A New Model for Preparing Students for Active Concerned Citizenship and Ethical Leadership* (Ithaca, NY: Cornell University Press, 2016).

3. Daniel M. Fogel and Elizabeth Malson-Huddle, eds., *Precipice or Crossroads: Where America's Great Public Universities Stand and Where They Are Going Midway through Their Second Century* (Albany, NY: SUNY Press, 2012).

4. Roger L. Geiger and Nathan M. Sorber, eds., *The Land-Grant Colleges and the Reshaping of American Higher Education* (New York: Routledge, 2013).

5. Alan I. Marcus, ed., *Science as Service: Establishing and Reshaping American Land-Grant Universities, 1865–1930* (Tuscaloosa: Alabama University Press, 2015); Alan I. Marcus, ed., *Science as Service: How American Land-Grant Universities Shaped the Modern World, 1920–2015* (Tuscaloosa: Alabama University Press, 2015).

6. Scott J. Peters et al., eds., *Engaging Campus and Community: The Practice of Public Scholarship in the State and Land-Grant University System* (Dayton, OH: Kettering Foundation Press, 2005).

7. George R. McDowell, *Land-Grant Universities and Extension into the 21st Century: Renegotiating or Abandoning a Social Contract* (Ames: Iowa State University Press, 2001).

8. Adrianna J. Kezar, Tony C. Chambers, and John C. Burkhardt, eds., *Higher Education for the Public Good: Emerging Voices from a National Movement* (San Francisco: Jossey-Bass, 2005).

9. Michael N. Bastedo, Philip G. Altbach, and Patricia J. Gumport, eds., *American Higher Education in the Twenty-First Century*, 4th ed. (Baltimore: Johns Hopkins University Press, 2016); Donald E. Heller, ed., *The States and Public Higher Education Policy: Affordability, Access, and Accountability*, 2nd ed. (Baltimore: Johns Hopkins University Press, 2011).

## Chapter 1 · The Land-Grant Study, Campus–Community Relationships, and the Servant University

1. Stephen M. Gavazzi, *The Optimal Town–Gown Marriage: Taking Campus–Community Outreach and Engagement to the Next Level* (Charleston, SC: Create Space, 2016).

2. Kellogg Commission on the Future of State and Land-Grant Universities, *Returning to Our Roots: The Engaged Institution* (Washington, DC: Association of Public and Land-Grant Universities, 1999), www.aplu.org/library/returning-to-our-roots-the-engaged-institution/file.

3. Michael Barone, "The New/Old Politics of the Capital versus the Countryside," *Washington Examiner*, April 28, 2017, www.washingtonexaminer.com/the-newold-politics -of-the-capital-versus-the-countryside/article/2621529.

4. Dante J. Scala and Kenneth M. Johnson, "Political Polarization along the Rural-Urban Continuum? The Geography of the Presidential Vote, 2000–2016," *Annals of the American Academy of Political and Social Science* 672, no. 1 (2017): 162–84.

5. "Sharp Partisan Divisions in Views of National Institutions," Pew Research Center, July 10, 2017, www.people-press.org/2017/07/10/sharp-partisan-divisions-in-views-of-national -institutions.

6. Urich Baer, "What 'Snowflakes' Get Right about Free Speech," *New York Times*, April 24, 2017, www.nytimes.com/2017/04/24/opinion/what-liberal-snowflakes-get-right -about-free-speech.html?ref=opinion&_r=1.

7. David French, "It's Time to Crush Campus Censorship," *National Review*, April 24, 2017, www.nationalreview.com/article/446999/free-speech-campus-censorship-congress -must-punish-universities-indulging-student-mob.

8. Colleen Flaherty, "Words Fly on Free Speech Bill," *Inside Higher Education*, May 15, 2017, www.insidehighered.com/news/2017/05/15/critics-proposed-legislation-first-amendment -rights-wisconsin-public-universities.

9. Justin Carissimo, "1 Dead, 19 Injured after Car Plows into Protesters in Charlottes-ville," *CBS News*, August 12, 2017, www.cbsnews.com/news/1-dead-19-injured-after-car -plows-into-protesters-in-charlottesville.

10. Peter Schmidt, "Charlottesville Violence Sparks New Worries about Safety during Campus Protests," *Chronicle of Higher Education*, August 15, 2017, www.chronicle.com/article /Charlottesville-Violence/240927.

11. Chris Quintana, "It's Been a Messy Semester for Free Speech on Campus: What's Next?," *Chronicle of Higher Education*, May 9, 2017, www.chronicle.com/article/Its-Been -a-Messy-Semester-for/240030?cid=wcontentgrid_6_1b.

12. Kellogg Commission, *Returning to Our Roots*.

13. Andrew Small, "The Ultimate 2016 Presidential Map?," *CityLab*, April 3, 2017, www.citylab.com/politics/2017/04/is-this-the-ultimate-2016-presidential-election-map /521622/?utm_source=SFTwitter.

14. Ryne Rohla, "The Most Liberal and Conservative College Neighborhoods," *Decision Desk HQ*, May 10, 2017, http://rynerohla.com/index.html/data.

15. Stephen M. Gavazzi, Michael Fox, and Jeff Martin, "Understanding Campus and Community Relationships through Marriage and Family Metaphors: A Town–Gown Typology," *Innovative Higher Education* 39 (2014): 361–74; Stephen M. Gavazzi and Michael Fox, "A Tale of Three Cities: Piloting a Measure of Effort and Comfort Levels within Town–Gown Relationships," *Innovative Higher Education* 40 (2015): 189–99.

16. John F. Cuber and Peggy B. Harroff, *The Significant Americans: A Study of Sexual Behavior among the Affluent* (New York: Appleton-Century-Crofts, 1965).

17. David French, "We're Not in a Civil War, but We Are Drifting toward Divorce," *National Review*, June 8, 2017, www.nationalreview.com/article/448385/americans-left-right -liberal-conservative-democrats-republicans-blue-red-states-cultural-segregate.

18. Tony C. Chambers, "The Special Role of Higher Education in Society: As a Public Good for the Public Good," in *Higher Education for the Public Good: Emerging Voices from a National Movement*, ed. Adrianna J. Kezar, Tony C. Chambers, and John C. Burkhardt (San Francisco: Jossey-Bass, 2005).

19. See Jeremy D. Penn, John D. Hathcoat, and Sungah Kim, "Undergraduate Academic Experience," and Jean Van Delinder and Sheryl A. Tucker, "Graduate Academic Experi-

ence," both in *The Modern Land-Grant University*, ed. Robert J. Sternberg (West Lafayette, IN: Purdue University Press, 2014).

20. Stephen M. Gavazzi, "Engaged Institutions, Responsiveness, and Town–Gown Relationships: Why Deep Culture Change Must Emphasize the Gathering of Community Feedback," *Planning for Higher Education* 43 (2015): 1–9.

21. Robert K. Greenleaf, *The Servant as Leader* (Westfield, IN: Greenleaf Center for Servant Leadership, 1970).

22. Robert K. Greenleaf, *Servant Leadership: A Journey into the Nature of Legitimate Power and Greatness*, 25th anniversary ed. (New York: Paulist, 2002).

23. Peter G. Northouse, *Leadership: Theory and Practice*, 6th ed. (Thousand Oaks, CA: Sage, 2013).

24. Stephen R. Covey, foreword to Greenleaf, *Servant Leadership*.

25. Larry C. Spears, "Servant Leadership and Robert Greenleaf's Legacy," in *Servant Leadership: Developments in Theory and Research*, ed. D. van Dierendonck and K. Patterson (New York: Palgrave Macmillan, 2010).

26. John E. Barbuto and Daniel W. Wheeler, "Scale Development and Construct Clarification of Servant Leadership," *Group and Organizational Management* 31 (2006): 1–27.

27. Robert K. Greenleaf, *The Institution as Servant* (Westfield, IN: Greenleaf Center for Servant Leadership, 1972); Larry C. Spears, "Tracing the Past, Present, and Future of Servant Leadership," in *Focus on Leadership: Servant Leadership for the 21st Century*, ed. L. C. Spears and M. Lawrence (New York: John Wiley and Sons, 2002); Daniel W. Wheeler, *Servant Leadership for Higher Education: Principles and Practices* (San Francisco: Jossey-Bass, 2012).

## Chapter 2 · The Land-Grant Institution and Mission in Service to Communities

1. "A Century of Lawmaking for a New Nation: U.S. Congressional Documents and Debates, 1774–1875," Library of Congress, accessed April 18, 2017, http://memory.loc.gov/cgi-bin/ampage?collId=llsl&fileName=012/llsl012.db&recNum=535.

2. "What Is ROTC?," Reserve Officer Training Corps, accessed April 18, 2017, www.rotcprograms.net/what-are-rotc-programs.

3. "Sea Grant Program," National Oceanographic and Atmospheric Administration, accessed April 18, 2017, http://seagrant.noaa.gov; "Sun Grant Program," US Department of Agriculture, National Institute of Food and Agriculture, accessed April 18, 2017, https://nifa.usda.gov/funding-opportunity/sun-grant-program; "About the Space Grant Program," National Aeronautics and Space Administration, accessed April 19, 2017, www.nasa.gov/offices/education/programs/national/spacegrant/about/index.html.

4. Committee on the Future of the Colleges of Agriculture in the Land Grant System, *Colleges of Agriculture at the Land Grant Universities: A Profile* (Washington, DC: National Academies Press, 1995).

5. Coy F. Cross, "Democracy, the West, and Land-Grant Colleges," in *Precipice or Crossroads: Where America's Great Public Universities Stand and Where They Are Going Midway through Their Second Century*, ed. Daniel M. Fogel and Elizabeth Malson-Huddle (Albany, NY: SUNY Press, 2012).

6. Daniel M. Fogel, "Challenges to Equilibrium: The Place of the Arts and Humanities in Public Research Universities," in Fogel and Malson-Huddle, *Precipice or Crossroads*.

7. Charles I. Abramson et al., "History and Mission," in *The Modern Land-Grant University*, ed. Robert J. Sternberg (West Lafayette, IN: Purdue University Press, 2014).

8. Jane Smiley, *Moo* (Toronto: Knopf Canada, 1995).

9. "Pacific Railroad Acts," Central Pacific Railroad Photographic History Museum, accessed April 20, 2017, www.cprr.org/Museum/Pacific_Railroad_Acts.html; "Homestead Act (1862)," accessed April 20, 2017, www.ourdocuments.gov/doc.php?flash=true&doc=31.

10. Carolyn R. Mahoney, "The 1890 Institutions in African American and American Life," in Fogel and Malson-Huddle, *Precipice or Crossroads*.

11. Association of Public and Land-Grant Universities, *The Land-Grant Tradition* (Washington, DC: Association of Public and Land-Grant Universities, 2012), www.aplu.org/library/the-land-grant-tradition/file.

12. "NIFA Land-Grant Colleges and Universities," US Department of Agriculture, National Institute of Food and Agriculture, accessed May 15, 2017, https://nifa.usda.gov/sites/default/files/resource/lgu_map_6_25_2014_0.pdf.

13. Michael M. Crow and William B. Debars, "University-Based R&D and Economic Development: The Morrill Act and the Emergence of the American Research University," in Fogel and Malson-Huddle, *Precipice or Crossroads*.

14. Jorge H. Atiles et al., "Service, Cooperative Extension, and Community Engagement," in Sternberg, *Modern Land-Grant University*.

15. George R. McDowell, *Land-Grant Universities and Extension into the 21st Century: Renegotiating or Abandoning a Social Contract* (Ames: Iowa State University Press, 2001).

16. Howard P. Segal, "Reengineering the Land-Grant University: The Kellogg Commission in Historical Context," in *Engineering in a Land-Grant Context: The Past, Present, and Future of an Idea*, ed. A. Marcus (West Lafayette, IN: Purdue University Press, 2005).

17. Nathan M. Sorber and Roger L. Geiger, "The Welding of Opposite Views: Land-Grant Historiography at 150 Years," in *Higher Education: Handbook of Theory and Research*, vol. 29, ed. Michael B. Paulson (New York: Springer, 2014).

18. Roger L. Geiger and Nathan M. Sorber, eds., *The Land-Grant Colleges and the Reshaping of American Higher Education* (New York: Routledge, 2013).

19. Nathan M. Sorber, *The Morrill Act in Yankeedom: A History of the Origins and Early Years of the Land-Grant College Movement* (Ithaca, NY: Cornell University Press, 2017).

20. Tony C. Chambers, "The Special Role of Higher Education in Society: As a Public Good for the Public Good," in *Higher Education for the Public Good: Emerging Voices from a National Movement*, ed. Adrianna J. Kezar, Tony C. Chambers, and John C. Burkhardt (San Francisco: Jossey-Bass, 2005).

21. Mark G. Yudof and Caitlin Callagan, "Commitments: Enhancing the Public Purposes and Outcomes of Public Higher Education," in Fogel and Malson-Huddle, *Precipice or Crossroads*.

22. David E. Schulenberger, "Challenges to Viability and Sustainability: Public Funding, Tuition, College Costs, and Affordability," in Fogel and Malson-Huddle, *Precipice or Crossroads*.

23. Clark Kerr, *Troubled Times for American Higher Education* (Albany, NY: SUNY Press, 1998).

24. Derek Bok, *Universities in the Marketplace: The Commercialization of Higher Education* (Princeton, NJ: Princeton University Press, 2003).

25. Adrianna J. Kezar, "Challenges for Higher Education in Serving the Public Good," in Kezar, Chambers, and Burkhardt, *Higher Education for the Public Good*.

26. E. Gordon Gee, "The Modern Public University: Its Land-Grant Heritage, Its Land-Grant Horizon," in Fogel and Malson-Huddle, *Precipice or Crossroads*.

27. Robert J. Sternberg, "Epilogue: Values Underlying the Activities of Land-Grant Universities," in Sternberg, *Modern Land-Grant University*.

28. Earnest L. Boyer, *Scholarship Reconsidered: Priorities of the Professoriate* (San Francisco: Jossey-Bass, 1990).

29. Hiram E. Fitzgerald et al., "The Centrality of Engagement in Higher Education," *Journal of Higher Education Outreach and Engagement* 16, no. 3 (2008): 7–28.

30. Scott J. Peters et al., eds., *Engaging Campus and Community: The Practice of Public Scholarship in the State and Land-Grant University System* (Dayton, OH: Kettering Foundation Press, 2005).

31. Kellogg Commission on the Future of State and Land-Grant Universities, *Returning to Our Roots: Executive Summaries of the Reports of the Kellogg Commission on the Future of State and Land-Grant Universities* (Washington, DC: National Association of State Universities and Land-Grant Colleges, 2001); "Carnegie Community Engagement Classification," New England Resource Center for Higher Education, accessed April 29, 2017, http://nerche.org/index.php?option=com_content&view=article&id=341&Itemid =618; "Innovation and Economic Prosperity Universities," Association of Public and Land-Grant Universities, accessed April 29, 2017, www.aplu.org/projects-and-initiatives /economic-development-and-community-engagement/innovation-and-economic -prosperity-universities-designation-and-awards-program/index.html.

32. Kellogg Commission on the Future of State and Land-Grant Universities, *Renewing the Covenant: Learning, Discovery, and Engagement in a New Age and Different World* (Washington, DC: Association of Public and Land-Grant Universities, 2000), www.aplu.org /library/renewing-the-covenant-learning-discovery-and-engagement-in-a-new-age-and -different-world/file.

33. Kellogg Commission on the Future of State and Land-Grant Universities, *Returning to Our Roots: The Student Experience* (Washington, DC: Association of Public and Land-Grant Universities, 1997), www.aplu.org/library/returning-to-our-roots-the-student -experience/file; Kellogg Commission on the Future of State and Land-Grant Universities, *Returning to Our Roots: Student Access* (Washington, DC: Association of Public and Land-Grant Universities, 1998), www.aplu.org/library/returning-to-our-roots-student -access-1998/file; Kellogg Commission on the Future of State and Land-Grant Universities, *Returning to Our Roots: A Learning Society* (Washington, DC: Association of Public and Land-Grant Universities, 1999), www.aplu.org/library/returning-to-our-roots-a-learning -society/file; Kellogg Commission on the Future of State and Land-Grant Universities, *Returning to Our Roots: Toward a Coherent Campus Culture* (Washington, DC: Association of Public and Land-Grant Universities, 2000), www.aplu.org/library/returning-to-our-roots -toward-a-coherent-campus-culture/file; Kellogg Commission on the Future of State and Land-Grant Universities, *Returning to Our Roots: The Engaged Institution* (Washington, DC: Association of Public and Land-Grant Universities, 1999), www.aplu.org/library /returning-to-our-roots-the-engaged-institution/file.

34. Center for Advances in Public Engagement, "Public Engagement: A Primer from Public Agenda," *Essentials*, January 2008, www.publicagenda.org/files/public_engagement _primer.pdf.

35. "About Us," Association of Public and Land-Grant Universities, accessed May 17, 2017, www.aplu.org/about-us.

36. Elena Silva, Taylor White, and Thomas Toch, *The Carnegie Unit: A Century-Old Standard in a Changing Education Landscape* (Stanford, CA: Carnegie Foundation for the Advancement of Teaching), www.carnegiefoundation.org/wp-content/uploads/2015/01 /Carnegie_Unit_Report.pdf.

37. Alexander C. McCormick and Chun Mei Zhao, "Rethinking and Reframing the Carnegie Classification," *Change: The Magazine of Higher Learning* 37, no. 5 (2005): 51–57.

38. "Brown University's Swearer Center for Public Service Assumes Leadership for Carnegie's Community Engagement Classification," Carnegie Foundation for the Advancement of Teaching, January 30, 2017, www.carnegiefoundation.org/newsroom/improvement

-voices/brown-universitys-swearer-center-for-public-service-assumes-leadership-for
-carnegies-community-engagement-classification/.

39. Amy Driscoll, "Carnegie's Community-Engagement Classification: Intentions and Insights," *Change: The Magazine of Higher Learning* 40, no. 1 (2008): 38–41.

40. John Saltmarsh et al., "Rewarding Community-Engaged Scholarship," in "Institutionalizing Community Engagement in Higher Education: The First Wave of Carnegie Classified Institutions," ed. Lorilee R. Sandmann, Courtney H. Thornton, and Audrey J. Jaeger, special issue, *New Directions for Higher Education*, no. 147 (2009): 25–35; Robert G. Bringle and Julie A. Hatcher, "Innovative Practices in Service-Learning and Curricular Engagement," *New Directions for Higher Education*, no. 147 (2009): 37–46; Andrew Furco and William Miller, "Issues in Benchmarking and Assessing Institutional Engagement," *New Directions for Higher Education*, no. 147 (2009): 47–54; David Weerts and Elizabeth Hudson, "Engagement and Institutional Advancement," *New Directions for Higher Education*, no. 147 (2009): 65–74; Lorilee R. Sandmann and William M. Plater, "Leading the Engaged Institution," *New Directions for Higher Education*, no. 147 (2009): 13–24.

41. Lorilee R. Sandmann, Courtney H. Thornton, and Audrey J. Jaeger, "The First Wave of Community-Engaged Institutions," *New Directions for Higher Education*, no. 147 (2009): 99–104.

42. "Innovation, Competitiveness and Economic Prosperity," Association of Public and Land-Grant Universities, accessed March 6, 2018, www.aplu.org/members/commissions /innovation-competitiveness-and-economic-prosperity/.

43. "Economic Engagement Framework," Association of Public and Land-Grant Universities, accessed May 4, 2017, www.aplu.org/projects-and-initiatives/economic -development-and-community-engagement/economic-engagement-framework.

44. "Higher Education Engagement in Economic Development: Foundations for Strategy and Practice," Association of Public and Land-Grant Universities, accessed June 1, 2017, www.aplu.org/CICEPtaxonomy.

45. "IEP University Designation & Award Process," Association of Public and Land-Grant Universities, accessed March 6, 2018, www.aplu.org/projects-and-initiatives/economic -development-and-community-engagement/innovation-and-economic-prosperity -universities-designation-and-awards-program/submission-process.html.

46. Association of Public and Land-Grant Universities, *Assessment Tools for Examining the Role of Universities in Economic Development* (Washington, DC: Association of Public and Land-Grant Universities, 2014), www.aplu.org/projects-and-initiatives/economic -development-and-community-engagement/economic-engagement-framework/related -resources/cicep-assessment-tools_201405.pdf.

## Chapter 3 · Land-Grant Strengths, Weaknesses, Opportunities, and Threats

1. Larry Goldstein, *College and University Budgeting: An Introduction for Faculty and University Administrators*, 3rd ed. (Washington, DC: National Association of College and University Business Officers, 2005).

2. Robert E. Dixon et al., "Financing and Fiscal Accountability," in *The Modern Land-Grant University*, ed. Robert J. Sternberg (West Lafayette, IN: Purdue University Press, 2014).

3. Jonathan S. Gagliardi et al., *American College President Study 2017* (Washington, DC: American Council on Education, 2017).

4. "25 Years of Declining State Support for Public Colleges," *Chronicle of Higher Education*, March 3, 2014, www.chronicle.com/interactives/statesupport.

5. Karin Fischer and Jack Stripling, "An Era of Neglect," *Chronicle of Higher Education*, March 3, 2014, www.chronicle.com/article/An-Era-of-Neglect/145045.

6. Rick Seltzer, "Health Care vs. Higher Ed," *Insider Higher Education*, April 12, 2017, www.insidehighered.com/news/2017/04/12/medicaid-funding-changes-pressure-state -higher-ed-funding.

7. Sara Hebel, "From Public Good to Private Good," *Chronicle of Higher Education*, March 2, 2014, www.chronicle.com/article/From-Public-Good-to-Private/145061.

8. David Longanecker, "State Governance and the Public Good," in *Higher Education for the Public Good: Emerging Voices from a National Movement*, ed. Adrianna J. Kezar, Tony C. Chambers, and John C. Burkhardt (San Francisco: Jossey-Bass, 2005).

9. Christopher Newfield, *The Great Mistake: How We Wrecked Public Universities and How We Can Fix Them* (Baltimore: Johns Hopkins University Press, 2016).

10. William F. Massy, *Reengineering the University: How to Be Mission Centered, Market Smart, and Margin Conscious* (Baltimore: Johns Hopkins University Press, 2017).

11. D. Alan Tree, "Research and Other Scholarship," in Sternberg, *Modern Land-Grant University*.

12. Michael M. Crow and William B. Debars, "University-Based R&D and Economic Development: The Morrill Act and the Emergence of the American Research University," in *Precipice or Crossroads: Where America's Great Public Universities Stand and Where They Are Going Midway through Their Second Century*, ed. Daniel M. Fogel and Elizabeth Malson-Huddle (Albany, NY: SUNY Press, 2012).

13. Melanie C. Page et al., "Teaching and Learning," in Sternberg, *Modern Land-Grant University*.

14. See https://engagementscholarship.org.

15. Venkatesh Narayanamurti and Toluwalogo Odumosu, *Cycles of Invention and Discovery: Rethinking the Endless Frontier* (Cambridge, MA: Harvard University Press, 2016).

16. James J. Duderstadt, "Creating the Future: The Promise of Public Research Universities for America," in Fogel and Malson-Huddle, *Precipice or Crossroads*.

17. Jung Cheol Shin and Robert Toutkoushian, *University Rankings: Theoretical Basis, Methodology, and Impacts on Global Higher Education* (New York: Springer, 2011).

18. Laura B. Barnes and Christie Hawkins, "Role of Institutional Rankings," in Sternberg, *Modern Land-Grant University*.

19. David Campbell and Gail Feenstra, "Community Food Systems and the Work of Public Scholarship," in *Engaging Campus and Community: The Practice of Public Scholarship in the State and Land-Grant University System*, ed. Scott J. Peters et al. (Dayton, OH: Kettering Foundation Press, 2005).

20. George R. McDowell, *Land-Grant Universities and Extension into the 21st Century: Renegotiating or Abandoning a Social Contract* (Ames: Iowa State University Press, 2001).

21. Steven J. Diner, *Universities and Their Cities: Urban Higher Education in America* (Baltimore: Johns Hopkins University Press, 2017).

22. G. Edward Schuh, "Revitalizing Land Grant Universities," *Choices* 1, no. 2 (1986): 6.

23. Philip G. Altbach, *Global Perspectives on Higher Education* (Baltimore: Johns Hopkins University Press, 2016).

24. Lou Anna K. Simon, "World Grant Universities: Meeting the Challenges of the Twenty-First Century," *Change: The Magazine of Higher Learning* 42, no. 5 (2010): 42–46.

25. John Hudzik and Lou Anna K. Simon, "From a Land-Grant to a World-Grant Ideal: Extending Public Higher Education Core Values to a Global Frame," in Fogel and Malson-Huddle, *Precipice or Crossroads*.

## Chapter 4 · The Impact of Governing Boards, Elected Officials, and Accrediting Bodies

1. Peter D. Eckel and Adrianna Kezar, "The Intersecting Authority of Boards, Presidents, and Faculty," in *American Higher Education in the Twenty-First Century*, 4th ed., ed. Michael N. Bastedo, Philip G. Altbach, and Patricia J. Gumport (Baltimore: Johns Hopkins University Press, 2016).

2. Robert Birnbaum, *How Academic Leadership Works: Understanding Success and Failure in the College Presidency* (San Francisco: Jossey-Bass, 1992).

3. James J. Duderstadt and Farris W. Womack, *The Future of the Public University in America: Beyond the Crossroads* (Baltimore: Johns Hopkins University Press, 2003).

4. Richard Novak and Susan Whealler Johnston, "Trusteeship and the Public Good," in *Higher Education for the Public Good: Emerging Voices from a National Movement*, ed. Adrianna J. Kezar, Tony C. Chambers, and John C. Burkhardt (San Francisco: Jossey-Bass, 2005).

5. See www.agb.org.

6. Association of Governing Boards of Universities and Colleges, *Free Speech on Campus: Guidelines for Governing Boards and Institutional Leaders* (Washington, DC: AGB Press, 2017), www.agb.org/store/freedom-of-speech-on-campus-guidelines-for-governing -boards-and-institutional-leaders; Natalie Krawitz, *The Board's Role in Financial Oversight* (Washington, DC: AGB Press, 2015), www.agb.org/store/the-boards-role-in-financial -oversight.

7. Association of Governing Boards of Universities and Colleges, *The Business of Higher Education* (Washington, DC: AGB Press, 2017), www.agb.org/sites/default/files/report _2017_guardians_business_higher_ed_0.pdf.

8. See www.ncsl.org and www.alec.org.

9. See www.nga.org.

10. "Education Division Strategic Plan: September 2017–December 2020," National Governors Association Center for Best Practices, accessed October 16, 2017, www.nga.org /files/live/sites/NGA/files/pdf/strategicplans/Center-Edu-StrategicPlan1720.pdf.

11. Fiscal Responsibility in Higher Education Academy, American Legislative Exchange Council, October 16–18, 2017, George Mason University, Arlington, VA.

12. "Accreditation in the United States: Regional and National Institutional Accrediting Agencies," US Department of Education, accessed September 8, 2017, www2.ed.gov/admins /finaid/accred/accreditation_pg6.html.

13. "About the Higher Learning Commission," Higher Learning Commission, accessed September 8, 2017, https://hlcommission.org/About-HLC/about-hlc.html.

14. "Policy Title: Criteria for Accreditation," Higher Learning Commission, accessed March 6, 2018, www.hlcommission.org/Policies/criteria-and-core-components.html.

15. Jodi S. Cohen, "State Budget Impasse Puts Schools' Accreditation at Risk," *Chicago Tribune*, February 5, 2016, www.chicagotribune.com/news/ct-illinois-colleges-budget -accreditation-20160205-story.html.

16. Monique Garcia and Kim Geiger, "With a Week to Go, Rauner and Madigan Can't Even Agree on Meeting," *Chicago Tribune*, June 25, 2017, www.chicagotribune.com/news /local/politics/ct-illinois-legislature-leaders-meetings-met-0625-20170623-story.html.

## Chapter 5 · The Critical Role of the Faculty

1. "1940 Statement of Principles on Academic Freedom and Tenure," American Association of University Professors, accessed October 9, 2017, www.aaup.org/report/1940 -statement-principles-academic-freedom-and-tenure.

2. Tami L. Moore et al., "Promotion and Tenure," in *The Modern Land-Grant University*, ed. Robert J. Sternberg (West Lafayette, IN: Purdue University Press, 2014).

3. Philip G. Altbach, "Harsh Realities: The Professoriate in the Twenty-First Century," in *American Higher Education in the Twenty-First Century*, 4th ed., ed. Michael N. Bastedo, Philip G. Altbach, and Patricia J. Gumport (Baltimore: Johns Hopkins University Press, 2016).

4. Sheila A. Slaughter, "Retrenchment in the 1980s: The Politics of Prestige and Gender," *Journal of Higher Education* 64 (1993): 250–82; Peter Schmidt, "Wisconsin Regents Approve New Layoff and Tenure Policies over Faculty Objections," *Chronicle of Higher Education*, March 10, 2016, www.chronicle.com/blogs/ticker/wisconsin-regents -approve-new-layoff-and-tenure-policies-over-faculty-objections/109380.

5. Jack H. Schuster and Martin J. Finkelstein, *The American Faculty: The Restructuring of Academic Work and Careers* (Baltimore: Johns Hopkins University Press, 2006).

6. Adrianna Kezar and Cecile Sam, "Understanding the New Majority of Non-Tenure-Track Faculty in Higher Education: Demographics, Experiences, and Plans of Action," *ASHE Higher Education Report* 36, no. 4 (2010): 1–133.

7. Allison Nichols, "The Effect of Tenure and Promotion Policy on Evaluation and Research in Extension," *Journal of Extension* 42, no. 2 (2004), https://joe.org/joe/2004april /rb1.php.

8. "Precipice or Crossroads: A Symposium on the Future of Public Research Universities," accessed April 28, 2017, www.uvm.edu/~ues/precipice-or-crossroads/?Page =presentations.html; Daniel M. Fogel and Elizabeth Malson-Huddle, eds., *Precipice or Crossroads: Where America's Great Public Universities Stand and Where They Are Going Midway through Their Second Century* (Albany, NY: SUNY Press, 2012).

9. Hameed Ahmed Khan, "Scientific and Technological Research: An Imperative for Development," in *Basic Research and Industrial Applications*, ed. Hameed Khan et al. (Islamabad, Pakistan: Commission on Science and Technology for Sustainable Development in the South, 2005).

10. Lesley Cooper and Janice Orrell, "University and Community Engagement: Towards a Partnership Based on Deliberate Reciprocity," in *Educating the Deliberate Professional: Preparing for Future Practices*, ed. Franziska Trede and Celina McEwen (New York: Springer, 2016).

11. Victor Bloomfield, "Public Scholarship: An Administrator's View," in *Engaging Campus and Community: The Practice of Public Scholarship in the State and Land-Grant University System*, ed. Scott J. Peters et al. (Dayton, OH: Kettering Foundation Press, 2005).

12. Barbara A. Holland, "Factors and Strategies That Influence Faculty Involvement in Public Service," *Journal of Public Service and Outreach* 4 (1999): 37–43.

13. Barbara A. Holland, "Institutional Differences in Pursuing the Public Good," in *Higher Education for the Public Good: Emerging Voices from a National Movement*, ed. Adrianna J. Kezar, Tony C. Chambers, and John C. Burkhardt (San Francisco: Jossey-Bass, 2005).

14. Barbara A. Holland, "Analyzing Institutional Commitment to Service," *Michigan Journal of Community Service Learning* 4 (1997): 39–41.

15. Earnest L. Boyer, *Scholarship Reconsidered: Priorities of the Professoriate* (San Francisco: Jossey-Bass, 1990).

16. Donald A. Schön, "The New Scholarship Requires a New Epistemology," *Change* 27, no. 6 (1995): 26–34.

17. Association of Public and Land-Grant Universities and University Economic Development Association, *Higher Education Engagement in Economic Development: Foundations for Strategy and Practice* (Washington, DC: Association of Public and

Land-Grant Universities and University Economic Development Association, 2015), www .aplu.org/library/higher-education-engagement-in-economic-development-foundations -for-strategy-and-practice/file. See also http://universityeda.org.

18. Robert G. Bringle and Julie A. Hatcher, "Student Engagement Trends over Time," in *Handbook of Engaged Scholarship: Contemporary Landscapes, Future Directions*, vol. 2, *Community–Campus Partnerships*, ed. Hiram E. Fitzgerald, Cathy Burack, and Sarena D. Seifer (East Lansing: Michigan State University Press, 2011), 411–30.

19. Hiram E. Fitzgerald et al., "The Centrality of Engagement in Higher Education," *Journal of Higher Education Outreach and Engagement* 16, no. 3 (2012): 7–28.

20. Miles A. McNall et al., "Systemic Engagement: Universities as Partners in Systemic Approaches to Community Change," *Journal of Higher Education Outreach and Engagement* 19, no. 1 (2015): 1–26.

21. See https://engagementscholarship.org.

## Chapter 6 · Our Students: Vanguard in the Community

1. Joseph Epstein, "Who Killed the Liberal Arts? And Why We Should Care," *Weekly Standard*, September 17, 2012, www.weeklystandard.com/who-killed-the-liberal-arts/article /652007.

2. E. Gordon Gee, "The Modern Public University: Its Land-Grant Heritage, Its Land-Grant Horizon," in *Precipice or Crossroads: Where America's Great Public Universities Stand and Where They Are Going Midway through Their Second Century*, ed. Daniel M. Fogel and Elizabeth Malson-Huddle (Albany, NY: SUNY Press, 2012).

3. Pamela Fly, "Liberal Studies, Undergraduate Curriculum, and the Land-Grant Idea," in *The Modern Land-Grant University*, ed. Robert J. Sternberg (West Lafayette, IN: Purdue University Press, 2014).

4. Patricia Gumport, "Graduate Education and Research," in *American Higher Education in the Twenty-First Century*, 4th ed., ed. Michael N. Bastedo, Philip G. Altbach, and Patricia J. Gumport (Baltimore: Johns Hopkins University Press, 2016).

5. Jean Van Delinder and Sheryl Ann Tucker, "Graduate Academic Experience," in Sternberg, *Modern Land-Grant University*.

6. Marcia C. Linn et al., "Undergraduate Research Experiences: Impacts and Opportunities," *Science* 347, no. 6222 (2015): 627–28.

7. Michael J. Rizzo and Ronald G. Ehrenberg, "Resident and Non-resident Tuition and Enrollment at Flagship State Universities," in *College Choices: The Economics of Where to Go, When to Go, and How to Pay for It*, ed. Caroline M. Hoxby (Chicago: University of Chicago Press, 2004).

8. Richard V. Adkisson and James T. Peach, "Non-resident Enrollment and Non-resident Tuition at Land Grant Colleges and Universities," *Education Economics* 16, no. 1 (2008): 75–88.

9. Robert G. Bringle and Julie A. Hatcher, "A Service-Learning Curriculum for Faculty," *Michigan Journal of Community Service Learning* 2 (1995): 112.

10. Aaron Einfeld and Denise Collins, "The Relationships between Service-Learning, Social Justice, Multicultural Competence, and Civic Engagement," *Journal of College Student Development* 49, no. 2 (2008): 95–109.

11. Robert G. Bringle and Julie A. Hatcher, "Innovative Practices in Service-Learning and Curricular Engagement," *New Directions for Higher Education* 147 (2009): 37–46.

12. Stephen M. Gavazzi and Michael Fox, "A Tale of Three Cities: Piloting a Measure of Effort and Comfort Levels within Town–Gown Relationships," *Innovative Higher Education* 40 (2015): 189–99.

13. Stephen M. Gavazzi, *The Optimal Town–Gown Marriage: Taking Campus–Community Outreach and Engagement to the Next Level* (Charleston, SC: Create Space, 2016).

14. Francis L. Lawrence, *Leadership in Higher Education: Views from the Presidency* (New Brunswick, NJ: Transaction, 2006).

15. David J. Weerts, "Toward an Engagement Model of Institutional Advancement at Public Colleges and Universities," *International Journal of Educational Advancement* 7 (2007): 79–103.

16. David J. Weerts and Elizabeth Hudson, "Engagement and Institutional Advancement," in "Institutionalizing Community Engagement in Higher Education: The First Wave of Carnegie Classified Institutions," ed. Lorilee R. Sandmann, Courtney H. Thornton, and Audrey J. Jaeger, special issue, *New Directions for Higher Education*, no. 147 (2009): 65–74.

17. David J. Weerts and Justin M. Ronca, "Examining Differences in State Support for Higher Education: A Comparative Study of State Appropriations for Research Universities," *Journal of Higher Education* 77, no. 6 (2006): 935–65.

18. Bradford Richardson, "Protests 101: College Civics Classes Focus More on Demonstrations Than Citizenship," *Washington Times*, January 11, 2017, www.washingtontimes.com/news/2017/jan/11/college-civics-classes-focus-more-on-demonstration.

19. See https://compact.org.

## Chapter 7 · Charting the Future of American Public Education

1. Brian Jacob, Brian McCall, and Kevin M. Stange, "College as Country Club: Do Colleges Cater to Students' Preferences for Consumption?" (NBER working paper no. 18745, National Bureau of Economic Research, 2013), www.nber.org/papers/w18745.pdf.

2. Michael Mumper and Melissa L. Freeman, "The Continuing Paradox of Public College Tuition Inflation," in *The States and Public Higher Education Policy: Affordability, Access, and Accountability*, 2nd ed., ed. Donald E. Heller (Baltimore: Johns Hopkins University Press, 2011).

3. Donald E. Heller, "Trends in the Affordability of Public Colleges and Universities: The Contradiction of Increasing Prices and Increasing Enrollment," in Heller, *States and Public Higher Education Policy*.

4. Robert A. Petrin, Kai A. Schafft, and Judith L. Meece, "Educational Sorting and Residential Aspirations among Rural High School Students: What Are the Contributions of Schools and Educators to the Rural Brain Drain?," *American Educational Research Journal* 51, no. 2 (2014): 294–326.

5. Laura Pappano, "Colleges Discover the Rural Student," *New York Times*, January 31, 2017, www.nytimes.com/2017/01/31/education/edlife/colleges-discover-rural-student.html.

6. "Precipice or Crossroads: A Symposium on the Future of Public Research Universities," accessed April 28, 2017, www.uvm.edu/~ues/precipice-or-crossroads/?Page=presentations.html; Daniel M. Fogel and Elizabeth Malson-Huddle, eds., *Precipice or Crossroads: Where America's Great Public Universities Stand and Where They Are Going Midway through Their Second Century* (Albany, NY: SUNY Press, 2012).

7. Nancy L. Zimpher and Jessica Fisher Neidl, "Statewide University Systems: Taking the Land-Grant Concept to Scale in the Twenty-First Century," in Fogel and Malson-Huddle, *Precipice or Crossroads*; John Hudzik and Lou Anna K. Simon, "From Land-Grant to a World-Grant Ideal: Extending Public Higher Education Core Values to a Global Frame," in Fogel and Malson-Huddle, *Precipice or Crossroads*.

8. Randall Woodson et al., "Reconsidering Mr. Lincoln's Land-Grant Universities: Taking Back the Future of American Public Higher Education" (panel session at the 2017

Association of Public and Land-Grant Universities Annual Conference, Washington, DC, November 13, 2017).

9.  Aims C. McGuiness Jr., "The States and Higher Education," in *American Higher Education in the Twenty-First Century*, 4th ed., ed. Michael N. Bastedo, Philip G. Altbach, and Patricia J. Gumport (Baltimore: Johns Hopkins University Press, 2016).

10.  See http://collegeaffordability.blogspot.com/.

11.  Richard K. Vedder, *Going Broke by Degree: Why College Costs So Much* (Washington, DC: American Enterprise Institute Press, 2004).

12.  Michael M. Crow and William B. Dabars, *Designing the New American University* (Baltimore: Johns Hopkins University Press, 2015).

13.  Robert K. Greenleaf, *Servant Leadership: A Journey into the Nature of Legitimate Power and Greatness*, 25th anniversary ed. (New York: Paulist, 2002).

14.  Daniel W. Wheeler, *Servant Leadership for Higher Education: Principles and Practices* (San Francisco: Jossey-Bass, 2012), 130–31.

15.  Michael Fabricant and Stephen Brier, *Austerity Blues: Fighting for the Soul of Public Higher Education* (Baltimore: Johns Hopkins University Press, 2016).

16.  Robert J. Sternberg, *What Universities Can Be: A New Model for Preparing Students for Active Concerned Citizenship and Ethical Leadership* (Ithaca, NY: Cornell University Press, 2016).

17.  Chad Wellmon, *Organizing Enlightenment: Information Overload and the Invention of the Modern Research University* (Baltimore: Johns Hopkins University Press, 2015).

18.  Martin J. Finkelstein, Valerie Martin Conley, and Jack H. Schuster, *The Faculty Factor: Reassessing the American Academy in a Turbulent Era* (Baltimore: Johns Hopkins University Press, 2016).

19.  Sternberg, *What Universities Can Be*.

20.  Jennifer Kavanaugh and Michael D. Rich, *Truth Decay: An Initial Exploration of the Diminishing Role of Facts and Analysis in American Public Life* (Santa Monica, CA: Rand Corporation, 2008).